G000141660

RIVERS, MEMORY, AND NATION-BUILDING

The Environment in History: International Perspectives

Series Editors: Dolly Jørgensen, *Umea University;* David Moon, *University of York;* Christof Mauch, *LMU Munich;* Helmuth Trischler, *Deutsches Museum, Munich*

ENVIRONMENT AND SOCIETY

Rivers, Memory, and Nation-Building

A History of the Volga and Mississippi Rivers

Dorothy Zeisler-Vralsted

berghahn
NEW YORK · OXFORD
www.berghahnbooks.com

Published by

Berghahn Books

www.berghahnbooks.com

©2015 Dorothy Zeisler-Vralsted

Library of Congress Cataloging-in-Publication Data

Zeisler-Vralsted, Dorothy.
 Rivers, memory, and nation-building : a history of the Volga and Mississippi rivers /
Dorothy Zeisler-Vralsted.
  pages cm. -- (The environment in history : international perspectives ; volume 4)
 Includes bibliographical references and index.
 ISBN 978-1-78238-431-1 (hardback : alkaline paper) -- ISBN 978-1-78238-432-8 (ebook)
 1. Volga River (Russia)--History. 2. Mississippi River--History. 3. Rivers--Social aspects-
-Russia 4. Rivers--Social aspects--United States. 5. Collective memory--Russia--History.
6. Collective memory--United States--History. 7. Nationalism--Russia--History. 8.
Nationalism--United States--History. 9. Human ecology--Russia--History. 10. Human
ecology--United States--History. I. Title.
 DK511.V65Z44 2014
 947.4--dc23

                                                                    2014018770

British Library Cataloguing in Publication Data

A catalogue record for this book is available from the British Library

Printed on acid-free paper

ISBN: 978–1-78238-431-1 hardback
ISBN: 978–1-78238-432-8 ebook

I've known rivers:
I've known rivers ancient as the world and older than the flow
          of human blood in human veins
My soul has grown deep like the rivers.
I bathed in the Euphrates when dawns were young
I built my hut near the Congo and it lulled me to sleep.
I looked upon the Nile and raised the pyramids above it.
I heard the singing of the Mississippi when Abe Lincoln went
          down to New Orleans, and I've seen its muddy bosom turn
          all golden in the sunset.
I've known rivers:
Ancient, dusky rivers.
My soul has grown deep like the rivers
                    —Langston Hughes, *The Negro Speaks of Rivers* (1922)

Their silhouettes show white in the air,
Their towers loom dark like a forest
Oh how much I love the evening time, full of fascination
Listen attentively, oh majestic Volga!
Poetic voice of your sacred waves,
They echo the glory of ancient Russia
                    —Petr Vyazemsky, *Evening on the Volga River* (1815)

The fate of the Volga may serve as a lesson for the study of destiny.
The day the Volga riverbed was sounded was the day of its subjugation,
its conquest by the powers of sail and oar, the surrender of the Volga to mankind.
                    —Velimir Khlebnikov, *The Tables of Destiny* (1922)

Contents

Illustrations

Preface

This book is the outcome of a professional career in water that spans academic and field work. My introduction to the multifaceted role of rivers began with the legendary K. Ross Toole, a history professor at the University of Montana, who prompted me to study and research what was euphemistically known as the "Big Ditch" in the Bitterroot Valley; an early-twentieth-century irrigation project whose promoters believed that through the manipulation of water, university professors could leisurely grow apples during the summer. The Big Ditch was my first introduction to the intersection of twentieth-century engineering and a riverine environment where engineers and their promoters had a messianic faith in the ability of technology to transform landscapes. After an academic initiation to water in the arid West, I had an opportunity to work in the Engineering Bureau of the Montana State Department of Natural Resources and see how farmers related to water when it was an everyday necessity for their livelihoods. In this setting, I worked on an irrigation project with farmers and residential irrigators in recording and researching their water rights. The outcome of this field work—which offered hands-on experience into the world of headgates, fluctuating river flows based on snowmelt and rainfall, and the ever-present desire to redesign the riverine landscape—lead ultimately to the establishment of an irrigation district in the Bitterroot Valley. As a result, I experienced firsthand the importance of water in an arid environment as irrigators vied—often pitting neighboring farmers against each other—to secure their appropriations. After that, I was hooked and the relationship between water and human communities has never ceased to fascinate. More academic research followed although the geographical location changed to the Yakima River Basin; another arid environment in the American West.

Although still studying water and specifically, rivers, my geographical focus changed from the American West to Russia after my first visit in the late 1990s. As part of a university exchange, I was fortunate to meet Oleg Kuznetsov, president of the Russian Academy of Natural Sciences and former rector of Dubna International University for Nature, Society and Man. A keen observer, Oleg was the first to recognize the similarities between the Volga and Mississippi Rivers and the benefits that might be derived from a comparative history. He encouraged further study and supported travel to his university, located near the Dmitrov Archives, on several occasions. Along with Oleg, many others supported my research and travel in a number of ways. Judith L. Kuipers, former chancellor of the University of Wisconsin–La Crosse, deserves special thanks as it was under her administration that I was first introduced to Russia and its subsequent research opportunities. Another chancellor from the same institution, Douglas N. Hastad, also lent support to my research interests and broadened my network of contacts for both Mississippi and Volga River expertise. While still a professor at the University of Wisconsin–La Crosse, I was fortunate to receive a Fulbright award for six months of lecturing and research at the Dubna International University for Nature, Society and Man. At this juncture, I acquired intellectual debts to many. First, Ilya Shatunovsky, former head of the Linguistics Department at Dubna University, provided the ideal working environment without which this book would never have been started. Second, my tutor and translator, Zhenya Tkachenko, was invaluable as she orchestrated visits to the Dmitrov Archives and museums, arranged interviews, and translated numerous 1930s Soviet texts. Third, the Pipenko family, who offered sustenance when sorely needed but also historical, literary, and artistic insights to the materials I was researching. These are only a few of the many who offered their time and expertise.

Another academic institution that offered timely financial support was the University of the United Arab Emirates where former dean Donald N. Baker lent his interest and support to this project. Through his support, I was able to spend time in archives in Russia and the United States. In addition to resources provided by the Fulbright Association and other academic institutions, other organizations that contributed include the German Historical Institute, Washington, D.C. for its travel support to a workshop that allowed me to further develop this comparative study. After the workshop, organizers published the text *Rivers in History: Perspectives on Waterways in Europe and North America,* in which my chapter, "Cultural and Hydrological Development of the Mississippi and Volga Rivers," considered the initial ideas that are one of the themes of the following book. While there were many other opportunities to discuss and refine my ideas about this comparative study, another conference warrants special mention as it also led to a publication. Special thanks to Marco Armiero and Wilko Von Hardenberg for organizing the first "Nature and Nation" conference, and for their subsequent work as editors of a special issue of *Environment and History.* Through their efforts, I was fortunate to publish still another aspect of my work in the article, "Aesthetics of the Volga and National Narratives in Russia." Finally, my present institution, Eastern Washington University, lent support in numerous ways from financial to flexible scheduling to the administrative support of Nita Holbert.

More informal but equally important contributions were the many conversations with colleagues, of which several edited earlier versions of this manuscript. The list is long and includes Vincent Langendijk, Victoria Penziner, Sarah Trainer, Fekri Hassan, Jim Wiener, Ron Rada, Cynthia Ruder, and David Bell. Adding to these scholars' contributions were those of George Ceffalo and his sources on the Mississippi River. My former colleagues at the International Water History Association—where I served as secretary for five years—provided numerous opportunities to engage in discussions regarding water and its role in the historical past. A few of these former colleagues include Heather Hoag, Johann Tempelhoff, Carol Fort, Maurits Ertsen, and Bob Varady.

Of course, none of my efforts would be successful without the keen editing and encouragement of David Moon. Despite what I know is a busy schedule, David closely reviewed my early submissions, offering critical insights at several junctures. With my academic background primarily in American history, David's expertise in Russian history was invaluable. His time with this work will always be appreciated. I also thank Adam Capitanio and Elizabeth Berg of Berghahn Books for their willingness to accommodate requested extensions, prompt responses, and ultimately overseeing the process.

Finally, there are four people who have shown amazing patience and support throughout this whole process. My husband, Jim; children, Robert and Nora; and daughter-in-law, Amanda, were always understanding when my work sometimes interfered with family life. Jim never lost faith in this work, for which I will always be grateful. For with each visit to the Mississippi and Volga River Basins my belief in the universal nature of river systems and the human communities that depend upon them was reinforced. But working with water, however, in all my past capacities taught me that rivers are more than facilitators of a nation's greatness; instead, their role with human history is a more intimate one as I hope the following chapters will reveal.

Introduction

On 21 July 2013, *The New York Times* featured a story about the revival of Newark, New Jersey, a city long associated with urban decline and decay. Newark's decline, in part a result of deindustrialization and the loss of jobs, also stemmed from environmental ills such as the earlier disposal of dioxin into the Passaic River, which runs alongside the city. Today, the river is central to Newark's recovery and reclamation efforts include a new sewage treatment plant and a highly visible boardwalk, reconceptualizing the use of riverfronts. The Passaic, in turn, becomes symbolic of a renewed Newark. But the article is quick to point out that Newark's recovery, represented through the reclamation of the Passaic River, is not unique. Instead, "It's a common approach these days, from Seoul to Madrid to San Francisco: upgrading cities by revamping ravaged waterfronts." The article goes on to say, "The idea is to make the Passaic a point of pride."[1] Urban rivers and the once-industrialized riverfront spaces have become fashionable as revitalized cities find new uses for urban space turning riverscapes into aesthetically pleasing areas full of potential for recreation and community building.

Historically, however, rivers have long been a means to cultivate regional or local pride of place as numerous mythologies, folk tales, and visual images reveal, offering rich collective memories. For example, Egyptians revered the Nile and often sang the river's praises, early Hindu cultures sanctified the Ganga with a colorful and provocative creation story, and Mid-Columbia Indians in the Columbia River Basin valued water as the "first sacred food."[2] These earlier homages to rivers, however, were not as purposeful as twenty-first-century efforts to enlist rivers in urban renewal strategies and instead were the product of daily experiences living and working alongside the rivers. As a result, individual rivers emerged as a source of pride, unifying the surrounding population. Always critical to ecological health, today rivers are enjoying a renaissance from a social and cultural perspective. As seen in the example of Newark, many cities in the throes of revitalization are relying upon urban rivers to serve as centerpieces for their revivals. Complementing the new appreciation for urban riverfronts, recent scholarship on rivers recognizes the centrality of rivers in the human past. In the academic realm, the literature on rivers progressed from earlier celebratory accounts on major rivers such as the popular 1940s series on American rivers, edited by Constance Skinner, to an array of environmental histories such as Christopher Morris's work on the Mississippi River or Mark Cioc's eco-biography of the Rhine.[3]

The growing body of scholarly works reveals the multidisciplinarity of river research as the field widened from mid-twentieth-century works that were primarily descriptive where rivers were valorized for their aesthetics while acknowledged for their utility and contribution in civilization-building. For example, texts such as Gordon Cooper's *Along the Great Rivers* in which he rhapsodized "Rivers, like clarions, sing to the ocean of the beauty of the earth, the fertility of plains, and the splendor of cities" were common paeans to major rivers.[4] Adding to the literature were institutional and administrative histories in which the development of a river was chronicled through the lens of a federal agency such as the U.S. Army Corps of Engineers. A number of works fall under this category such as Martin Reuss's examination of the Atchafalaya Basin or the exhaustive study of the Grand Coulee Dam by Paul Pitzer. Journalists have expanded the field with lively accounts of a single river, such as Marq de Villiers recalling his trip down the Volga after the collapse of the Soviet Union. De Villiers parlayed his journey into a running commentary on the post-Soviet environment. Other journalists, such as Ray March with his account of a California river in *River in Ruin* or Philip Fradkin's *A River No More* exemplify the contributions targeted for general audiences.[5]

Adding to the chorus of historical studies are contemporary journalistic works that address the environmental degradation of the world's rivers and water resources through years of rampant industrialization and modernization. Attracting a popular audience, the theme of environmental decline can be found in works such as Fred Pearce's *When the Rivers Run Dry* where he wrote of the deterioration of the Mekong and Rio Grande Rivers and Aral Sea, among others. Other popular books warning of the pending water crisis and the despoliation of major rivers include Steven Solomon's *Water: The Epic Struggle for Wealth, Power, and Civilization* and Patrick McCully's *Silenced Rivers*, to name a few from a burgeoning field. Although written from the perspective of impending environmental catastrophe, these texts complement academic efforts in that both reflect the consensus that rivers and water resources—critical to human existence—are threatened by contemporary resource practices. Further, works such as McCully's provide another context in which to understand the twentieth century drive to modernize, with the corresponding manipulation of rivers, and the subsequent effects upon major river systems.[6]

Growing in complexity are studies such as Sara Pritchard's book on the Rhône in which she drew upon methodologies from several disciplines including science, technology, and society (STS) and environmental history and provided an in-depth examination of post–World War II development of the

Rhône. Pritchard categorized her work as an enviro-technical approach, evidence of a maturation and sophistication in the study of rivers. In her findings, she demonstrated that the Rhône's development was motivated, in part, to recapture the past grandeur of a nation devastated by war. A common theme in river studies, Pritchard revealed how rivers are employed to enhance national prestige. Throughout the twentieth century, engineering feats on major rivers—such as the Grand Coulee, Aswan, and Three Gorges Dams—were testimonies to a nation's ascent and a source of national pride. Another sampling of the multidisciplinarity and increased sophistication of river scholarship can be found in a 2010 dissertation by Randall Dills on the Neva River and its part in the history of St. Petersburg. Dills considered his research as serving a number of audiences, including urban, Russian, and environmental historians. He credited the Neva with providing a lens through which to understand St. Petersburg as it evolved into a modern city. In his words, "water, particularly the meaning and use of the watered environs of the city, is the best lens to trace these disputes as the battle over capital was fought again and again."[7] More singular in purpose are books such as that of art historian Tricia Cusack whose *Riverscapes and National Identities* analyzed the role of five major rivers in the emergent nationalism of the nineteenth century. Cusack's study adds another dimension to the historiography of rivers and challenged scholars of nationalism to consider riverscapes when theorizing about the construction of nationalist discourse. By relying upon visual imagery such as the artwork of Isaak Levitan portraying the Volga River, Cusack presented a convincing thesis how rivers valorized through these nineteenth-century portraits contributed to a growing national ethos. She also demonstrated that visual culture, in this instance riverscape imagery—frozen in time through the landscape art of Levitan and Repin—retained its influence on national identity.[8]

Adding to the historical record and another comparative study is Peter Coates's comprehensive work, *A Story of Six Rivers*. His approach, however, differed from Cusack in that he selected less well-known rivers—the Danube, Spree, Po, Mersey, Yukon, and Los Angeles—while the scope of inquiry was more extensive. In the introduction, Coates emphasized his was not the familiar story of environmental degradation as he showed how rivers were an integral part of the human past and, quoting from an environmental classic, contended that despite human alterations rivers "retain 'unmade' attributes." To Coates, "Rivers are works in progress." As an environmental historian, he presented contemporary perceptions of rivers as cultural constructions and furthers an understanding of the role of rivers by looking at ancient and ongoing associations with rivers such as "river of life," "river of riches," "river of recreation," "river of peril," and "river of inspiration." These associations revealed the cultural construction of nature and rivers as well as the multiple layers of human interaction with rivers. (The discussion of river associations complements Cusack's argument that visual imagery lends a constancy to nationalist ideals with their incorporation of riverscapes.) Coates even tackled the question of agency that so often plagues environmental historians and concluded that "Environmental history calls a river a river. It makes the river a leading participant, if not overwhelming protagonist." Coates's study, not only offered a theoretical framework, but also illustrated the dramatic shifts in river scholarship since the early twentieth century.[9]

A less obvious association with the scholarship on rivers but still adding to the growing recognition that rivers played pivotal roles in the human past are the works of two Russian historians and their findings into overlooked aspects of Russia's imperial past. In Catherine Evtuhov's *Portrait of a Russian Province: Economy, Society and Civilization in Nineteenth Century Nizhnii Novgorod*, although an examination of a specific province, she demonstrated the centrality of the Volga and Oka Rivers in the province's history and success. In her retelling of this provincial history, Evtuhov's study is unusual on two counts. First, most Russian histories of the nineteenth century have been preoccupied with how the era led to the Bolsheviks and their ultimate failure. But in Evtuhov's study, she was concerned with what existed in the nineteenth century not what went wrong. Second, within this departure from traditional Russian scholarship in which Evtuhov focused on the history of one province, she included the role of the two rivers. By breaking down provincial history into its discrete parts, she revealed a Russian past that was more diverse with multiple leading participants. In her history, the Volga and Oka Rivers and Nizhnii Novgorod residents intersect at multiple junctures, producing the world-renowned Nizhnii Novgorod Fair and an economy dependent upon an extensive trade down to the Caspian Sea. In other words, Evtuhov recognized the importance of the Volga and local ecology in shaping the powerful merchant class. The role of the rivers became increasingly significant when her study highlighted how much the merchant class dictated Russian life. Evtuhov supplied further evidence of the two rivers' importance with her discussion of Russian words used specifically to describe the Volga's hydrological regime. For example, the Russian word *staritsa* referred to an earlier river course while the term *polovodie* indicated the annual May floods. The evolution of a vocabulary for a specific fluvial regime indicated an immediacy with the Volga, suggesting the river's presence in everyday lives. Still her history remained the story of how provincial life offered a valuable glimpse into nineteenth-century Russia revealing a powerful merchant class along with the province's other occupations. While the Volga and Oka Rivers played key supporting roles in this history, Evtuhov unlike Coates and Cusack did not portray the rivers as the principal actors.[10]

Similar to Evtuhov's work is Robert E. Jones's book, *Bread Upon the Waters*. Jones questioned the prevailing views regarding Russia's imperial past and in so doing, he illustrated the primacy of rivers, such as the Volga in Russia's past.

In his account— while the rivers served a strictly utilitarian role—the shift in emphasis for this time period and documentation that Russia was an imperial nation in the same mold as her European counterparts revealed the contributions of Russian waterways and the worlds they created. Rich in detail, he discussed these internal waterways which the government persisted in funding in order to ship grain from the central Volga region to St. Petersburg and its Baltic port. Jones, like Evtuhov, changed the focus of Russian scholarship and disclosed a society with a bustling grain trade and an economic outlook mirroring Europe. His evidence supported "Boris Mironov's contention that imperial Russia was a normal country following the same path to modernity as other European countries." The Volga, with its access to Eastern markets as well as Russia's grain-producing regions, was key to this shifting perspective.[11]

In the same vein are the studies by historians Thomas C. Buchanan with his *Black Life on the Mississippi* and Walter Johnson's *River of Dark Dreams* that both examine African-American life during the time of slavery. In these texts, the Mississippi River figures prominently. For African-Americans the river intersected with their lives on a number of levels as the river offered freedom, oppression, escape, sustenance, renewal, disease, and displacement. While Buchanan emphasized the world of steamboat travel and its liberating effect upon free and enslaved Blacks, Johnson revealed an "agro-capitalist landscape" where the Mississippi represented both a means of escape and an avenue into the bowels of slavery. But similar to Evtuhov and Jones, the river is not the principal actor but instead remained in a supporting role. Still other recent contributions to riverine literature, complementing the scholarship of Buchanan and Johnson, can be found in literary studies such as Lee Joan Skinner's examination of the Pastaga River. In her study, she analyzed the power of the Pastaga as shown in the novel *Cumandà* by Juan Leon Mera that featured internal social and racial strife in post-independence Ecuador. Using the methodology of ecocriticism and cultural geography, Skinner perceived the river as one of the main actors in the drama as lives and identities are influenced by its dynamic presence. The river, like the Mississippi in Buchanan's and Johnson's studies, is a mediated space between cultures and in Skinner's analysis of Mera's work, the river was a central figure. In Skinner's words, the "river is a space of mediation between humans and the natural world, a landscape that both supports humans and is inimical to them." In Skinner's probing critique of Mera's work, she revealed his personification of the river through his identifying the river as "king" and "sovereign" even endowing the river's tributaries with the ability to fight in battle. Skinner's article and her use of eco-criticism and cultural geography broadens the discourse in river scholarship further supporting the case for rivers as historical actors.[12]

Anchoring the twenty-first-century outpouring of river scholarship are the classics beginning with Richard White's *Organic Machine,* which perhaps more than any other study reconceptualized the way environmental historians perceived rivers. In White's words, "Nature, at once a cultural construct and a set of actual things outside of us and not fully contained by our constructions, needs to be put into human history." He succeeded in this with his portrayal of the Columbia River. In *The Organic Machine*, he brought the river alive with a history where earlier memories of the river were retrieved and integrated into the river that exists today—departing from previous environmental histories that emphasized decline and loss and placed nature outside the human drama. (Mentioned earlier, Peter Coates cited White's conclusions regarding the Columbia River and how although changed the river still kept certain attributes.) Another classic is Donald Worster's *Rivers of Empire*, in which he utilized Karl Wittfogel's hydraulic empire thesis to argue that rivers, as a source of power, continue to be appropriated and manipulated to serve the interests of a few in a capitalist system. Different approaches, to be sure, yet both scholars acknowledged the centrality of rivers in history. With these texts, White and Worster—founders of the field of environmental history—lent credibility to the scholarship of rivers.[13]

Given the multitude of books written on rivers, endowing them with numerous representations and functions, how is the following study different and what does it add to the scholarship of rivers? First, this is a comparative study of two major rivers—the Volga and Mississippi. Although multiple volumes on rivers exist, none offer a historical comparison of two major rivers from ancient times to the early twentieth century. Second, by looking at the past from the vantage point of these two rivers, multiple narratives emerge resulting in a history that is diverse, comprehensive, and rich in comparisons. For example, the Volga's story includes early empires such as the medieval Khazars, who long before the advent of the global market used the Volga to carry on a brisk trade with their neighbors to the east, west, and south. Or another story with Vikings camped on the middle stretches of the Volga hoping to capture prized silver dirhams through trade with Arab merchants. Along with trade, however, the Volga sustained numerous agricultural populations, such as the descendants of Slavic groups, with its riverbanks offering the best land and bounty. Several centuries after the Vikings, the story expands with the Mongol conquest of Russia during the winter—a singular feat unmatched by the armies of Napoleon and Hitler. After their victories, the Mongols made the Volga riverbanks their home with camps that included Kazan and Sarai. When the Mongols were routed by Ivan IV, also known as Ivan the Terrible, the river was an actor again as folklore celebrates Ivan's whipping and ultimately, taming the river in preparation for battle. Still another story commemorates the trials and tribulations, evoked through song and folklore, of the barge haulers or burlaki, who worked endless hours pulling barges over the shallow waters of the Volga before the arrival of the steamship. But the river had another story of the burlaki. At nightfall along the riverbanks, they lived an existence free of constraints, again captured through song and folklore. Still, the Volga was witness to more suffering as the riverbanks were a breeding ground for cholera with major epidemics in the 1800s.

By the nineteenth century, the Volga's story parallels another history: the advent of modernization. Steamships, navigational canals, and hydropower—tools of the modern nation-state—all become part of the Volga's history. Throughout these multiple narratives, one constant emerges. Whether during the long history of Imperial Russia or the brief Soviet Union interlude, the Volga's role in defining Russia is recognized as artists portray the riverine landscape and Soviet songs extol the nation's debt to the river. Thus, the Volga River was integral to the success of empires, the livelihood and identity of so many, and Russia's identity and emergence as a modern nation-state.

For the Mississippi, similar stories can be told. A robust Indian trade network saw the exchange of status goods ranging from copper found in the north by Lake Superior to shells and alligator teeth found in the Lower Mississippi River Basin and Gulf of Mexico—all by way of the river. Or by C.E. 1100, the existence of Cahokia, an empire on the banks of the middle stretches of the river, which saw the construction of pyramid-shaped mounds, lining a riverine landscape. From its vantage point on the river, Cahokia became the administrative center of an extensive mound-building empire with sites in present-day Oklahoma, Georgia, and Alabama. But the river also witnessed the advance of European missionaries and traders, competing for Indian souls and markets. As the river accommodated a growing trade between Indians and Europeans, waves of new populations from Britain, England, and Spain arrived. At the river's mouth, Indian populations who lived well off the bounty of a rich riverine environment saw the establishment of trading posts, and ultimately cities. In the upper reaches of the Mississippi, trade persisted in the eighteenth and nineteenth centuries, as the market in furs governed relations between Europeans and Indians. Other arrivals to the Mississippi River Valley were African slaves who also lent their stories to the river. For some, the river offered a means of escape as renegade communities in the delta swampland were established in the seventeenth century. For other African slaves, the river offered a respite and a measure of freedom from a plantation economy. Freedom also came to the flatboatmen whose lives, living on the margins, mirrored the burlaki. But the Mississippi, like the Volga, was a conduit for disease. As goods were traded up and down the river, smallpox also found its way into Native American communities, decimating populations. Cholera outbreaks occurred on board steamships with the deceased thrown overboard into the Mississippi. For the first European settlers, they chose locations in the Delta region that were often havens for disease as high mortality rates reveal.

But similar to its counterpart, a change occurred during the nineteenth and twentieth centuries when the Mississippi becomes a partner in America's story of modernization. Like the Volga, travel on the Mississippi is dominated first by steamships with later transportation facilitated by the construction of navigational canals—all contributing to the nation's success. Underlying that success, the Mississippi was part of an emergent national narrative, crafting an identity depicted in song, art, poetry, and prose that is both nostalgic and forward looking.

By viewing the past through these two rivers, which in itself differed from earlier cited works, history is not circumscribed by the boundaries of nations or the political actions of a few. Political ideologies become conflated as the historical similarities overwhelm any national differences. Instead, from the starting point of the Volga and Mississippi Rivers, a more nuanced history is revealed as the rivers diminish the traditional markers that shape the history of cultures and nations. When the river becomes the organizing theme, a different story evolves. For example, new questions of race and class are raised when looking at the intersection of humans and these two rivers. For the African-American community, the Mississippi River alternated between liberator and oppressor informing the social construct of an identity that was at times lamented, celebrated, demeaned, and feared. By looking at the lower Mississippi River in the eighteenth and nineteenth centuries, a world is revealed that allowed for a freedom of movement for African slaves not permissible in the surrounding plantations. Yet the river also served for many African slaves as a reminder of past lives or what the future held. Spirituals, such as "Roll, Jordan, Roll" could be heard on the river, suggesting a connection that went beyond the everyday world of work. A similar experience can be found in the lives of the earlier-mentioned burlaki, men who pulled barges up and down the river by way of leather harnesses strapped across their chests. For them, the Volga offered a freedom not experienced by the land-bound serfs. Again, their lives on the river were punctuated by song; work songs to be sure that often reflected the rhythmic pulling of the barges. Still, the songs bound them to the river. Songs from both communities—the burlaki and African-Americans—offered cultural artifacts that revealed the construction of an identity closely tied to the rivers.

The lives of the burlaki and African slaves were shaped by their work on the Volga and Mississippi. Both groups through their labor on these rivers experienced a freedom that their counterparts did not have. This freedom, evoked in song and folklore, contributed to a cultural identity as well. But more importantly, by viewing the past through the history of these two rivers, a new historical relationship between the environment and labor is uncovered. In both cases, the rivers not only oppressed but also liberated. Further, the songs, folklore, print, and visual culture that emanated from the experience of the burlaki and African slaves capture the constraints and freedom of their labor on the rivers. In the same vein, the rivers presented a frontier experience, which again had a liberating effect on certain classes. In the United States, the Mississippi offered a "rough and tumble" existence for flatboatmen, depicted in the art of George Caleb Bingham. In Imperial Russia, the Volga, particularly the southern reaches far away from the seat of power, was often a refuge for bandits as travelers were often warned about their safety in these areas. Once again, it was the rivers that provided an environment where humans experienced a freedom unknown in other settings.

But a study of the rivers reveals even more about race and class when looking at the outbreak of disease, such as the cholera epidemics that plagued Imperial Russia throughout the nineteenth century. For Russia, cholera outbreaks persisted after being eradicated in other modern nations and the poor suffered the most with each occurrence. The disease, a product of poor drinking water, originated along the riverbanks where housing was substandard and poorer populations lived. For inhabitants of the Mississippi River Valley, smallpox in particular found its way into Native American tribes via trade on the river. Even today, there is a correlation between disease and the river as a number of petrochemical plants are located along the river from Baton Rouge to New Orleans in areas with large, poor Black and Latino populations. The term "Cancer Alley," refers to this stretch of the river as many from academic and activist communities contend there is an unusually high incidence of cancer, stillbirths, and asthma. The multifaceted nature of the rivers endures as both were and are conduits for trade while simultaneously conveying a sense of freedom inherent in the flowing rivers. Yet at the same time, the riverbanks were the homes of the very poor and breeding grounds for epidemic diseases. For African-Americans and the burlaki, their oftentimes immediacy with the Volga and Mississippi Rivers, in turn fostering a more conscious level of the river's workings, produced knowledge and an identity that differed from the mainstream societies.

By the nineteenth century, however, both rivers were reimagined and integrated into a metaphorical rather than a physical space. This transition was experienced differently by those living in the emerging nation-states of Russia and the United States. Although each country possessed its own symbolic representations, the move to appropriate these distinguishing characteristics mirrored an emergent nationalism found throughout the West in the nineteenth century. Scholars, such as Benedict Anderson, Ernest Gellner, and Anthony Smith, have traced the rise of nationalism with different conclusions as to its causes and definition. For example in a 2013 article by Anthony Smith, he recognized the contributions of landscape artists in building a nationalist consensus. While his study was limited to the artwork of Britain and France, some of his findings applied to the United States and Russia such as a growing nineteenth-century tourism in the British Isles with an increased appreciation for British landscapes.[14] Both the United States and Russia experienced a similar outcome as the tourist trade grew with steamboat cruises on the Volga and Mississippi Rivers in the nineteenth century. Nationalist sentiment reinforced the notion of exceptionalism for both countries. Each country touted their uniqueness through a litany of landscape references. Concomitant with the Volga and Mississippi as primary symbols, each advancing a unity unknown in earlier centuries, were other riverscapes or landscape features distinguishing each country and forming a distinct national identity. In the United States and Russia, the argument for exceptionalism was based upon a comparison with European landscapes. In the United States the Hudson River represented American perceptions about being at the "center of the world" in art and prose that touted the riverscape's superiority.[15] For Russia, in addition to the Volga, other images long associated with Russian identity were the forest and steppes. But landscape and national identity were not limited to these countries as comparisons can be drawn with the German search for identity found in the idea of heimat. Or in Italy, another analogy was the association of its mountains with national identity as explored by Marco Armiero in his groundbreaking work, to cite a few examples.[16]

Among the cacophony of images, however, the Volga and Mississippi as national rivers enclosed within the border of each country, became key to crafting national identity. Further, long after the rivers served the emergent nation-states, their roles as national icons persisted. For the elite, although the rivers had been valorized earlier through myth, by the nineteenth century the rivers became a cerebral experience as they occupied a spiritual place in Russian and American iconography, and represented a part of the historical memory. In the 1800s, when both the United States and Russia sought to distinguish themselves from a dominant Western European tradition, the unique landscapes of the Volga and Mississippi Rivers figured prominently. "Mother Volga" and "Old Man River" became select epithets associated with each country's sustenance, wealth, and of course, aesthetics. But for the Russian peasant or Midwestern settler, who lived at the mercy of each river's capriciousness—whether through floods, challenging navigation routes, or the carrier of disease—the aesthetics of the river did not resonate in the same fashion. This is not to say that the growing body of mythology surrounding each river was not celebrated by all classes, as it was, and all knew the legends and songs memorializing each river. But the daily experiences with the rivers differed, resulting in different narratives. This gap in experience persisted into the twentieth century even while those representing the elite changed; particularly in what became the Soviet Union. In either the United States or the Soviet Union, the class that labored on the river, whether constructing dams for hydropower or building locks to improve navigation experienced the river in all its facets, especially when trying to harness these once magnificent, free-flowing rivers.

To the elite, the technological accomplishment could not be overstated as rivers were bridled, tamed, and rerouted in order to modernize. Nineteenth-century imagery of the rivers, commemorating their beauty and strength, framed a discourse that further enhanced twentieth-century engineering feats. While all citizens benefitted from the results of these technological and engineering feats as improved transportation meant cheaper goods and hydropower meant electricity, the laborers who took part in the construction, realizing the technological achievements, saw in the river a far different taskmaster. This proved especially true for those in the Soviet Union who were forced to work in the icy waters of the Volga to build the Moscow-Volga Canal in record time. Even laborers on the locks and dams of the Upper Mississippi River faced dangers and undoubtedly perceived the river much differently than the political leaders celebrating the completion of a new nine-foot channel.

Despite the duality of associations, the rivers unified as well as separated. By the nineteenth century, Russia and the United States were crafting national identities that unified populations by drawing upon the historical memory of the Volga and Mississippi. As each country sought distinguishing characteristics to celebrate, the rivers with all their attendant mythology, folklore, prose, poetry, art, and song offered a rich repository in which to shape a national narrative. For Imperial Russia, through art, the Volga was part of a trilogy of symbols that included the bordering steppes and the onion-shaped dome of the Russian Orthodox Church. (The Volga as seen from the vantage point of the Russian village was another traditional Russian portrait.) For the United States, the Mississippi symbolized a frontier, where free agents such as the flatboatmen, realized a life free from convention. "Mother Volga" and "Old Man River" each became a source of national pride while at the same time aided in both countries' drive to modernize. The unique riverscape of each became a cause to celebrate as the rivers assumed iconic status. With imagery ranging from the pastoral to utilitarian, Russian and American populations early on reconciled the duality of the rivers. Steamboats not only altered the riverine habitat as snags were removed and riverbank forests cut down but also became part of the growing mythology of the river anchored in an earlier pastoralism. The twin images persist as both rivers are still depicted as nineteenth-century icons while increasingly becoming engineered rivers—modern-day super bargeways.

Using rivers as a starting point, however, brings into question what is historically important or significant. By viewing early-twentieth-century histories of the United States and Soviet Union, through the vantage point of the Mississippi and Volga Rivers, a different story emerges than the one steeped in political history or limited to social histories of the era. By the 1920s, engineers and political leaders in the Soviet Union and United States, like their predecessors, perceived the rivers as avenues to modernization. For the Soviet Union, the dream of linking Moscow to the Volga, first envisioned by Peter the Great in the 1700s, became a reality in 1937. Through a series of locks and dams, river barges traveled from Astrakhan to Moscow six months out of the year. For the United States, constructing the nine-foot channel on the Upper Mississippi River had been a long-standing dream as "improvements" to the river began in the early 1800s. By the late 1930s, agricultural goods from the Upper Mississippi could be shipped economically to the Gulf Coast. Contemporary histories in the 1930s focused on the engineering successes of each project, extolling the technological prowess each country demonstrated. In addition, credit was placed upon the governments of each that facilitated these projects and others. To the Soviets, only a communist system with a centralized economy could successfully facilitate major hydro-projects. To American political leaders, only a democracy could undertake these engineering marvels. Always part of the each country's national narrative, the rivers were later incorporated into a Cold War rhetoric that defined each nation for fifty years.

What is missing, however, from the narratives is that in both instances the outcome for each river was the same. Instead of free-flowing rivers, a series of slack water ponds dotted the riverscapes with environmental consequences for the Volga and Mississippi. From the perspective of the rivers, political ideology mattered little. The bigger story is the one about the health of riverine environments, regardless of rhetoric. Granted, major rivers have always served utilitarian purposes, and river traffic—whether birchbark canoes, rafts, steamships, or barges—on the Mississippi and Volga Rivers has been present since humans arrived. But in the twentieth century, the scale of use changed dramatically. With the aid of technology to enlarge channels, build navigational locks, and ensure an even depth for barges, the utility of the rivers entered a new dimension; one that affected habitat, water quality, and species. These consequences will have long-lasting effects that will shape human history in all its dimensions.

Yet while there have been numerous books recounting the history of major rivers, few, if any, have viewed the past from the comparative perspective of two major rivers from pre-modern times to the twentieth century. Those that have, such as Tricia Cusack's work, placed each river in the context of the nineteenth century and the relationship between riverscapes and national identity, and Peter Coates's work did not include the Volga and Mississippi in his vignettes of five lesser-known rivers. Many noteworthy individual river histories have been written with landmark texts such as Mark Cioc's work on the Rhine River, or the forthcoming scholarship of David Pietz as he reveals the role of the Yellow River in China's long history, or more commercial texts, such as Peter Ackroyd's work on the Thames, to name a few. But these works examine a single river without the comparative analysis that chronicles similarities and reveals certain constants that rivers have played in the past. By comparing these two major rivers, a dialectic emerges that can be applied to other river systems that demonstrates the connections between ideology and nature, power and state control. In summary, several themes surfaced that might be applicable in understanding other major river systems.

First, each river is enshrined in the collective memory through mythology, folklore, and song. Second, the rivers persisted in the historical memory through the nation making of the nineteenth century. Both the Volga and Mississippi Rivers contributed to Russia's and the United States' emergent national narrative with evidence of each river's iconic status found in art, prose, poetry, and song. Earlier renditions of the rivers whether through mythology, folklore, or the arts, were enlisted to serve the modern nation-state. Third, the rivers revealed the gaps in race and class through the lens of labor and disease. Several laboring classes (African slaves, the burlaki, and frontiersmen) all experienced the river differently than their counterparts and those more economically advantaged. Fourth, as modernization became the rallying cry in the twentieth century, the rivers were a critical part in realizing the modern nation-state whether through navigation and/or hydropower. Case studies of the Moscow-Volga Canal and the Upper Mississippi River locks and dams are testimonies to twentieth-century modernization. Yet even as the rivers are harnessed, bridled, and subdued—becoming part of each nation's modernization ethos—past images of the rivers were drafted into use as the Mississippi and Volga evolved into the engineered rivers we see today. The duality of the rivers persists as both are icons of a revered past and symbols of a dynamic future. Fifth, in revealing the history of the rivers and their similarities, the competing ideologies of the United States and Soviet Union mattered little. Despite political rhetoric extolling each nation's hydro-projects—constructed to serve either a greater democratic or socialist state—differing political ideologies were inconsequential. The outcome for both rivers was the same as each was rerouted, bridled, harnessed, and ultimately, subdued. Sixth, both rivers' development became models for export as hydro-projects in the 1930s became the symbols for modernization in developing countries. While not universal, these themes may be found when studying other major river systems, adding to a growing body of knowledge regarding race and class, the role of historical memory, nation-making and national identity, modernization and the environment.

Now a few words about methodology—in telling a story about two major rivers, the problem of scale and sources challenged this project from the beginning and I beg the reader's pardon for any omissions. In trying to chronicle as complete a history as possible, I have drawn from multiple disciplines and worked with both print and visual culture. The disciplines I relied upon most include history, archaeology, art history, architectural history, political science, and geography. But despite including such a vast range of subject areas, there are omissions. No one better than the author realizes that greater attention to Native American settlements along the Mississippi or the work of geographers on the Volga, for example, would have resulted in a more thorough account. But given the time span covered and the importance of a balanced coverage, choices were made about what to include and leave out. The more immediate goal, however, of broadening our understanding of the past through the perspective of two major river systems was met through a diverse array of sources. For the early chapters, primary sources included folklore, mythology, travelers' accounts, and archaeological findings. Beginning with chapter 2, sources in print and visual culture were used with artwork and photographs cited. In the use of artwork portraying each river and the surrounding landscape, these images became part of the river's past and integral to the historical memory of each country. So by the 1930s, the images, or waterscapes—the historical building blocks—were part of the story that enhanced the transformation of each river.

In addition to visual culture, primary print sources included memoirs by a host of actors, such as Gulag survivors, writers, and political leaders, whose lives intersected with either the Volga or Mississippi Rivers. Secondary sources, such as those found in a number of archives (among them the National Archives at Kansas City, the Smithsonian, Russian State Library, Dmitrov History and Regional Museum and Archives, and the Museum of the Moscow-Volga Canal, University of Wisconsin–La Crosse Archives, and Winona State University) included newspapers, testimonies and bureaucratic reports published at the Moscow-Volga Canal work camps, 1930s promotional publications by the Soviet Union, engineering bulletins by the U.S. Army Corps of Engineers, and newspaper articles from a number of small communities located along the Upper Mississippi River. These were the principal sources for chapters 3 through 5. Supplementing the sources were several oral history interviews with Russian scholars who either researched the Moscow-Volga canal or had family members affected firsthand by its construction. Secondary sources by prominent scholars in Russian and U.S. history, cultural studies, art history, architectural history, archaeology, and political science were used throughout the text.

In an effort to capture the most pressing themes in a chronological framework, the chapters were divided as follows. In chapter 1, the early history of each river was explored through the lens of select Native Americans that lived in the Mississippi River Valley along with the first European explorers to travel the Mississippi. (Given the multiple Native American tribes that lived in the river basin, only a few were chosen to represent these early intersections with the river.) When looking at the Native American experience, mythology, folklore, and archaeological findings were used. For the Volga, early mythologies from the Kievan period along with accounts from groups, such as Arab and Viking traders, were examined. From the folklore and mythologies generated by these early riverine experiences, the Mississippi and Volga Rivers became intrinsic to the cultural and historical past. A brief physical geography of each river was recounted in the chapter.

In chapter 2, each river's role in the emerging national narratives of the nineteenth century was explored. The literature is dense regarding the representative role of landscape with contributions from scholars such as Denis Cosgrove, Martin Warnke, and Simon Schama. The chapter utilized their arguments (and others) in illustrating each river's part in advancing a nationalism that touted a unique, exceptional landscape. Through literary texts, music, and art the earlier celebratory images of "Mother Volga" and "Old Man River," also known as "Father of Waters," were expressed to serve burgeoning national identities. But there were differences between the portrayals of each river. In the case of the Mississippi, the river was memorialized not only for a scenic beauty, one that rivaled and often surpassed the Alps, but as a liberator. The American artist George Caleb Bingham popularized this view of the Mississippi with his well-known works, "The Jolly Flatboatmen" and "Raftsmen Playing Cards." In both paintings, the stereotypical American frontiersman as rugged individual was celebrated. In contrast, while the Volga was noted for its aesthetic value, with comparisons to the Rhine and other major rivers, the river was also seen as an oppressor. One of the most famous paintings in nineteenth-century Russia, Ilya Repin's "The Barge Haulers," depicted a world where the Volga was part of the tyranny that the burlaki faced. Still, both rivers, evidenced by print and visual culture, contributed to the national narratives that emerged in the nineteenth century and distinguished Russia and the United States from other nations.

Entering the twentieth century, chapter 3 examined the discourse regarding nature and the subsequent consequences for the Volga and Mississippi Rivers, offering a context for the case studies to follow in chapters 4 and 5. Throughout the industrialized West, political leaders and the new league of professionals, including engineers and planners, were mesmerized by the potential through technology to reshape the natural world. In the United States, multiple purpose water projects become one of the means to conquer new regions of the country. In Lenin's Soviet Union, electrification became the panacea and symbol for "catching up" with the industrialized West. The literature during this period of utopian visions was rich with references on how to enlist nature in developing an industrialized, modernized society. Harnessing the Volga and Mississippi Rivers was one of the principal means by which this modernization occurred. By looking at the political writings of Lenin, Trotsky, Franklin Delano Roosevelt, David Lilienthal, and other well-known American and Russian political thinkers, the similarities between the two nations was striking. Further support can be found in the exchange between the Russian and American community of engineers and scientists. (One of the first major hydropower projects, Dneprostroi, was constructed through the assistance of American engineers.) Chapter 3 articulates the shared vision of modernization and how the vision subsumed differing political ideologies, despite rhetoric to the contrary. For both rivers, however, the outcome was the same.

In chapters 4 and 5, the story of two major engineering projects on the upper reaches of the Volga and Mississippi Rivers is retold. These projects, the Moscow-Volga Canal, a 128-kilometer-long canal linking Moscow to the Volga River, and the Mississippi River Channel Project with its construction of twenty-eight locks and dams, were undertaken in the 1930s. Both illustrated the technological prowess of each country as major navigation channels were constructed and additional power sources were acquired. But the projects revealed more than engineering feats as the nationalist rhetoric surrounding both touted achievements in labor, providing jobs for unskilled, often illiterate workers, and securing a future for the disenfranchised, to name two. In the Soviet Union, the Moscow-Volga Canal was one of the hallmarks in Stalin's second Five Year Plan and the project was a showpiece with its own journals, theater, artists, and architects. In the United States, the locks and dams were built during the Depression Era by the Corps of Engineers using New Deal public employment. Similar to the Moscow-Volga Canal, every phase of the project's construction was documented with thousands of photographs, journals, and news accounts publicizing the undertaking. The symbolism of transforming these major rivers was not lost on the promoters of each project. For example, one of the journals for the Mississippi River project was called "Old Man River" and upon completion of the Moscow-Volga Canal, journalists declared that "Mother Volga was constrained." One of the ongoing themes will be the persistence of river mythology, encased in the ongoing national narrative, enhancing the engineered transformation of both rivers while also keeping alive the treasured aesthetics of each river.

In ending the text, the epilogue briefly chronicled the subsequent history of the Volga and Mississippi Rivers up to the present. In retelling this history, the rivers were placed within the broader context of hydro-modernization and how what happened to the rivers in the 1930s became a model for export throughout the developing world. The consequences of this on a local and global scale were discussed. In conclusion, seeing the past through the prism of the Volga and Mississippi Rivers continues to enlighten and enrich our understanding of history as I hope the following chapters will reveal.

Notes

1. *The New York Times,* 21 July 2013, 1, 19.

2. Eugene S. Hunn, *Nch'i-Wàna, "The Big River": Mid-Columbia Indians and Their Land* (Seattle: University of Washington Press, 1990), 91.

3. For a discussion of the popularity of the Rivers of America series see Nicolaas Mink, "A Narrative for Nature: Constance Lindsay Skinner and the Making of Rivers of America" *Environmental History* 1, no. 4 (October 2006): 751–774; Christopher Morris, *The Big Muddy: An Environmental History of the Mississippi and Its Peoples from Hernando de Soto to Hurricane Katrina* (Oxford: Oxford University Press, 2012); Mark Cioc, *The Rhine: An Eco-biography, 1815–2000* (Seattle: University of Washington Press, 2002).

4. Gordon Cooper, *Along the Great Rivers* (New York: Philosophical Library, 1953), 11.

5. Martin Reuss, *Designing the Bayous: The Control of Water in the Atchafalaya Basin, 1800–1995* (College Station: Texas A&M University Press, 2004); Paul C. Pitzer, *Grand Coulee: Harnessing a Dream* (Pullman: Washington State University Press, 1994); Marq de Villiers, *Down the Volga: A Journey Through Mother Russia in a Time of Troubles* (New York: Viking, 1992); Ray A. March, *River in Ruin: the Story of the Carmel River* (Lincoln: University of Nebraska Press, 2012); Philip L. Fradkin, *A River No More: The Colorado River and the West* (New York: Alfred A. Knopf, 1981). This is only a sampling of the numerous texts on rivers with certain rivers such as the Hudson, Amazon, Mississippi, to name a few, having multiple publications from varying perspectives.

6. Fred Pearce, *When the Rivers Run Dry: Journeys into the Heart of the World's Water Crisis* (Toronto: Key Porter Books, 2006); Steven Solomon, *Water: The Epic Struggle for Wealth, Power, and Civilization* (New York: HarperCollins, 2010); Patrick McCully, *Silenced Rivers: The Ecology and Politics of Large Dams* (London: Zed Books, 2001).

7. Sara B. Pritchard, *Confluence: The Nature of Technology and the Remaking of the Rhône* (Cambridge: Harvard University Press, 2011); Randall Dills, "The River Neva and the Imperial Façade: Culture and Environment in Nineteenth Century St. Petersburg Russia" (Ph.D. diss., University of Illinois at Urbana-Champaign, 2010), viii.

8. Tricia Cusack, *Riverscapes and National Identities* (Syracuse: Syracuse University Press, 2010).

9. Peter Coates, *A Story of Six Rivers: History, Culture and Ecology* (London: Reaktion Books, 2013), 22–23, 27.

10. Catherine Evtuhov, *Portrait of a Russian Province: Economy, Society, and Civilization in Nineteenth-Century Nizhnii Novgorod* (Pittsburgh: University of Pittsburgh Press, 2011), xvi, 36–38.

11. Robert E. Jones, *Bread Upon the Waters: The St. Petersburg Grain Trade and the Russian Economy, 1703–1811* (Pittsburg: University of Pittsburgh Press, 2013), 222.

12. Walter Johnson, *River of Dark Dreams: Slavery and Empire in the Cotton Kingdom* (Cambridge: The Belknap Press of Harvard University Press, 2013); Thomas C. Buchanan, *Black Life on the Mississippi: Slaves, Free Blacks, and the Western Steamboat World* (Chapel Hill: University of North Carolina, 2004); Lee Joan Skinner, "Identity, Engagement, and the Space of the River in *Cumandà,*" in *Troubled Water: Rivers in Latin American Imagination,* ed. Elizabeth M. Pettinaroli and Ana Maria Mutis, *Hispanic Issues On Line* 12 (2013), 131. Web.

13. Richard White, *The Organic Machine: The Remaking of the Columbia River* (New York: Hill and Wang, 1995), x; Coates, *A Story of Six Rivers*, 22; Donald Worster, *Rivers of Empire: Water, Aridity, and the Growth of the American West* (New York: Oxford University Press, 1985).

14. Multiple studies regarding the origins and characteristics of nationalism are available with leading works including Benedict Anderson, *Imagined Communities: Reflections on the Origin and Spread of Nationalism* (London: Verso Books, 1983); Ernest Gellner, *Nations and Nationalism* (Ithaca: Cornell University Press, 1983); Anthony Smith, *National Identity* (London: Penguin, 1991); Smith, "'The Land and its People': Reflections on Artistic Identification in an Age of Nations and Nationalism," *Nations and Nationalism* 19, no. 1 (2013): 87–106.

15. R.H. Boyle, *The Hudson River* (New York: W.W. Norton & Co., 1969). For an example of the perceived Hudson River distinctness, see the quote by American naturalist John Burroughs on page 62.

16. For an excellent discussion of Russians' changing ideas about nature in the nineteenth century, see Christopher Ely, *This Meager Nature Landscape and National Identity in Imperial Russia* (DeKalb: Northern Illinois University Press, 2002); Jane T. Costlow, *Heart-Pine Russia: Walking and Writing the Nineteenth-Century Forest* (Ithaca: Cornell University Press, 2012); Alon Confino's work, *The Nation as a Local Metaphor: Wurttemberg, Imperial Germany, and National Memory, 1871–1918* (Chapel Hill: University of North Carolina Press, 1997) convincingly argues that only through the symbol of the *heimat*, roughly translated as homeland, and its integration of certain aspects of German nature, was a common identity for the German Empire solidified; Marco Armiero, *A Rugged Nation: Mountains and the Making of Modern Italy* (Cambridge: The White Horse Press, 2011).

 CHAPTER 1

The Early Years

Rivers have always served utilitarian purposes and history is rich with examples of rivers as highways, boundaries, irrigators, and ultimately, unifiers. Mythologies beautified these pedestrian roles with accounts ranging from a river's birth to its central place in the afterlife. In recent centuries, rivers assumed another function as they contributed to emergent national narratives.[1] For the Mississippi and Volga Rivers their niche in the historical memory is not only through myths but later revealed through epithets. The Mississippi River, known as the "Wicked River" to the early voyageurs, challenged those who tried to navigate an unknowable geography with hidden sandbars and snags, all subordinate to an unpredictable flow. At times swift moving, submerging all in its way, while in other instances the river became the slow, lazy Mississippi. For the Volga, "Mother Volga," is a sobriquet that persists as the river with its surrounding rich fertile plains sustained the population.[2] Although a more nurturing image and certainly not as threatening as the "Wicked River," the Volga also tested the skills of navigators with the river's shallows and uneven depth.[3]

Whether nurturer or tormentor, however, both rivers conveyed impressions of power captured through the tales of travelers and folklore. When the Jesuit missionary and explorer, Father Jacques Marquette traveled downstream the Mississippi in 1673, looking for the river's outlet, he described the confluence of the Missouri and Mississippi Rivers in the following passage: "[S]ailing gently down a beautiful, still, clear water, we heard the noise of a rapid into which we were about to fall. I have seen nothing more frightful; a mass of large trees, entire, with branches, real floating islands, came rushing from the mouth of the river Pekitanoui (Missouri), so impetuously, that we could not, without great danger, expose ourselves to pass across. The agitation was so great that the water was all muddy and could not get clear."[4]

The Volga, in turn, which "swells like the Egyptian Nile in the summer," was immortalized in a Russian folktale. In admiration of the river's prowess, the folktale recounts the tale of two river sisters, Vazuza and Volga, and their quarrel over which "is the wiser, the stronger, and the more worthy of high respect." To resolve this, they decide whichever one reaches the Caspian Sea first is the winner. The Volga, through her calm demeanor, triumphs, as the following passage reveals: "When Volga awoke, she set off neither slowly nor hurriedly, but with just befitting speed. At Zubtsof she came up with Vazuza. So threatening was her mien, that Vazuza was frightened, declared herself to be Volga's younger sister, and besought Volga to take her in her arms and bear her to the Caspian Sea."[5]

Contributing to the iconic status of these rivers is their size and topography. According to early French accounts, the name Mississippi comes from the Algonquin, *Missi* meaning great and *sepe* a river. First-time visitors, the Talon brothers, during their trip with the La Salle expedition in 1698, remarked upon the Mississippi's size with a claim that its width was at least two musket shots. For comparison purposes, they described another river in the area as "about a musket-shot wide." Length and course also define the river. Once called, "the crookedest river in the world," the Mississippi is the longest river on the North American continent with a length of 3,705 kilometers from its source in northern Minnesota (Lake Itasca) to its mouth in the Louisiana Delta. Overshadowing its length, however, is the size of the river basin as it includes 4.76 million square kilometers, making it the third largest watershed in the world. Cutting through a diverse terrain, the river begins in the north woods of Minnesota, winds through midwestern farmland, and ends in the hot, subtropical Gulf of Mexico. The habitats the river supports are equally rich including wetland, open-water, and floodplain; all providing sustenance for numerous fish species and wildlife.[6]

Three major divisions further identify the river and are referred to as the headwaters, the Upper Mississippi River Basin, and the Lower Mississippi River. The headwaters begin at Lake Itasca, flowing southward to an area by Minneapolis, Minnesota, where the Upper Mississippi River Basin begins and runs downstream to Cairo, Illinois, where the Ohio River empties into the Mississippi. Finally, the Lower Mississippi begins at Cairo and ends in the Gulf of Mexico. In addition to the Ohio River, the other major tributary is the Missouri River, which joins the Mississippi near St. Louis, Missouri. Each of the divisions are bordered by very different landscapes—in the north, the Mississippi winds through bluffs that often dwarf the river's course; in the middle, the Mississippi runs through wider, open expanses, once heavily forested as part of the Yazoo-Mississippi Floodplain; and in the lower, southern end, the vegetation is thicker with swamps and the impressive delta.

The Volga shares similar defining characteristics as it courses through diverse terrain—a central part of multiple landscapes, mimicking Russia's rich cultural diversity. Like the Mississippi, early impressions of the river's size reveal surprise. When in 1253, Friar William of Rubruck saw the mouth of the Volga (also known as Etilia), he claimed "this is the largest river I have ever seen" and that the lower reaches of the river were "almost twice as large as the

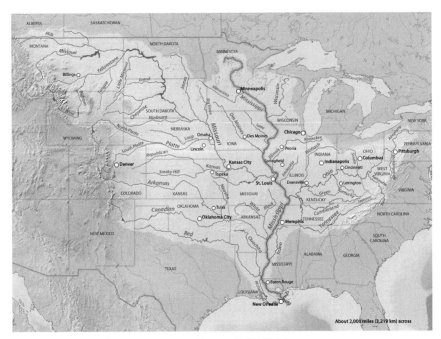

Figure 1.1. Map of Mississippi River. *Source:* DEMIS Mapserver.

river of Dalmietta" (also known as the Lower Nile) and "four times wider than the Seine."[7] The Volga River is the largest river in Europe with a length of 3,700 kilometers.

Starting in the Valdai Hills (located northwest of Moscow), the river flows in a southeastern direction with one turn northward before returning to a southeastern flow and empties near Astrakhan; bridging the cultures of Europe and Eurasia. The Valdai Hills also house the headwaters of the Dnieper and Western Dvina Rivers, along with some smaller rivers, but the Volga River Basin covers the greater area with a watershed that extends more than 1,450 million square kilometers or 8 percent of the country's territory including 151,000 rivers and brooks. Of the 2,600 rivers to flow into the Volga, the principal tributaries include the Kama, Samara, Oka, and Vetluga Rivers. The Volga is also divided into three parts: the upper, middle, and lower. The Upper Volga begins at the source near the village of Volgaverkhovye in the Valdai Hills and continues until the present-day Rybinsk Dam, specifically at the confluence of the Sheksna River. Below the Rybinsk Dam, the Middle Volga flows to the site of the dam that impounds the Zhiguli Reservoir where the Lower Volga begins and subsequently empties into the Caspian Sea. The terrain of the river basin ranges from a forested zone of southern taiga in the north to forest-steppe to the arid delta area in the south, supporting a heterogeneous ecology. Similar to

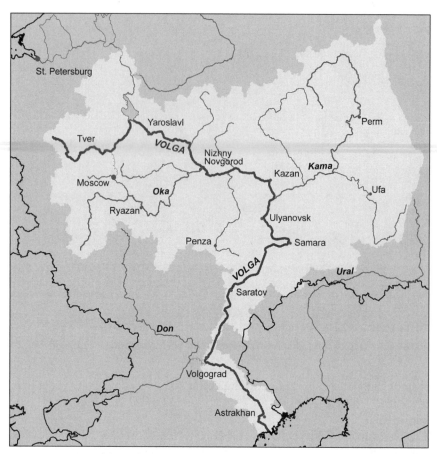

Figure 1.2. Map of the Volga River system. Created by Karl Musser based on USGS data.

the Mississippi, the habitat sustained by the river includes seventy-four species of fish that contribute to a large commercial fishing industry.

In introducing both rivers, parts of their entire basins will be discussed offering a glimpse of the diversity of each. For each river covered broad expanses—with histories distinct as their parts—and opened up the surrounding regions to vast trade networks. As major transportation arteries, the rivers were key to emergent cultures and the riverine environments were home to multiple cultures. But development along each river was uneven. For both, the upper reaches were slower to develop while the lower and middle regions saw populations living by the rivers earlier. In the case of the Volga, trade exposed the European West to the Asian East and the Baltic North to the Middle Eastern South. In later years, commerce went primarily from south to north while the Mississippi carried goods from north to south. Both rivers, however, were much more than trade routes. The Volga served multiple roles, including historical marker such as when Ivan IV, also known as Ivan the Terrible, unified Russia in 1552 by defeating the last Mongol stronghold on the Volga, thereby paving the way for a Russia beyond the Volga. A new frontier, and subsequently, a new chapter in Russian history, resulted as "beyond the Volga" conveyed an imagery and meaning familiar to all Russians. But the river also served as a line of retreat for shrinking empires such as the Khazar or as an avenue to invasion—and even disease—as the Mongols waited for the river to freeze before launching their attacks on empires west of the Volga, eventually bringing the dreaded plague. The Mississippi, in turn, represented a dividing line in the historical past. Empires, such as the Spanish and French, claimed lands either east or west of the Mississippi. Disease-ridden environments in the delta region also challenged early European settlers. Before the arrival of the Europeans, however, earlier cultures, such as the Winnebago, saw crossing the river as part of the journey to the afterlife much like the Egyptians who in their pilgrimage to the afterlife crossed the Nile. Thus in the historical memory, each river offered a landmark, a rallying point, by which to organize a history rich with a diversity representing nomadic and sedentary cultures.

For the Volga, however, its entry into the human past occurred long before the Mongol presence or the existence of a unified Russia under Ivan IV as the river supported a multiethnic culture with Arabs, Bulghars, Norsemen, Pechenegs, and Khazarites all relying upon the Volga as one of their most valued trade routes.[8] Thus by the dawn of the seventh century an array of nomadic and seminomadic cultures populated the Volga River Basin, all sustained by the river. For the Volga River Basin, one of the first prominent empires was the Khazar Khaganate. Established by the seventh century, the Khazars occupied an expanse ranging from the Ukraine to a large part of the steppe in South Russia with boundaries in the east as far as Kazakhstan and to the south into parts of Georgia. The empire evolved from a nomadic to urban culture, revealing a cosmopolitan environment with markets extending into the Middle East, Central Asia, and Northern Europe. Through the Volga River, trade was lucrative with furs such as marten, sable, and squirrel along with honey and other prized goods finding their way downstream to the Khazar capital of Itil, located at the Volga River estuary. By the eighth century, a brisk trade was established with Arab and Jewish merchants as they supplied exotic goods from the south in exchange for northern furs.[9] The Khazar Khaganate, which lasted until the tenth century, eventually controlled several other cultures living on the Volga who paid tribute to the Khaganate while benefitting from the Khazar trade network. For the Khazarites, their history mirrored others that evolved from a nomadic to agricultural and ultimately, an urban existence.[10] While groups living along the Volga, such as the Volga Bulghars, paid tribute to the

Khazar Empire, the empire was always subject to attacks by nomadic groups such as the Pechenegs and later, the Rus—both invaders looking for plunder from the rich trade network. In addition to the trade network, the Khazar Khaganate, by way of their location, protected other empires including the Byzantine by serving as a buffer to raiding nomadic groups, such as the Pechenegs. The Volga was central to these raids as the empire was most vulnerable in the winter when nomadic groups waited for the river to freeze and launch their attack while during summer months, the empire enjoyed freedom from the attacks.[11]

Lying above Khazaria, at the confluence of the Kamas and Volga Rivers was another empire, the Volga Bulghars. Established by the mid eighth century, the Bulghars monopolized the Middle Volga trade, and supplied the Khazar Empire with goods from the north—furs, wax, and honey—in return for silver. Immortalized by Ibn Fadlan, an Arab envoy from the Abbasid Caliphate in Baghdad, who traveled from Baghdad to visit the Bulghar king in 921 in what is today Tatarstan, his writings revealed an extensive trade network on the Volga linking cultures from Northern Europe to Central Asia to the Near East. His journey followed caravans traveling from Khwarazm located in Central Asia to the Volga River in contemporary Russia. Recording his visit—the purpose of which was never clear although believed in part to spread Islam—Ibn Fadlan described meeting the king who lived by the river Itil (an earlier name for the Volga). In recalling the location, Ibn Fadlan spoke "of a market, which takes place periodically, in which much precious merchandise is sold." For the Bulghars, while they practiced some agriculture and grazing, their primary income came from trade. During his stay, Ibn Fadlan also visited the Rus (descendants of Scandinavian tribes) who traveled down the Itil, encamping on the river for trade. The Rus had a particular interest in capturing the silver found in the dirhams that were circulating as a result of the Arab trade for furs. While Ibn Fadlan considered the Rus barbaric, he described their presence as such: "They come from their own country, moor their boats on the strand of the Itil, which is a great river, and build on its banks large houses out of wood." He also described their trading practices—reinforcing his perception of their barbaric ways—in which slaves were part of the trade.[12]

The Bulghar market oversaw the exchange of Central Asian silver goods and currency for the prized Northern Russia furs, amber, ivory, birch bark, and dried fish. At this time, trade along the Volga was so lucrative that accounts exist of a merchant in the eleventh century who not only had warehouses on the Volga in the Bulghar region but another one in India. The Volga was the means to all of this. As an integral part of early Russian history, the Volga facilitated an internal commerce that contributed to a diversity that overshadowed any one identity. This diversity, in turn, has characterized Russia throughout its history up to the twenty-first century when Russia is still recognized as a multiethnic empire. From the beginning the river was a lens through which to understand Russia.[13]

Meanwhile, far to the north of the Khazar, the empire later known as Kievan Rus was emerging. Giving more credence to the role of rivers—at least in the extant literature—Kievan Rus had its origins in the Valdai Hills, known in the *Primary Chronicle* as Okovskii Forest, where the Dvina, Dnieper, and Volga Rivers all begin. In *The Primary Chronicle,* called by its authors *The Tale of Bygone Years,* and written around 1040 to 1118, the Volga is described as a river that "rises in this same forest but flows to the east, and discharges through seventy mouths into the Caspian Sea." (During the same period, the Mississippi River Basin, near present-day St. Louis, was also experiencing the birth of a short-lived empire, Cahokia, which boasted an urban area rivaling the size of London from C.E. 1050 to 1200.) In this northern part of present-day Russia, however, the initial settlers were eastern Slavs who lived around the various river valleys that flowed into the Dnieper River. The Vikings began to arrive in the eighth century attracted by the prospect of northern Russian rivers to establish trade networks. Drawn by the trade that the Slavs enjoyed with the Bulghars and the silver found in the Arab dirhams from southern trade routes, the Vikings began exploring northern sites beginning with Lake Ladoga. Dirham hoards have been found near the site indicating the extent of the Arab trade from the southern reaches of the Volga. The Vikings became a presence in the area, using the riverine highways of the Dnieper, and later the Volga, to launch attacks against the Byzantine and Khazar Empires. But as Ibn Fadlan observed, they were also part of the broader trade network, supplying the Bulghars with furs, as seen in his characterization of the Bulghars.[14] Eventually, the Slavs and Vikings allied, and with cultural elements from each, the well-known Kievan Rus emerged by the second half of the ninth century with its locus shifting to the south and the city of Kiev. Its borders included the "Baltic Sea to the north, the steppe bordering the Black Sea in the south and from the Carpathian Mountains in the west almost to the Volga in the East." One of the cultural capitals of Eastern Europe, Kievan Rus is "still regarded as the ancient seat of Russian culture." Included in Kievan Rus was the city of Novgorod, which through the Volkhov River gave residents access to the Volga and subsequently, the Caspian Sea. A commercial hub, Novgorod's trade afforded Kievan Rus with exposure to a vast trade network.[15]

Kievan Rus, however, was not without threats from its neighbors. A common occurrence throughout the ancient world was the plunder of urban areas by nomadic groups. In the case of Kievan Rus, after Prince Sviatoslav defeated the city of Itil (near present-day Astrakhan) in the late tenth century thereby securing entry into Khazars' trade routes, the Pechenegs wrested control from Kievan Rus. The Pechenegs were attracted by the rich trade in furs, particularly those from the northern region and their prized fox furs. But nomadic groups also contributed to the cultures they invaded as in the case of the Pech-enegs, who through their presence along the Volga introduced the unjointed snaffle—a horse rein—to the Western world. The Pechenegs, however, were not the only threat to Kievan Rus in the eleventh century as the Kipchaks, also known as the Cumans or Polovtsy, were another invading nomadic group in the area.[16]

Concomitant with trade goods and technological advances was a growing body of mythology and folklore regarding each major river in Kievan Rus. Central to the culture, stories about the Volga included the tale of the river sisters, Vazuza and Volga, and their rivalry in reaching the Caspian Sea first. Still another one, "The Metamorphosis of the Dnieper, the Volga, and the Dvina," explains how the three transformed from earlier human forms to rivers.[17] In *The Primary Chronicle*, more folklore acknowledging the importance of the Volga and other Russian rivers can be found. An accounting of Kievan Rus, thereby legitimizing the empire and in the words of one scholar "providing a vision," the *Chronicle* was written by a number of authors with annual excerpts dating from 852. In the beginning of the text, called the prolegomenon, the author states "This is the tale of bygone years from whence came the Russian land, who first ruled in Kiev, and from which source the Russian land had its beginning." Similar to other creation stories, the prolegomenon tells of a flood and after the waters subside, Noah's three sons, Shem, Ham, and Japeth, separate the earth amongst themselves. The first mention of the Volga is here as "To the lot of Japeth fell the northern and the western sections … and he likewise acquired dominion over other rivers, among them the Desna, the Pripet', the Dvina, the Volkhov, and the Volga, which flows eastward into the portion of Shem."[18]

In another Kievan-era story, "The Lay of Igor's Campaign," considered by many to be the best Russian writing during this period, the power of the Don and Volga Rivers are recognized through homage to one of the Kievan princes: "Great prince Vsevolod! Do you not intend to come from far away to watch over your paternal golden throne? For you, with the oars (of your fleet), can scatter the river Volga into droplets. With the helmets (of your army) you can pour out the river Don."[19] Using the rivers as an indicator of strength will be a common refrain in Russian history persisting up to Stalin's time when he touted the Soviet Union's greatness by reference to its constraint of the Volga. But the Volga served as a reference point in other instances as it represented a political boundary for tenth-century Kievan Russia, under Sviatoslav, with borders extending from the "Volga to Dnieper to Danube Rivers and from Kiev to Novgorod."[20] These stories reflected the importance of the Volga as it was part of a trade network included in the Northern Hanseatic League in which the bustling city of Novgorod exchanged goods by way of the rivers connecting the city to the north and south. Mentioned earlier, nearby Novgorod were the Volga headwaters, which ultimately gave Novgorod access to the Caspian Sea. The Volga waterway was one of the keys to the economic success of Kievan Rus—a role the river repeated in succeeding empires.[21]

But the landscape of Russian history changed with the arrival of the Mongols, who radically altered the trajectory of Russian history, occupying lands once part of Kievan Rus, the Bulgar Empire, and territory farther south. Later called the Golden Horde, the Mongols affected the emerging Russian Empire in several ways. For purposes here, the most significant change was their reliance upon the Volga to expand trade—exposing the Kievan Empire to new cultures along with exotic goods. The Mongol conquest occurred quickly. In 1237, they crushed the Bulghar capital of Bolgar near present-day Kazan. The capital, located at the confluence of the Kama and Volga Rivers, was extensive according to medieval standards as the city covered an estimated 500 hectares compared to Kiev with 380 hectares. The Mongols went on to conquer other Volga populations, including the Kipchaks, so by 1237 in a singular winter campaign that included crossing the icy Volga, all those living in the Volga basin had been defeated. After these victories the Mongols turned their attention to Kievan Rus, embarking on a winter campaign. Brutal in their submission of native populations, the Mongols occupied much of the Volga region until 1552 when Ivan IV defeated the Tatar capital, Kazan.[22]

During the Mongols' tenure, commerce persisted with "the Volga, chief water highway of the era." Some cities on the trade route, such as Bolgar, were rebuilt and a revitalized, if not expanded; trade began with china and celadon from China and pottery from Iran. With trade, a number of cities appeared along the Volga, including Sarai, Astrakhan, and Kazan. After gaining control, the Mongols divided up their conquered territories according to the rivers and the Volga River Basin fell under the rule of Batu Khan. Once in power, he built the capital of Sarai during the 1240s, near where the Volga empties into the Caspian. (His successor, Berke, later moved the capital to another location on the Lower Volga but kept the name, Sarai.) In archaeological findings, both locations reveal rich urban environments and evidence of "the dynamic commercial contacts with the neighboring European regions, and with the Oriental areas in particular." Throughout this early history, the Volga facilitated the rise of a Eurasian market, a preliminary to contemporary global markets.[23]

When Ivan IV finally routed the Mongols by capturing Kazan in 1552, and within a few years took over the Khanate of Astrakhan in the Volga Delta, he expanded Muscovite Russia's borders to the south and east. The Volga becomes further etched in the historical memory as local legends about Ivan's final victory over the Mongols declare that he whipped the Volga into submission as his men almost drowned trying to cross the river. According to the story, Ivan called out to the river:

Don't be stupid, river, calm down, or it'll be worse for you! The Volga did not abate, but raged worse than before. Send the executioner here? Yelled the tsar, I'll teach you a lesson! The executioner arrived, a mighty man—and the tsar ordered him to whip the river with his knout, to teach it not to rebel against the tsar and his army. The executioner took his knowt, rolled up the sleeves of his red shirt, took a run, and as he whipped the Volga, the blood sprayed upwards a yard in height, and a bloody wound appeared in the water, as thick as a finger. The waves in the river went calmer, but the tsar yelled, "Show no mercy, strike harder!"[24]

After one more flogging, the river was subdued and all Ivan's men successfully crossed the Volga. But the legend does not end here as the river is remembered further:

And now, they say, at the spot where the crossing took place, you can see three bloody wounds on the Volga, especially on a summer evening, if you look into the sun when it is setting behind the hills.[25]

With complete control of the Middle and Lower Volga region, trade grew and expanded in these new directions. Dominating the Volga, Russian merchants could be found in Astrakhan and the eastern cities established by the Mongols. The trade was lucrative with furs and salt remaining main exports for Russia while exotic goods were imported from the East. The Volga and Don were the principal routes for the trade that grew after Ivan unified the country. For the Volga, the main commercial hubs were Iaroslavl and Nizhni Novgorod. Yet despite what was a brisk commercial trade, travel and shipping on the Volga remained unchanged for the next two and a half centuries. Until the arrival of steam, a typical trip down the Volga from Nizhni Novgorod might not begin until the middle of July as ships would become grounded if they left before the river swelled with the inflow of the northern tributaries. But even after waiting, ships still became grounded as the account of Adam Olearius, a German traveler in seventeenth-century Russia, relays: "[W]hen the wind subsided somewhat, we lifted anchor, hoping to make better progress this day. However, we had hardly gone a quarter of a league when we were grounded again, at Teliatinskii Island, and soon again, at Sobshchinskii Island. On the latter, a large ship had been grounded during high water [sic], and it still stood there, intact. Here we remained nine full hours, until the ship got afloat again."[26] Throughout Olearius's trip down the Volga, they encountered shallow places and on one particularly challenging day, they traveled only a half league. On that day, Olearius said all he heard was "Pull! Row! Back!"[27]

Complementing Olearius's account is one by a British observer, Laurence Oliphant, who also visited the fair at Nizhni Novgorod in 1852 and upon his trip downstream remarked upon the Volga's threatening shallows, called pericartes. According to Oliphant, who believed the Volga was the most challenging European river to navigate, the shallows not only prolonged the voyage but traffic on the river could result in accidents with ships colliding and other navigational perils. Yet Oliphant recognized the beauty of the river as he remarked "nothing could exceed the magnificence of the Volga, as it stretched away like some inland sea, which the strong breeze, as it hurried us down its mighty stream, rippled into tiny waves."[28]

Adding to the trials of river travel was the fear of meeting with brigands along the way. Before starting his voyage, Olearius mentions the warning he received regarding the pillaging Cossacks. But piracy and banditry had long been associated with the river as Ivan IV, after routing the Mongols, had to contend with piracy on the lower reaches of the Volga. Up until the nineteenth century piracy and banditry were linked to the Volga. Only with the arrival of steamships and tourism did this perception—often rooted in reality—change. Peasants, displaced by economics, politics, or plague outbreaks, migrated to the Volga basin where their livelihoods depended upon the river through fishing or shipping. But in some instances they "joined the robber bands that infested that region."[29] In one well-known Russian folk lyric, an orphan who lived near Astrakhan talks about his early life and becoming a robber. He includes the Volga in the following verse:

> Tell us, tell us, orphan, who bore you?
> My own Mama bore me, an orphan,
> I was nursed and fed by Mother Volga,
> I was brought up by a light boat of white willow,
> I was rocked by nana and mama, the fast waves,
> I was raised by the strange far-off land of Astraxan,
> And from this land I went to become a robber.[30]

Cossacks, living along the lower stretches of the river, were also associated with piracy, as one song about Ermak Timofeevich, also known for his part in the conquest of Siberia, reveals. In the song, Ermak tells his fellow Cossacks "We cannot stay in Astrakhan, If we stay on the Volga, we shall be called pirates." Regardless of which groups committed acts of piracy, from the tsars' perspective, the further away from the center of power in Moscow, the more likely the occurrence of bandit attacks as overseeing the empire's broad expanse was a challenge to all the tsars. The Volga, similar to the Mississippi, often provided freedom for one population at the expense of another.[31]

Threats also came from neighboring countries. In the late 1560s, Turkey looked with interest at Astrakhan and even sent an expedition to the area with the idea of building a canal from the Don River to the Volga (an idea that Peter the Great also tried in the 1700s and was realized during the Soviet Union). Unaware of the topographical challenges, the Turkish force soon gave up and returned home but not without Russia's notice. The Russians, in turn, remained sensitive to Turkey's political ambitions for the next century and the importance of the Volga River. In the words of one scholar, Turkey's "'Astrakhan' campaign represented another act in the 'drama' of the struggle for mastery of the Volga, and as such its importance is undeniable."[32]

Thus by the late sixteenth century, the Volga River was an integral part of Muscovite Russia's history. Not only did the river contribute economically and strategically to Russia but the river bridged a historical memory that includes the trials and tribulations of Don Cossack revolts, the struggles of peasants who lived by the river, the burlaki who worked the river, and a refuge for unhappy lovers, to name a few. In one of Russia's more famous ballads, "Stenka Razin," the Volga is a central character. The ballad popularized the story of a Don Cossack, Stenka Razin, who led insurgents in 1670–71 against their masters along the Volga. A firsthand account of Razin's actions, known for their "ferocious brutality," can be found in the account of the Dutch traveler, Jean Struys. Present during Razin's raids, Struys contributes to the account that forever links Razin's legendary acts to the Volga for in the course of these attacks, the Don Cossack is said to have sacrificed his beautiful Persian bride to the Volga. His gift to the Volga is immortalized through a well-known ballad in which Razin makes reference to Mother Volga, an epithet that persists into the twentieth century:

> Volga, Volga, Mother Volga
> Wide and deep beneath the sun
> You have never seen such a present
> From the Cossacks of the Don

In the nineteenth century, Pushkin remembered the incident in a poem and Razin continued to be celebrated during the Soviet era. The lyrics of the popular "Song about the Volga" state how before Razin, the country was oppressed.[33]

The group, however, that had the closest connection to the river were the burlaki, also known as the barge haulers, who often began their lives as serfs working on the land. Sometimes they left the land in the summer to work on the river or ran away from the landed estates. Their backbreaking work on the river, for which they received little pay, consisted of pulling barges upstream by means of wide straps harnessed around their chests. Similar to Stenka Razin and the Cossacks, a rich folklore evolved about their lives, capturing their exploits, triumphs, and sorrows. Discussed in chapter 2, the burlaki represented varying images throughout Russia's history. Initially they were perceived as lawless characters—sometimes runaway serfs, bandits, or robbers—frequently given to drunken evenings followed by days of arduous labor. By the late nineteenth century, the image changed and the burlaki were seen as victims of an oppressive tsarist state. The river, in this instance, was part of the oppression as its unforgiving terrain of shallows and sandbars constantly challenged the efforts of the burlaki. For example, on a day without wind, a ship might only travel two leagues. In describing such a day, one traveler observed "When the wind is not directly behind them, the Russians do not go under sail. Instead, they carry the anchors, one after another, a quarter of a league ahead in a small boat; then, using the bast [anchor] ropes, a hundred or more men, standing one behind another, pull the boat against the current. However, by this means they cannot go more than two leagues a day. The boats, which are flat on the bottom, can haul 400 to 500 lasts of freight." Still, Russia's economy grew from the eighteenth to nineteenth centuries as the state built more canals linking their numerous rivers with shipments of timber and grain.[34]

Given the poor state of Russia's roads, water transportation was critical for the country and long before the construction of twentieth-century projects such as the Moscow-Volga Canal, giving Moscow access to the Caspian Sea, or the Volga-Don Canal connecting the Volga to the Sea of Azov and the Black Sea, earlier tsars began the work of canal building. (The United States would also experience a period of canal building in the early 1800s in efforts to connect interior waterways with the coast and Great Lakes.) For the Volga, however, one of the more significant projects began during the Petrine period when Peter the Great sought to connect the river to the Baltic Sea. Motivated by the necessity of providing grain to St. Petersburg as well as entering Russian surplus goods such as grain and timber on the world market, Peter realized the importance of an extended Volga waterway. (The Mississippi River served a similar role in the nineteenth century as the principal means for the shipment of grain from the Gulf of Mexico.) Known as the Vyshniy Volochek system, the canal succeeded in connecting St. Petersburg with the Middle Volga region. Serious problems, however, plagued the waterway from the start including shallow streams and inclement weather. Although Peter had tried to improve the system, after his death in 1725 few advances were made until Catherine the Great's reign. Still the eighteenth century saw an expanded grain market in Russia. So by the late 1770s, when Aleksandr Nikolaevich Radishchev recorded his travels including a stop in Vyshniy Volochek, he commented on the canal's brisk business transporting grain and other goods. Radishchev also recognized the importance of water transportation in Russia, giving credit to the "first man to whom it occurred to emulate nature in her benefactions and to put a river to work." But Peter the Great's efforts extended beyond the Vyshniy Volochek Canal as he sought to build a canal connecting Moscow to the Volga River. Not until the nineteenth century, however, did Russia begin new efforts in canal building with attempts to link the Volga to the White Sea and a return to Peter's earlier ambition of a Moscow-Volga link. Although the advent of the railroad halted an active canal-building agenda, canals were an integral part of the imperial transportation network. The Volga was always key to these early attempts to expand a commercial network and Russia's exposure to the West and East.[35]

Halfway across the world, however, was another equally important riverine highway—the Mississippi River. Contributing to the growth of a number of diverse cultures, the Mississippi River facilitated trade from areas as far north as Lake Superior to perhaps as far south as Mesoamerica. Similar to the Volga, the Mississippi River Valley was where a number of cultures intersected and exchanged far more than trade goods. For example, beginning around 500 B.C.E., archeologists found evidence of an extensive trade network along the Upper Mississippi and its tributaries with an exchange that included copper from Lake Superior's Isle Royale, pipestone originating in southwestern Minnesota, lead ore from Illinois and Iowa, and obsidian from Yellowstone. This network subsided around C.E. 500 but flourished again with the advent of Cahokian civilization.[36]

Still open to varying interpretations, much of Cahokia's history remains a mystery to archaeologists. Paralleling the ascendency of Kievan Rus in the mid eleventh century, Cahokia was a complex culture with a vast trading network and a level of sophistication that included woodhenges that served as an early observatory. Cahokia, the center of at least fifty surrounding communities, was located near present-day St. Louis in an area known as the American Bottoms, chosen because of a resource base that allowed for farming on the river bottoms and ridgetops. In fact the site had some of the richest alluvial land in the Mississippi River Valley. Early-nineteenth-century visitors recognized the abundance of the American Bottoms, as one visitor described the Cahokian site in the following glowing terms: "[E]xtending on the Mississippi, from the Kaskaskia to the Cahokia river, about eighty miles in length, and five in breadth; several handsome streams meander through it; the soil of the richest kind, and but little subject to the effects of the Mississippi floods. A number of lakes are interspersed through it, with high and fine banks; these abound in fish, and in the autumn are visited by millions of wild fowl. There is, perhaps, no spot in the western country, capable of being more highly cultivated, or of giving support to a more numerous population than this valley."

While the observation was made in the early 1800s before any scientific studies were undertaken, the opinion is accurate as members of Cahokia did find the best lands to support a culture that subsisted on maize, game (large and small), and fish. As a result, they first chose the highest wetlands because the drainage would be better and the elevation would protect against flooding. Because of these advantages scholars believe that Cahokia did not have to secure food from neighboring cultures.[37]

Cahokia was derived from earlier mound builders in the Arkansas River Valley. Part of an archaeological era known as the Mississippian in North American prehistory, Cahokia, which had a greater population than London in 1150, is believed to be one of four major mound systems. (In the preceding Hopewell era, the mounds were not flat topped as they were in the Mississippian.) The other three mound systems are Spiro, located in present-day Oklahoma, and where their specialization was engraved shells; Etowah, near Atlanta with a specialization in statuary; and Moundville, near the Black Warrior River in Alabama, known for their pottery and ceramics. Each of the mound systems was governed by powerful chiefdoms with Cahokia serving as the administrative center. In addition to trade with the other mound systems, Cahokia traded with other groups, such as the Winnebago, northern neighbors in present-day Wisconsin. Some scholars also contend that trade occurred with the Mesoamerica culture as they uncovered evidence of Aztec gods in Cahokia. Later, French, British, and Spanish explorers engaged in many of the same trade networks.[38]

When Europeans first arrived to the area and saw the mounds, their impressions conveyed a sense of wonder at the culture that built them. An early visitor in 1811, H.M. Brackenridge extolled Cahokian accomplishments in the following passage:

> When I reached the foot of the principal mound, I was struck with a degree of astonishment, not unlike that which is experienced in contemplating the Egyptian pyramids. What a stupendous pile of earth! To heap up such a mass must have required years, and the labors of thousands. — It stands immediately on the bank of the Cahokia, and on the side next it, is covered with lofty trees. Were it not for the regularity and design which it manifests, the circumstances of its being on alluvial ground, and the other mounds scattered around it, we could scarcely believe it the work of human hands. — The shape is that of a parallelogram, standing from north to south; on the south side there is a broad apron or step, about half way down, and from this, another projection into the plain about fifteen feet wide, which was probably intended as an ascent to the mound. By stepping round the base, I computed the circumference to be at least eight hundred yards, and the height of the mound about ninety feet.[39]

Numerous early visitors repeated this awe and admiration. For Brackenridge's description was of only one mound and at one time Cahokia included over one hundred earthen mounds, with the tallest, Monks Mound, reaching a height of 30.5 meters and covering 6.4 hectares or 16 acres. Perched on the banks of what is now a dry river channel of the Mississippi, Monks Mound revealed a culture intent on demonstrating its mastery, not only of its populace, but the surrounding landscape as well. Many of the ceremonies at Monks Mound occurred at night with large fire pits lighting up the towering mound, reinforcing its magnitude, predating later twentieth-century efforts to dominate the riverine landscape. Evidence points to other senior-ranking members of Cahokian society also building structures that oversee the landscape. On an everyday level, Cahokians manipulated their environment by farming the river bottoms and ridgetops as well as hunting migrating waterfowl. While archaeologists continue to revise their conclusions about Cahokia, some contend that the structures they built were more similar to pyramids than mounds. Regardless of its origins, Cahokia introduced a new era in the Mississippi Valley with cities the size of old Mesopotamian city-states and trade routes that stretched up to northern Minnesota, east to the Ohio River Valley, and west to the Missouri River. In places such as present-day Trempealeau, Wisconsin, archaeologists suggest the Cahokians established either outposts or colonies in their expansive trade network. Mentioned earlier, one of the more widely held interpretations holds that Cahokia was one of several major chiefdoms and acted as the administrative center, with parallel cultures established at Spiro and Etowah.[40]

Contact between the Cahokians and the Midwestern, Southern, and Plains tribes undoubtedly occurred by way of a trade network stretching throughout the Mississippi and Missouri River Basins. Evidence of trade and cross-cultural exposure can be found through the remains of a popular game known as chunky in which players rolled a "chunky stone" across the ice or ground and spears were thrown to mark the stone's resting stop. The player whose spear landed the closest was the winner. Through chunky, new ideas regarding "politics and religion" were spread. The Mississippi River was the conduit for all of this as the "Cahokians ... probably traveled hundreds of miles up the Mississippi and Missouri rivers to trade, read or convert the peoples in those places on a semiregular basis." Anticipating later Mississippi River travel, a petroglyph near the confluence of the Ohio and Mississippi Rivers was found recently which some archaeologists believe is a map. The map shows where "a constriction in the river required careful navigation by travelers." Despite the appearance of an entrenched, flourishing culture, reaching its peak around C.E. 1050, Cahokia society disappeared after C.E. 1200. Still the Mississippi Valley saw new groups migrating into the area and while scholars do not agree on the descendants of the Cahokians, among the eastern tribes are "vague origin stories of people who originated in the east, near big rivers." A widely held interpretation is that other chiefdoms rivaled Cahokia's power and their cultures persisted after Cahokia's population dispersed.[41]

But mound building was not limited to Cahokia and as settlers arrived in the Midwest in the early 1800s, their accounts included the existence of mounds throughout the upper Midwest. For example, in 1766 when Jonathan Carver traveled on the upper reaches of the Mississippi in present-day Wisconsin, near Lake Pepin he recounted seeing a rise on the open area bordering the west bank of the river. Upon closer inspection, he found this break in the prairie "had once been a breastwork of about four feet in height, extending the best part of a mile and sufficiently capacious to cover five thousand men. Its form was somewhat circular, and its flanks reached the river. Though much defaced by time, every angle was distinguishable, and appeared as regular, and fashioned with as much military skill, as if planned by Vauban himself."[42]

Around the same time the Cahokians were reaching their zenith, the Winnebago migrated northward from the Mississippi River Valley, settling in present-day Wisconsin. Identified by archaeologists as part of the Upper Mississippian Oneota archaeological tradition, the Winnebago reveal a mythology keenly aware of the natural world. Based on an oral tradition, their folklore documents a culture closely tied to a riverine environment. Surrounded by water with a territorial reach in 1600 that stretched from Green Bay, Wisconsin, to the Fox and Wisconsin Rivers and continued west to the Mississippi River, their world included "thunderbirds and water spirits, mythological creatures of great power ... either aiding or hindering the protagonist." Even their identity related to water as Winnebago identified as Hochangara, which according to scholars originates from the word *ho chunk* meaning Big Fish and Big Voice or True Voice. Similar to Volga River mythology, in the Winnebago world the water spirits could be good or bad. In their folktales, the Mississippi is called "Big Water" and through their descriptions of the river, they had traveled as far south as the confluence of the Missouri and Mississippi Rivers. Their stories showed a culture that traveled extensively in the upper Midwest as "The Journey of the Ghost to the Spiritland" illustrates. In the story, the afterlife is reached after the spirit passes over "perpendicular cliffs" that "at each end appear uncircumventable, at each end it will seem as if you would be stepping into the ocean." These cliffs, it is assumed are the bluffs lining the Upper Mississippi River. But the river also figured into everyday life as the Winnebago calendar refers to the twelfth moon as "Fish running." Later, the Winnebagos will be one of the tribes supplying French traders with furs in the late 1700s and early 1800s.[43]

The Winnebagos, however, were only one tribe who lived along the riverine corridor in the Upper Mississippi Valley. Two other large tribes, the Ojibway (also known as the Chippewa) and the Dakota, inhabited the upper stretches of the river beginning around the same time period. For the Ojibway, their oral history accounts credit their arrival around the sixteenth century to their search for food, which archaeologists believe refers to their diet of wild rice found on the lakes by the Mississippi headwaters. Their creation mythology mirrors that of many religions as they believe the earth rose from earlier flood-waters and, similar to the Winnebago, their journey to the afterworld includes crossing a large body of water before reaching land resembling prairies. At one time, the Ojibway occupied a vast amount of territory that included Lake Superior and much of the Mississippi River headwaters, and at times extended to St. Anthony Falls, near present-day St. Paul, Minnesota. Competing with the Ojibway for territory was the Dakota tribe as both relied on this part of the Mississippi River Valley for hunting, fishing, and limited agriculture. When the Europeans arrived, starting with the French fur traders, both tribes began an exchange of furs for European goods as the French eventually sought to claim the entire Mississippi River Valley.[44]

At the other end of the river lived a number of tribes also sustained by the bounty of the Lower Mississippi River Valley and delta. For example when Hernando de Soto and his armies entered the Lower Mississippi River Valley in the 1540s, near the Native American village of Quizquiz, he saw firsthand the bounty of rich bottomlands farming. As late as spring, the Indians had a surplus of maize from the year before, testimony to the richness of the alluvial plain. In another case, one delta tribe, the Bayogoulas, used the river to their advantage by living on a natural levee and enjoyed a diet of fish, seasonal game, and nuts and berries from the surrounding forest. Seminomadic, they also practiced limited agriculture with the cultivation of maize. Their familiarity with the river was impressive as one of the early French colonizers, Pierre Le Moyne d'Iberville, recounted how when showing them a map of the "Myssy-sypy" in order to find the east fork of the river, he realized later that they were trying to indicate how "they went to the Myssysypy by way of rivers that con-nect with one another." Their lives, however, changed dramatically with the arrival of the Europeans. In d'Iberville's *Journals,* he also recalled when en-countering the tribe in the beginning of the eighteenth century, there was still evidence of smallpox in the village which had already claimed a quarter of the population. Disease also struck the Ojibway but not to the same extent.[45]

Similar to the Volga's history, evidence suggests that most of these groups interacted through extensive trade networks with the Mississippi serving as the main artery. While evidence is sketchy as to the place of the Mississippi in early folklore, with the exception of the Winnebago, the importance of knowing the river was critical as early petroglyphs served as navigational maps. Further, even the types of boats used by the Indians indicated an intimate knowledge of the river. Early European explorers noted with admiration that the canoes used by Native Americans, whether birchbark or dugout, allowed for river pas-sage that often extended for hundreds of miles.

Dramatic change, however, came to the Mississippi River Valley in the mid sixteenth century with the arrival of the Europeans. The Lower Mississippi

River Valley, in particular, became a contested landscape as Spain, France, and Great Britain sought control of the region. In response to British encroachment and ultimate colonization, many of the tribes allied with the French. Mirroring the cosmopolitan milieu that often characterized the Volga, the Gulf South by the 1700s hosted a number of different empires, ethnicities, and cultures lending a vibrancy to the area often overlooked. Throughout this period, fraught with disease, removal, and other tragedies for the earlier inhabitants, the Mississippi River was the mainstay of an emergent multiethnic environment whether through transportation or sustenance. De Soto is believed to be the first European to see the Mississippi River, which the Spanish called "Espiritu Santo," in 1546. De Soto approached the river from an expedition that began in Florida and wound its way through what would be the southeastern United States. In the *De Soto Chronicles,* the river is first described when de Soto and his men have to cross the river by the Indian town of Chisca in eastern Tennessee. Again, the men are impressed by the size of the river as the following indicates: "It [the crossing] was nearly a half league wide, and if a man stood still on the other side, one could not tell whether he were a man or something else. It [the river] was of great depth and of very strong current. Its water was always turgid and continually many trees and wood came down it borne along by the force of water and current."[46]

By the 1600s, the French began arriving in significant numbers as the French government and traders tried establishing posts along the river in order to capture the lucrative fur trade. Initially early French explorations focused on the Mississippi River as a passage to the Far East. In 1673, the governor of French Canada, charged the explorer and Jesuit missionary, Father Jacques Marquette, "either to seek a passage from here [Lake Superior] to the China sea by the river which empties into the California or Red sea [Gulf of California]." Marquette, accompanied by fellow explorer Louis Joliet, began the voyage down the Mississippi which concluded with all explorers and competing nation-states accepting that the Mississippi's outlet was not the Pacific Ocean. Marquette's voyage also enlightened in other ways. In his journal, he described a river where size was never constant, observing: "On sounding, we have found ten fathoms of water. Its breadth is very unequal: it is sometimes three quarters of a league, and sometimes narrows in to three arpents (220 yards)." Coupled with varying depths, Marquette noted differing terrains with bluffs dotting the upper reaches, followed by flat land and eventually, land that is dense with vegetation. In addition to the assorted landscapes, suggesting a fertility the farther south they went, Marquette remarked upon the plentiful fish and game. For fish, he commented upon "monstrous fish … one of which struck so violently against our canoe, that I took it for a large tree abut to knock us to pieces." The game they saw along the river banks included deer, moose, and bustards, to name a few. The route they used, in their birchbark canoes, began by way of Lake Michigan to the Fox River and then on to the Wisconsin River for four days until they came to the Mississippi, became the standard for years to come for Upper Mississippi River travel. After their trip, which ended at the Arkansas River, fairly accurate maps were made of the Upper Mississippi River Valley as the river became the primary highway for all north-south commerce. Again a trade network, the river, like the Volga, carried a rich trade of furs and other goods south. Within the next decade in 1682, another French explorer, Robert Cavelier de La Salle, traveled all the way down the Mississippi, which he called the St. Louis River, to the river's mouth on the Gulf of Mexico. Upon successfully completing his voyage, La Salle claimed all the territory in the Mississippi River Basin for King Louis XIV.[47]

For the first half of the eighteenth century, France dominated the Mississippi River Valley leading one historian during the period to call the Mississippi a French river. The French colonial period, however, was brief, lasting from 1718 to 1769. Aggressive in their pursuit for territory and trade, Britain and France along with their Indian allies, competed for the interior of the continent, each seeing the importance of the Mississippi River Basin. Trade was the driving force as furs, in particular beaver, were commanding high prices. In comparing the approaches of the different European nations to the North American continent and its inhabitants, French relations contrasted sharply with the British. First, the French and Indians intermarried. Second, because the robust fur trade prompted and sustained the French presence, it was in their interest to maintain the existing environment as much as possible. The inside of the beaver pelt was used for the felt in hats and was in high demand. Europeans also prized beaver pelts because they could be converted into a material for waterproofing. Much like earlier traders on the Volga, furs in the northern reaches of what would be the United States, were prized for their quality. With the mania for beaver hats in the early nineteenth century, beavers were almost trapped to extinction as traders sent their goods downstream the Mississippi.[48]

As a result, the Mississippi River and the interior of the continent became more and more valued as the French first established a colony near the river's mouth followed by Sieur de Bienville establishing New Orleans in 1718. French influence was further buttressed by "a string of posts and settlements from the Great Lakes down the Mississippi Valley." But the Seven Years War (also known as the French and Indian War) put an end to French claims as the 1763 treaty concluding the war ceded Britain possession of all the land east of the Mississippi, with the exception of New Orleans. Spain was given possession of New Orleans, along with land west of the Mississippi in return for Spain's allying with France. By this time, all three colonial powers had introduced a frontier economy to the Gulf Coast and with that economy came the introduction of slave labor; first Indian slaves followed by the importation of African slaves. Another dynamic resulted as African slaves embarked on their own history informed by the Mississippi River. As slavery evolved in the Gulf Coast and Lower Mississippi River Valley, there were instances of slaves escaping and forming their own communities in the delta; living off the river's resources. But the river affected the lives of African slaves in another way. As a plantation economy grew, African slaves found a life far less encumbered working on the steamships as opposed to the plantations or town work. Similar to the burlaki, work on the river offered a freedom unknown to the other slaves.[49]

All three European powers—Great Britain, France, and Spain—relied on a frontier economy in which the Indians participated through trade and wartime alliances and African slaves through their labor. So, by 1789 when the United States was established, an expansive economy was in place that undoubtedly contributed to U.S. interest in navigation on the Mississippi. For American settlers living in the territories such as Kentucky, navigation on the Mississippi was especially important as indicated by one of their Fourth of July toasts: "The Navigation of the Mississippi, at any price but that of Liberty," as reported in local newspapers. Working through diplomatic channels, by 1795, Spain acknowledged American claims to navigation on the Mississippi. But the most important agreement, from an American perspective, occurred in 1803 when President Thomas Jefferson authorized the Louisiana Purchase from France for $15 million. Now the United States could count New Orleans and all of Louisiana among its holdings, insuring unimpeded (at least from European powers) navigation on the Mississippi.[50]

With the Louisiana Purchase, all of the Mississippi River Valley became a part of the recently formed United States and the area became associated with an emergent national narrative. The Lewis and Clark exploration of the area resulted in more definitive answers regarding the once-hoped-for passage to India as well as further knowledge about the richness of the interior. Expeditions up the river were launched looking for the river's source. In 1806 Zebulon Pike claimed that Upper Red Cedar Lake was the river's source. Following Pike's discovery, in 1823 an Italian self-styled explorer, Giacomo Costantino Beltrami, traveling alone in what is now northern Minnesota, also claimed to have located the source at a lake he named Julia. In tortured prose, he wrote, "I have discovered the place of his origin in space, but who can disclose to us his origin in point of time? Did the first beams of the sun constitute also the first of his days? Does he belong to incalculable antiquity or to modern ages?" But Beltrami also begins associating the river with certain traits, when he touts "Judge whether the Mississippi be not the first river of the world!" He goes on to say that "what confers on the latter [the Mississippi] a decided superiority is, that along the whole extent of its banks man can breathe the air of liberty, and industry meets with no restriction." Despite his claims, Beltrami's discovery was not considered credible.

It was not until 1832 when Henry Rowe Schoolcraft, Indian agent and scientist, began his search that the source of the river was located. In his journals detailing the expedition and ultimate discovery, Schoolcraft provides a geographical explanation of why earlier explorers mistook the Upper Red Cedar Lake for the river's source. But his most compelling passage regarded the discovery itself. He wrote, "we followed our guide down the sides of the last elevation, with the expectation of momentarily reaching the goal of our journey. What had been long sought, at last appeared suddenly. On turning out of a thicket, into a small weedy opening, the cheering sight of a transparent body of water burst upon our view. It was Itasca Lake—the source of the Mississippi."[51] By this time, the Mississippi like the Volga, was already beginning a new role as the United States sought to distinguish the country from other nations.

In concluding, throughout the early years of human history the Mississippi and Volga Rivers were instrumental whether through the migrations of nomadic people, facilitating trade networks, or providing sustenance. This centrality was remembered by way of folklore, mythology, and other means of accounting, such as poetry and song—laying a foundation for the rivers to become an integral part of the nation-building that occurred in later centuries. Thus by the beginning of the nineteenth century, the Volga and Mississippi Rivers were entrenched in narratives about the Russian and American past. In analyzing these narratives—constructing the past through the prism of each river—the history of the Mongols or Cahokia, for example, takes on a different perspective. These empires become in part, riverine civilizations resulting not only in lucrative trade networks but cultures where the rivers are part of a larger discourse whether as boundaries, place markers, or the repository for folklore—in short, frames of reference. Integral to the historical past, the rivers evolved into more than merely functional assets in nation-building. Instead, a historical memory was transpiring that brooked the ancient world where the rivers had a pragmatic and spiritual niche to the beginnings of a modern-day mentality where the mysteries of the waterways could be explained and ultimately, subdued.

These foundational years, when the rivers became etched in a memory based upon the tangible and intangible, were key to the nineteenth-century search for a national identity. Always part of a dynamic that included the utilitarian and metaphorical, the rivers with their past roles as major waterway, unifier, and folk hero, occupied a significant niche in the nation-building discourse of the nineteenth and twentieth centuries. Through these multiple roles, the rivers deflected the diversity that always threatened to separate Russian and American attempts at nation-building. Appropriated in the emergent nationalist discourse in the nineteenth century, the historical memories of Mother Volga nurturing her citizens, joining a landscape that touted space and the calm Volga waters, or the Father of Waters fascinating American settlers with his volatility while cultivating the rugged individual of American lore, revealed each river's centrality and provided a rallying point for nations eager to craft a distinct identity. The following chapter recounts the transition—through art, prose, and poetry—of early river mythology and folklore into symbols of the modern nation-states of Russia and the United States that transcended discrete identities based upon geographical, economic, and ethnic differences.

Notes

1. Evidence of rivers contributing to cultural identity dates back thousands of years as Herodotus noted that while traveling in Egypt, Egyptians were identified as those who drank the waters of the Nile. See Herodotus, *The History of Herodotus*, trans. George Rawlinson (Garden City: The International Collector's Library, 1928), 87. For a further discussion on the influence of rivers upon culture and identity, see Dorothy Zeisler-Vralsted, "The Nile, Ganges, Volga and Mississippi Rivers: Their Portrayal in Art and Literature," in *Water History and Humanity*, vol. 1, *UNESCO History of Water and Civilization* (Paris: UNESCO, 2014 scheduled publication). A recent publication connecting rivers and national identity is Tricia Cusack, *Riverscapes and National Identity* (Syracuse: Syracuse University Press, 2010). See citations in chapter 2, endnote 4.

2. In Lee Sandlin's popular history of the Mississippi River, he wrote: "While the voyageurs called it the wicked river, the plantation slaves called it Old Devil River, because of its habit of playing bizarre and malicious tricks." Sandlin, *Wicked River: The Mississippi When it Last Ran Wild* (New York: Pantheon Books, 2010), 24. An essay by Melissa K. Stockdale, argued that initially the terms "fatherland" and "motherland" were interchangeable but that after the revolution, the use of motherland became more an emotional, patriotic response while fatherland was associated with "the state and citizenship." Motherland also became tied to the land, a bond that superseded the state. See Stockdale, "What is a Fatherland? Changing Notions of Duty, Rights, and Belonging in Russia," in *Space, Place, and Power in Modern Russia: Essays in the New Spatial History,* ed. Mark Bassin, Christopher Ely, and Melissa K. Stockdale (DeKalb: Northern Illinois University Press, 2010), 23–49.

3. In his 1852 account of travel down the Volga, the British visitor, Laurence Oliphant, discussed the Russian word, *pericartes,* which was used to describe the shallows. According to Oliphant, "These shallows are called pericartes; and as they occur very frequently, either the barges or the steamer were constantly running aground." See Oliphant, *The Russian Shores of the Black Sea in the Autumn of 1852* (New York: Redfield, 1854), 35.

4. Claudius Dabon, "The Voyages and Discoveries of Father James Marquette in the Valley of the Mississippi," in *Discovery and Exploration of the Mississippi Valley with the Original Narratives of Marquette, Allouez, Membre, Hennepin, and Anastase Douay* by John Gilmary Shea, 2nd ed. (Albany: Joseph McDonough, 1903), 42.

5. "The Journey of William of Rubruck," in *Mission to Asia: Narratives and Letters of the Franciscan Missionaries in Mongolia and China in the Thirteenth and Fourteenth Centuries,* ed. Christopher Dawson (New York: Harper and Row, 1966), 125; W.R.S.

Ralston, *Russian Folk-Tales* (London: Smith, Elder & Co., 1873), 208. Throughout the folktale, since the Volga and Vazuza Rivers are sisters, they are referred to in the feminine, perhaps laying the foundation for the Volga's later characterization as "Mother Volga."

6. Numerous sources discuss the origin of the name, Mississippi, including Dabon, "Voyages and Discoveries," 7; R.T. Huntington and Wayne Franklin, "Expedition to the Mississippi River by Way of the Gulf of Mexico," *Iowa Review* 15, no. 2 (Spring–Summer, 1985): 122. For a comparison during the same expedition, the river that La Salle called the "Riviére des Cannes" or the River of Canes was described as being "about a musket-shot wide" (ibid., 102). Mark Twain, *Life on the Mississippi* (1883; repr., New York: Signet Classic, 1961), 1.

7. For an introduction to Russian geography see Dennis Shaw, "Russia's Geographical Environment," in *The Cambridge History of Russia*, vol. 1, ed. Maureen Perrie (Cambridge: Cambridge University Press, 2006), 19–43. "The Journey of William of Rubruck" in *Mission to Asia*, 116, 209, 124.

8. For a good general history and discussion of Russia's multiethnic culture, see Geoffrey Hosking, *Russia and the Russians: A History* (Cambridge: Belknap Press, 2001).

9. A brief overview of early Central Asian history can be found in Peter B. Golden, *Central Asia in World History* (Oxford: Oxford University Press, 2011). For different perspectives on the Khazar Empire, see Ravil Bukharaev, *Islam in Russia: The Four Seasons* (New York: St. Martin's Press, 2000); Arthur Koestler, *The Thirteenth Tribe: The Khazar Empire and Its Heritage* (New York: Random House, 1976); Victor Spinei, *The Great Migrations in the East and Southeast of Europe from the Ninth to the Thirteenth Century: Hungarians, Pechenegs, and Uzes*, vol. 1 (Amsterdam: Adolf M. Hakkert, 2006). Thomas S. Noonan documents the trade between the Arabs and Khazars through the arrival of dirhams in Russia around C.E. 800, which he concludes, "These coins were the fruit of a growing trade which at first involved the Arabs and Khazars." See Noonan, "Why the Vikings First Came to Russia," *Jahrbücher für Geschichte Osteuropas*, Neue Folge, Bd. 34, H.3 (1986): 340.

10. A discussion of the interactions between nomadic and sedentary groups in the steppe empires can be found in Tatiana Stefanova and Tsvetelin Stepanov, *The Bulgars and the Steppe Empire in the Early Middle Ages: The Problem of the Others* (Leiden: Brill, 2010).

11. The Pechenegs were defeated later by the Kipchaks in 1087, who Russians called Polovtsy and who occupied the steppe area between the Volga and Don Rivers. See A. Bruce Boswell, "The Kipchak Turks," *The Slavonic Review* 6, no. 6 (June 1927): 70. Spinei, *The Great Migrations*, vol. 1, 162.

12. A general history of the Volga Bulghars can be found in I. Zimonyi, *The Origins of the Volga Bulghars* (Szged, 1990). *Ibn Fadlan's Journey to Russia: A Tenth-Century Traveller from Baghdad to the Volga River*, trans. Richard Frye (Princeton: Markus Wiener Publications, 2005), 58, 99; Noonan, "Why the Vikings," ibid.; *Ibn Fadlan's Journey to Russia*, 64–65.

13. *Ibn Fadlan's Journey to Russia*, 16.

14. *The Russian Primary Chronicle, Laurentian Text*, trans. Samuel Hazzard Cross and Olgerd P. Sherbowitz-Wetzor (Cambridge: The Mediaeval Academy of America, 1953),

53. For an excellent history of Kievan Rus, see Simon Franklin and Jonathan Shepard, *The Emergence of Rus 750–1200* (London: Longman, 1996).

15. *An Anthology of Russian Folk Epics,* trans. James Bailey and Tatyana Ivanova (Armonk, New York: M.E. Sharpe, 1998), xvii, xix.

16. András Pálóczi-Horváth, *Pechenegs, Cumans, Iasians: Steppe Peoples in Medieval Hungary* (Corvina: Hereditas, 1989), 21; Boswell, "The Kipchak Turks," ibid.; Spinei, *The Great Migrations,* vol. 1–2. In Russian scholar Nicholas Riasanovsky's text, he not only emphasized that the "Kievan state encompassed ancestors of Russians" but also discussed the Kievan state's ever-constant threat from steppe invaders. See Riasanovsky, *Russian Identities: A Historical Survey* (Cambridge: Oxford University Press, 2005), 21, 29.

17. Ralston, *Russian Folk-Tales,* 218–221.

18. As contemporary scholars, such as Simon Franklin, Jonathan Shepard, and Dennis Shaw observe, Russia's history is bound by its rivers. In Shaw's words "Rivers thus seem to have been central to the identity of the early Russians." Shaw, "Russia's Geographical Environment," 32. An earlier account regarding the importance of the Valdai Hills and Russia's major rivers can be found in Robert J. Kerner's work, in which he writes "The Valdai Hills … may be described as embracing the most strategic and important portages of Europe and Asia. In fact, the region may be regarded as the single grand portage in itself and hence the key portage of the world." See Kerner, *The Urge to the Sea: The Course of Russian History, The Role of Rivers, Portages, Ostrogs, Monasteries, and Furs* (Berkeley: University of California Press, 1942), 1. Hosking, *Russia and the Russians,* 42; *The Russian Primary Chronicle,* 51–52.

19. Serge A. Zenkovsky, *Medieval Russia's Epics, Chronicles, and Tales,* trans. Serge A. Zenkovsky (New York: E.P. Dutton & Co., Inc., 1963), 152.

20. Ibid., 1.

21. For an excellent discussion of Novgorod during this period, see V.L. Ianin, "Medieval Novgorod," *The Cambridge History of Russia,* vol. 1 (Cambridge: Cambridge University Press, 2006): 188–210.

22. Spinei, *The Great Migrations,* vol. 2, 608. Spinei points out how the Mongols were unique in their successful winter campaigns, especially in light of the failures of Napoleon and Hitler when attempting winter invasions (ibid., 609–610). A good overview of the Mongol's campaign can be found in W. Bruce Lincoln, as he stressed that "Only the horsemen of Batu Khan, who were bred to thrive in the rough storms that lashed the high Asian plains along Siberia's Mongolian frontier, have ever fought a successful winter war in Russia." See Lincoln, *The Conquest of a Continent: Siberia and the Russians* (Ithaca: Cornell University Press, 1994), 17.

23. Jerome Blum, *Lord and Peasant in Russia: From the Ninth to the Nineteenth Century* (Princeton: Princeton University Press, 1961), 78; Spinei, *The Great Migrations,* vol. 2, 668; Bailey and Ivanova, *An Anthology of Russian Folk Epics,* xx; Spinei, ibid., 666. Accounts left by merchants, such as the Florentine, Francesco Balducci Pegolotti, credit the Mongols with securing a safe trade network in their territory. See Henry Yule and Henri Cordier, tr. and ed., *Cathay and the Way Thither, Being a Collection of Medieval Notices of China,* vol. 3 (London, 1916): 143–171, http://depts.washington.edu/silkroad/texts/pegol.html.

24. The river was a boundary in another sense in that after Ivan IV defeated the Mongols at Kazan, "local people who did not convert to Orthodox Christianity were expelled 30 kilometers from the capital and away from the banks of the rivers." See Helen M. Faller, "Repossessing Kazan as a Form of Nation-building in Tatarstan, Russia," *Journal of Muslim Minority Affairs* 22, no. 1 (2002): 82; N.Ya. Aristov's Tales, "The Punishment of the Volga," in Maureen Perrie, *The Image of Ivan the Terrible in Russian Folklore* (Cambridge: Cambridge University Press, 1987), 177.

25. Ibid., 177–178.

26. An excellent overview of Russia's changing boundaries after Ivan IV can be found in David Moon, "Peasant Migration and the Settlement of Russia's Frontiers, 1550–1897," *The Historical Journal* 40, no. 4 (December 1997): 859–893. Adam Olearius, *The Travels of Olearius in Seventeenth-Century Russia*, (Stanford: Stanford University Press, 1967), 295, 297. Another colorful description of early Russian commerce with the East can be found in Afanasy Nikitin, *Voyage Beyond the Three Seas, 1466–1472* (Moscow: Raduga Publishers, 1985). Nikitin was the first Russian to reach India and record his experiences down the Volga from Tver.

27. Nikitin, *Voyage Beyond the Three Seas*, 301.

28. Oliphant, *The Russian Shores of the Black Sea*, 55.

29. Olearius, *The Travels of Olearius*, 294; Blum, *Lord and Peasant in Russia*, 163.

30. *Down Along the Volga*, ed. Roberta Reeder (Philadelphia: University of Pennsylvania Press, 1975), 200.

31. Perrie, *The Image of Ivan the Terrible*, 243.

32. P.A. Warneck, "The Volga-Don Navigation Canal," *Russian Review* 13, no. 4 (October 1954): 285–291; A.N. Kurat, "The Turkish Expedition to Astrakhan in 1569 and the Problem of the Don-Volga Canal," *The Slavonic and East European Review* 40, no. 94 (December 1961): 23. For a brief but thorough overview of canal building during Russia's Imperial Period, see R.A. French, "Canals in Pre-revolutionary Russia" in *Studies in Russian Historical Geography* (London: Academic Press, 1983), 451–481.

33. Ralston, *Russian Folk-Tales*, 220; Nicholas V. Riasanovsky and Mark D. Steinberg, *A History of Russia*, 8th ed. (New York: Oxford University Press, 2011), 177.

34. Olearius, *The Travels of Olearius*, 297. For further insights into the Russian economy during this period, see David Moon, *The Russian Peasantry, 1600–1930: The World the Peasants Made* (Chicago: Addison Wesley Longman, 1999). An extended discussion about the burlaki can be found in chapter 2.

35. French, "Canals in Pre-revolutionary Russia," in *Studies in Russian Historical Geography*, 451–481; Robert E. Jones, *Bread Upon the Waters: The St. Petersburg Grain Trade and the Russian Economy, 1703–1811* (Pittsburgh: University of Pittsburgh Press, 2013), 1, 77; Aleksandr Nikolaevich Radishchev, *A Journey from St. Petersburg to Moscow* (Cambridge: Harvard University Press, 1958), 156–157. Although the Volga-Don Canal was never completed under Peter the Great, the account of a British hydraulic engineer hired to construct the canal provided interesting insights into Peter's ambitions and subsequent challenges. See John Perry, *The State of Russia under the Present Tsar* (London, 1716).

36. Calvin R. Fremling, *Immortal River, The Upper Mississippi in Ancient and Modern Times* (Madison: University of Wisconsin Press, 2005), 103, 104–111.

37. There are a number of works on Cahokia but several that provide excellent overviews are George R. Milner, *The Cahokia Chiefdom: The Archaeology of a Mississippian Society* (Washington: Smithsonian Institution Press, 1998); Timothy R. Pauketat, *Cahokia: Ancient America's Great City on the Mississippi* (New York: Viking Press, 2009); Timothy R. Pauketat and Thomas E. Emerson, eds., *Cahokia: Domination Ideology in the Mississippian World* (Lincoln: University of Nebraska Press, 1997). Additional background on Cahokian society was provided by Professor Jerry R. Galm, Professor of Anthropology, Eastern Washington University (March 2012). H.M. Brackenridge, *Views of Louisiana: Together with a Journal of a Voyage Up the Missouri River, in 1811* (Pittsburgh: Cramer, Spear, and Eichbaum, 1814) as quoted by Barnard Shipp, *The Indian and Antiquities of America* (Philadelphia: Sherman & Co., Printers 1897), 252.

38. Milner, *The Cahokia Chiefdom*; Galm, Interview (March 2012).

39. Brackenridge, *Views of Louisiana*, as cited in Shipp, *Indian and Antiquities*, 254.

40. Pauketat, *Cahokia: Ancient America's Great City*, 26; James Theler and Robert Boszhardt, *Twelve Millennia: Archaeology of the Upper Mississippi River Valley* (Iowa City: University of Iowa Press, 2003).

41. Pauketat, *Cahokia: Ancient America's Great City*, 39, 139, 154, 159.

42. William R. Smith, *The History of Wisconsin in Three Parts, Historical, Documentary, and Descriptive*, vol. 3 (Madison: Beriah Brown, Printer, 1854), 240.

43. Robert L. Hall, "Relating the Big Fish and the Big Stone: The Archaeological Identity and Habitat of the Winnebago in 1634," *Oneota Archaeology: Past, Present, and Future,* ed. William Green, Report 20, Office of the State Archaeologist (Iowa City: University of Iowa, 1995), 19–33. According to Hall, "Winnebago is a word of Algonquian origin that refers to water that is bad smelling or brackish" furthering the association with water. Ibid. For another superb introduction to the world of the Winnebago see Beatrice A. Bigony, "Folk Literature as an Ethnohistorical Device: The Interrelationships between Winnebago Folk Tales and Wisconsin Habitat" *Ethnohistory* 29, no. 3 (Summer 1982): 155–180. Bigony believes that the Winnebagos' "references to the elements reveal both their awe of the powerful natural forces as well as their presence in daily life" (ibid., 160).

44. One of the best early overviews of the Ojibway is William W. Warren, *History of the Ojibway People* (1885; repr., St. Paul: Minnesota Historical Society Press, 2009). For general information on the Ojibway and Dakota, see the Minnesota History Society website at http://www.historicfortsnelling.org/history.

45. Jeffrey P. Brain, "Late Prehistoric Settlement Patterning in the Yazoo Basin and Natchez Bluffs Regions of the Lower Mississippi Valley," *Mississippian Settlement Patterns,* ed. Bruce D. Smith (New York: Academic Press, 1978), 356–357, 364–365; *LeMoyne d' Iberville's Journals of Three Voyages to the Mississippi from December 31, 1698 to April 27, 1702* trans. Richebourg Gaillard McWilliams. (Alabama: University of Alabama Press, 1981), 63, 48. For an overview of Native American life in the Lower Mississippi, see Daniel H. Usner, Jr., *Indians, Settlers, and Slaves in a Frontier Exchange Economy: The Lower Mississippi Valley Before 1783* (Chapel Hill: University of North Carolina Press, 1992), 21–22.

46. For an excellent discussion of the Gulf South and its diversity in the eighteenth century, see *Coastal Encounters: The Transformation of the Gulf South in the Eighteenth*

Century, ed. Richmond F. Brown (Lincoln: University of Nebraska Press, 2007). *The De Soto Chronicles, The Expedition of Hernando de Soto to North America in 1539–1543,* vol. 1, ed. Lawrence Al Clayton, et al. (Tuscaloosa: University of Alabama Press, 1993), 113.

47. Dabon, "Voyages and Discoveries," 4, 54, 18–19; William Watts Folwell, *A History of Minnesota,* vol. 1 (1921; repr., St. Paul: Minnesota Historical Society Press, 1956), 33–34.

48. While numerous articles and books on the fur trade can be found, two excellent overviews are Jay Gitlin, "Empires of Trade, Hinterlands of Settlement," and Richard White, "Animals and Enterprise," in *The Oxford History of the American West,* ed. Clyde A. Milner II, et al. (New York: Oxford University Press, 1994), 79–115, 237–275. D.W. Meinig, *The Great Columbia Plain: A Historical Geography, 1805–1910* (Seattle: University of Washington Press, 1968), 34. Meinig cites Meriwether Lewis's comments regarding furs found in the Upper Missouri River Basin as "richer in beaver and Otter than any country on earth," although Lewis was looking to send the furs via the Columbia.

49. Elliott West, "American Frontier," in *The Oxford History of the American West,* 118. For a discussion of the frontier economy and all the participants, i.e. Indians, Europeans, and African slaves, in the Lower Mississippi River Valley, see Usner, *Indians, Settlers, and Slaves.* The best book on the relationship between African Americans and the Mississippi River is Thomas C. Buchanan, *Black Life on the Mississippi: Slaves, Free Blacks, and the Western Steamboat World* (Chapel Hill: University of North Carolina Press, 2004).

50. David Waldstreicher, *In the Midst of Perpetual Fetes: The Making of American Nationalism, 1776–1820* (Chapel Hill: University of North Carolina Press, 1997), 278. In an article by U.S. Western historian, Donald Pisani in which he focused on the contributions of rivers in American history, he considered President George Washington's perspective on the Mississippi River. According to Pisani: "To Washington and his contemporaries, the design of the continent seemed providential. The Atlantic Ocean connected the thirteen colonies, and the Mississippi promised to bind together the interior communities." Pisani, "Beyond the Hundredth Meridian: Nationalizing the History of Water in the United States," *Environmental History* 5, no. 4 (October 2000): 466–482.

51. Giacomo Costantino Beltrami, *A Pilgrimage in Europe and America, Leading to the Discovery of the Sources of the Mississippi and Bloody River. …* (London: Hunt and Clark, 1828), 542, 544. For an interesting perspective on Beltrami's ill-fated journey, see William H. Goetzmann, *New Lands, New Men: America and the Second Great Age of Discovery* (New York: Viking, 1986), 151–153. *Schoolcraft's Expedition to Lake Itasca: The Discovery of the Source of the Mississippi,* ed. Philip P. Mason (East Lansing: Michigan State University Press, 1958), 37, xix.

CHAPTER 2

Rivers as Nation-Builders

Embedded in a historical memory spanning centuries and cultures, the Volga and Mississippi Rivers entered a new era in the nineteenth century. Straddling two worlds—the pragmatic and aesthetic—the rivers were still celebrated for their physical prowess based on long-standing roles as transportation arteries, unifiers, nurturers, and oppressors. Juxtaposed with the pragmatic and utilitarian needs the rivers served, the aesthetic properties of each river grew more pronounced throughout the century. Already iconic presences in the United States and Russia through folklore and mythology, the Volga and Mississippi Rivers evolved into nationalist symbols by the mid nineteenth century as the twin forces of industrialization and modernization transformed the rivers. (Paradoxically, the shift to nationalist symbol was marked by a diminishing local knowledge of each river's regime with the advent of steamboats and railroads.) Paralleling the changes—prompted by technology and resulting in locks and dams, hydrostations, and improved navigation channels—was a visual and print culture that valorized the rivers. Artists, poets, writers, and musicians celebrated the rivers, leaving a cultural imprint in Russian and American society with nostalgic depictions of pastoral and idyllic rivers.

For artists, using the genre of landscape art, nature and space are controlled and rationalized, and in the instance of both rivers, by the nineteenth century competing images of a serene, unspoiled river contrasted with images of steamships plying through the placid waters. Thus the Mississippi might be depicted as the ancestral home of Native American villages or the harbinger of progress as steamships dominated river trade by the middle of the century. Other artists portrayed a river that nurtured a free spirit while retaining the idyllic images of a sleepy, rustic landscape. In Russia, artists shaped the national narrative as the expansive Volga was often depicted winding alongside the traditional onion-shaped dome and the vast steppe—a trilogy of national symbols. Contributing to the Volga's centrality in nation-building were those cities located on the banks of the Volga, along the Golden Ring, long associated with Russia's rise. Golden Ring cities such as Yaroslavl, situated at the confluence of the Volga and Kotorosl Rivers, or Kostroma, at the confluence of the Volga and Kostroma Rivers, represent a Russia considered traditional and still revered. Accompanying the images was prose or poetry inspired by national sentiment, further immortalizing the Volga and Mississippi Rivers as school children memorized verse by poets such as Henry Wadsworth Longfellow and his well-known poem, *The Song of Hiawatha*, a work that became part of the American canon. In Russia, the nineteenth-century poet A. Nekrasov paid homage to "Mother Volga," in verse still studied by Russian students. Musicians and writers also contributed to the growing body of literature that anchored both rivers in the national narrative. Not limited to the United States and Russia, landscape ideals participated in the nation-state mythology, ranging from the English garden, Italian Alps, Dutch canals, the Wild West, and the German Rhine. In each of these examples, a distinctive landscape contributed to an evolving national identity.

Thus as part of the larger landscape aesthetic, the Mississippi and Volga Rivers informed a nationalist discourse emerging in Russia and the United States. Reflecting nineteenth-century movements across Europe where a nascent nationalism was coming into full bloom, Russia and the United States looked to their unique, exceptional landscapes for contributions to the developing narrative. Unlike many European nations where a distinct landscape was already associated with the culture, such as the Italian Alps, the United States and Russia were discovering their landscapes in the nineteenth century. For both cultures, valorization of the rivers contributed to the discourse. As major arteries, the rivers were already cultural centerpieces and commemorated for their utilitarian as well as mythological status. Known as "Mother Volga" and the "Father of Waters," journalists, novelists, and poets drafted the rivers into the emergent national narrative and assigned attributes to each ranging from nurturer to liberator.

This reciprocal relationship between landscape and culture is an area explored by a number of scholars as many studies show. Using the prism of landscape, a broader context for social and political history is revealed as seen in the works of Denis Cosgrove, Martin Warnke, and Kenneth Robert Olwig. Adding to their conclusions is Simon Schama's work as he uncovers the existence and perseverance of a nature mythology in the nation's memory.[1] Building upon their arguments but also taking their conclusions a step further and singling out rivers—the Mississippi and Volga—in the dialectic, a more nuanced story emerges. For example, through the study of nineteenth-century Russian artwork, the Volga River worked in tandem with another major characteristic of Russian national identity, namely space, to forge an identity that incorporated the boundlessness and vastness of the Russian terrain. In the case of the Mississippi River, nineteenth-century artwork of the river moved the national identity westward and contributed to a growing frontier myth that shaped an American mentality. In studying the artwork of each, the inhabitants, at times, occupied very different roles. These differences were products of the culture's interactions with the river and ranged from the celebration of the individual as portrayed by George Caleb Bingham in his *Jolly Flatboatmen* to the oppression of the burlaki, or barge haulers, as seen in Ilya Repin's, *The Volga Boatmen*. Alternative portrayals, however, tout the barge hauler's freedom in contrast to the peasant farmer and lament the hardscrabble life of the flatboatmen. Regardless of the portrayal, however, the river influences the dominant narrative whether as nurturer, liberator, or oppressor.[2]

But the rivers also emerge as historical actors, informing a national discourse that is captured by artists, poets, and writers. Numerous illustrations of the Volga and Mississippi Rivers during the nineteenth century reveal more than an artist's aesthetic choice as the characterizations complement a singularity of place and an emergent national pride. This budding national identity incorporates earlier mythology and folklore that celebrated and valorized the rivers. The persistence of these earlier paeans to the rivers, despite an unreconciled relationship with the despoiling effects of industrialization and modernization, presents a new dynamic. Part of the awe that comes when witnessing hydro-modernization works and their subsequent harnessing of rivers can be attributed to the revered place that rivers occupied for centuries. This continuity, a refrain of awe, is based on a historical memory of the rivers dating back centuries as successive generations express their own understandings of the Volga and Mississippi Rivers as each evolve into national icons.

Yet before idealizing their own landscapes in the nineteenth century, particularly the waterscapes of the Volga and Mississippi Rivers, Russian and American landscape artists relied upon European images of landscapes as the predominant aesthetic. A relatively recent art form, beginning in the seventeenth century, landscapes and their celebration of the natural world replaced earlier views of nature as menacing and frightening. (For an example of this earlier imagery, see Gozzoli's *Trial by Fire*, painted in 1444, where nature is bleak and forbidding.) But by the end of the seventeenth century, the perceptions of nature went from threatening to serene and tranquil and during the transition art served as a medium in the process. Prompted in large part by the new technique of linear perspective, developed during the Renaissance, nature was framed and became the view. Dramatically changing the viewer's perception of the natural world, this new technique "glorifies the spectator by organizing everything in the picture in relation to the location of the eye of the beholder." Thus, with the arrival of linear perspective, the depiction of rivers changed radically. The technique allowed more freedom for the artist to craft a view while the observer, in turn, associated the view with an aspect of the landscape. In other words, by framing the image, perceptions can be shaped regarding the content. So, to paraphrase the landscape scholar Gina Crandell, in landscape portraits the viewer must be cognizant that what is termed nature has often been "mediated by pictorial activities such as appropriation, framing and re-presenting."[3]

Another result of this negotiated view is the distance that ensues between the viewer and nature. The depicted scene loses its independence and becomes a constructed view. Ownership of the scene belongs to the viewer, which in turn introduces a sense of control over the surroundings and ultimately, nature. Or in other words, "the spectator has moved inside and the landscape is outdoors." Crandell cites two excellent examples of these phenomena with Leonardo da Vinci's *Annunciation* (late 1470s) and Lorenzo di Credi's *Annunciation* in the late fifteenth century. The removal of the spectator and the coinciding sense of mastery over nature led to an objectification of resources, allowing a civilization to simultaneously valorize the river while exploiting it for hydropower. This is not to say that early Egyptian and Indian society, for example, did not see the Nile and Ganges in utilitarian terms, as they did, but the distance between utilitarian and sacred widened in the modern era. The artwork beginning in the eighteenth century is of special value in realizing the difference among these civilizations' ongoing dialectics with their rivers.[4]

As a result, the new genre of landscape painting, first popularized by Claude Lorrain with his scenic portraits of the Italian landscape, allowed another lens for the portrayal of water and rivers. Initially Claude's landscapes gave ascendancy to the Italian landscape which remained the predominant landscape aesthetic for many years.[5] But the depiction of landscapes evolved and was influenced by intellectual movements such as the Romantic Movement in the nineteenth century. For example, in the United States in the 1820s, poets called upon artists to paint the New World and part of this synergy no doubt produced the Hudson River School, which existed from 1825 to 1876. In many ways similar to what occurred in Russia, artists in the Hudson River School underscored the exceptionalism of the American environment. But in emphasizing American uniqueness, their points of comparison were always the European landscapes. Some of the more notable artists in this school included Thomas Cole, Frederic Edwin Church, and Martin Johnson Heade.

Further evidence of efforts to tout the American landscape and its superiority over its European counterpart, particularly through one of its most scenic rivers, can be found in the following commentaries. Beginning with William Cullen Bryant, a well-known nineteenth-century poet, he encouraged Americans to visit "the western shore of the Hudson" as "worthy of a pilgrimage across the Atlantic as the Alps themselves." This was during a period when the wealthy chose Europe as their destination for extended vacations. Another paean to the American landscape came from Thomas Cole, a prominent Hudson River School artist, who when visiting Italy and other parts of Europe said that he did not think Europe's scenery could compete with an American vista and that the Rhine was "infinitely inferior to the Hudson in natural magnificence and grandeur." Cole and Bryant worked together in producing *The American Landscape*, a collection of landscapes that in the words of one scholar "was an effort to capitalize on the growing taste for picturesque scenery in the context of cultural nationalism."[6]

Although the initial efforts of Bryant, Cole, and others to celebrate the American landscape began in the East, it was not long before the Mississippi River became part of the discussion distinguishing America's physical beauty. Complementing the work of the Hudson River School and its promoters were general histories of the new republic's geography, such as Timothy Flint's popular 1832 work, *The History and Geography of the Mississippi Valley*. Flint echoes Cole's words when he compensates for the perceived lack of American culture by comparing landscapes where the Mississippi and its tributaries figure prominently. In Flint's words:

> Our country has been described abroad, as sterile of moral interest. We have, it is said, no monuments, no ruins, none of the colossal remains of temples, and baronial castles, and monkish towers ... [but] when our thoughts have traversed rivers of a thousand leagues in length; when we have seen the ascending steamboat breasting the surge, and gleaming through the verdure of the trees; when we have imagined the happy multitudes, that from these shores will contemplate this scenery in days to come; we have thought, that our great country might at least compare with any other, in the beauty of its natural scenery.

In the same passage, Flint also pays tribute to the achievements of past Native American civilizations in the Mississippi Valley who would later be known as the mound builders. Together the Hudson River School, with its emphasis on American New World beauty, and histories, such as Flint's, set the stage for the Mississippi and its iconic place in American culture, reinforcing the celebration of what is perceived as American exceptionalism. Thus, in the nascent national narrative, rivers figured prominently in America's story.[7]

As Flint's history indicated, the Mississippi like the Hudson River became a bellwether for American exceptionalism as nineteenth-century artists produced numerous paintings of the waterscape. A popular art form in the mid nineteenth century was the panorama. Capturing the imagination of a mass public, the panoramas were part theater and part painting, requiring large areas for display. The topics were numerous and in England, one popular panorama entitled "Eidometropolis" by Girtin was the city of London along the Thames. In this panorama, the Thames "was the commercial artery signifying Britain's maritime prowess." In the United States, several artists painted panoramas of the Mississippi River with the first well-known one publicly identified as *Banvard's Panorama of the Mississippi, Painted on Three Miles of Canvas, exhibiting a View of Country 1200 Miles in Length, extending from the Mouth of the Missouri River to the City of New Orleans, being by far the Largest*

Picture ever executed by Man. According to one contemporary, John Putnam, Banvard was inspired by an article in a "foreign journal" that lamented while "America could boast the most picturesque and magnificent scenery in the world" the country did not have an artist to prove it. Not only did his panorama address this oversight and showcase American scenery but according to Putnam, Banvard's painting also reflected the superiority of the Mississippi over "the streamlets of Europe." Initially disinterested, the American public soon attended showings in large numbers. Following Banvard's painting was the panorama by Henry Lewis that was allegedly four miles long. He referred to his undertaking as the *Great National Work*. In contrast to Banvard, Lewis included part of the Upper Mississippi River in an area near Minneapolis. Both artists showed their panoramas to audiences in the eastern part of the United States and Europe. In addition to these two major panoramas, three others were painted during this period.[8]

As the panoramas of the Mississippi River drew large crowds, nationally and internationally, these creations also served educational and entertainment purposes. One beneficiary of the panoramas was America's first renowned poet, Henry Wadsworth Longfellow, who after seeing Banvard's work immortalized the river in poems, such as *The Song of Hiawatha*, one of the most well-known poems in the United States in the nineteenth century. In addition to seeing the panorama, Longfellow chose the setting of Minnehaha Falls on the Mississippi River after seeing a daguerreotype of the falls. The falls are memorialized in these famous lines from *The Song of Hiawatha*:

> "Hark!" she said; "I hear a rushing,
> Hear a roaring and a rushing,
> Hear the Falls of Minnehaha
> Calling to me from a distance!"

In another well-received Longfellow poem, *Evangeline,* part of the setting is again the Mississippi River Valley. He describes Evangeline's journey here:

> It was the month of May. Far down the Beautiful River,
> Past the Ohio shore and past the mouth of the Wabash,
> Into the golden stream of the broad and swift Mississippi,

In this epic poem, Longfellow goes on to describe the lower Mississippi Valley after studying its flora and fauna from Banvard's panorama. The importance of these poems, particularly *The Song of Hiawatha,* cannot be underestimated as every school child was expected to memorize sections of this work of Americana. As a result, the Mississippi River was becoming embedded in the historical memory associated with a national narrative that distinguished its landscape and heritage from the well-established Europe.[9]

Further contributing to the rich folklore surrounding the river was the Mississippi's role in shaping what became known as the frontier identity evidenced through doctrines such as Manifest Destiny that celebrated and rationalized the westward movement. One of the foremost nineteenth-century artists who immortalized the Mississippi in this arena was George Caleb Bingham. Not possessing the artistic ability of landscape artists associated with the Hudson School, Bingham was more of a popularizer in large part due to the support he received from the American Art-Union. This organization, although only in existence for twelve years during the mid nineteenth century, influenced American culture significantly. One of the Union's presidents was William Cullen Bryant (mentioned earlier for his belief in the singularity of the American landscape) who was a strong and vocal advocate for the American arts. Bryant was a likely spokesperson as the mission of the Union was "to accomplish a Truly National Object through the promotion, distribution and exhibiting of paintings and sculptures by native or resident artists." Inherent in the mission and often discussed in union publications was the claim that a republican society could cultivate an appreciation of the arts as the association sought to break with European models "by favoring native subjects." Many of the works promoted by the Union were landscapes, and in comparing American and European landscapes, one 1844 Union report asked, "Is not Nature's home everywhere? And does she not here spread forth landscapes lovely as those of Claude."[10]

Yet more evidence of the Union's mission to develop an American landscape aesthetic came in 1844 when the Union distributed the P.F. Rothermel work, *De Soto Discovering the Mississippi*. With that end in mind, namely the promotion of American art, the Union sponsored exhibits that were free and open to the public. Union activities were a success with large numbers attending their exhibits. Despite competition from other art organizations, such as the National Academy of Design (founded in 1825 with the goal to promote fine arts in the United States), the American Art-Union remained the most influential in the United States with memberships reaching 20,000 in 1849.

It was through the American Art-Union that several of Bingham's works became well-known in the late 1840s, including *Jolly Flatboatmen, Raftsmen Playing Cards,* and *Stump Orator,* although Bingham also exhibited with the National Academy of Design. The Union, however, provided him the greatest exposure through their wide distribution of engravings to members. In an 1849 Union bulletin discussing Bingham, his paintings were described as "thoroughly American in their subjects and could never have been painted by one who was not perfectly familiar with the scenes they represent." Despite later criticism of his work in a Union article entitled "Development of Nationality in American Art," the author still acknowledged that Bingham produced "some good studies of the western character."[11]

In Bingham's paintings, he depicted an image of the river that was already capturing the American imagination, namely the Mississippi River as the gateway to the West. In one of Bingham's more famous paintings, *Fur Traders Descending the Missouri* (the Missouri is a major tributary of the Mississippi), he portrays, in the words of one critic, "a historical past mingling with an almost mythical existence along the frontier riverbanks." In this painting, the waterscape shares an identity with corresponding nineteenth-century portraits of the Volga—the river is functional, serving the young nation's commercial needs. But the river as a boundary between civilization and the frontier is also the producer of a world fast disappearing—the fur trader and the opening of the Western frontier. A nostalgia and a sense of what the new country should be pervades Bingham's works, similar in many respects to the Russian artist, Isaak Levitan's depiction of the traditional Russian village situated alongside the Volga. In both, the rivers are a major part of the idealized past.

Another well-known Bingham work is his *Raftsmen Playing Cards*. This work shows the rough and tumble world of the raftsmen. A frontier actor, similar to the legendary Daniel Boone, the raftsman's marginal existence is

Figure 2.1. George Caleb Bingham, *Raftsmen Playing Cards,* 1847, oil on canvas.
Source: Saint Louis Art Museum, bequest of Ezra H. Linley by exchange 50:1934.

comparable to that of the burlaki in that both types were known for their law-lessness and living on the fringe of society. While the raftsman and burlaki led lives, punctuated by hard work with minimal material rewards, the raftsman's outsider status translated into an idealized image of rugged individualism or in the words of one contemporary critic the men possessed a "vitality," all made possible by the river. The wildness of the river and the frontier allowed for a freedom that marked American exceptionalism. In contrast, at certain historical points, the vastness of the steppes that surrounded the Volga pro-duced a labor force that was depicted as the oppressed burlaki, although prior to the nineteenth century the burlaki also enjoyed an outsider status separat-ing them from the land-bound serfs. In both instances, the frontier, whether the American West or the steppes, worked in tandem with the rivers to shape a labor force that shared an imagery of freedom at the cost of being outside tra-ditional society. Again, these were all popular images and while embedded in a budding national consciousness, the reality between American and Russian workforces, despite the celebration of an American individualism, may have been more similar than different. (For example, paintings of slaves working in the lower Mississippi, along with their numerous work songs, offer a compet-ing image to the flatboatmen and one much closer to those of the burlaki.) Still, the popularization of the freedom of the flatboatmen persisted as seen in another Bingham painting, *Jolly Flatboatmen*. As the title implies, the painting

Figure 2.2. George Caleb Bingham, *Jolly Flatboatmen in Port*, 1857, oil on canvas. *Source:* Saint Louis Art Museum, Museum Purchase 123:1944.

Figure 2.3. John Frederick Kensett, *View on the Upper Mississippi,* 1855, oil on canvas. *Source:* Saint Louis Art Museum, Eliza McMillan Trust 22:1950.

conveys the same message in that the flatboatmen are touted for their rugged individualism, which in turn contributed to a carefree existence that many Americans equated with the frontier identity.[12]

In studying Bingham's work, scholars surmised that many nineteenth-century Americans considered the world Bingham illustrated as passing and fueled by nostalgia, the paintings depicted a recent past that man wanted to commemorate. As a result, this is the river culture they wanted to remember. But Bingham's portrayals of the Mississippi River also revealed the evolution of a river initially perceived as wild and unpredictable to the present-day perceptions of a scenic, pastoral waterway. Other painters, such as Seth Eastman, John Frederick Kensett, and Ferdinand Richardt, followed Bingham and reinforced the image of a romantic, quiet river. Underlying these portraits, however, was the closely held belief that the United States, with its major rivers such as the Mississippi and Hudson, were distinct from Europe. American landscape painters of the American West, such as Albert Bierstadt, Thomas Moran, and John Mix Stanley reflected these convictions.

Coinciding with nineteenth-century representations of the landscape was a growing folklore of the exploits of various river pilots or the earlier keelboatmen such as the legendary Mike Fink. (The river pilots were the successors to the raftsmen in Bingham's paintings.) Stories about Fink's "rough and tumble" exploits, often mirroring the volatility and strength of the Mississippi, are renowned. Some of the most common accounts referred to his prodigious alcohol consumption—contemporaries claimed he could drink up to a gallon of whiskey a day without any effects—to the oft-told tale of his target shooting a bottle perched on his brother's head. According to one 1828 account, typical in its celebratory tone: "He was the hero of a hundred fights, and the leader in a thousand daring adventures. From Pittsburg to St. Louis and New Orleans, his fame was established. Every farmer on the shore kept on good terms with Mike—otherwise there was no safety for his property.... On the Ohio, he was known among his companions by the appellation of the 'Snapping Turtle'; and on the Mississippi, he was called 'The Snag.'"[13] Complementing the colorful stories about Fink and keelboatmen were songs that illuminated their reputations as roustabouts. One song described their lives: "Dance all night, till broad daylight / And go home with the gals in the morning."[14]

But inherent in the stories in which Fink represented the common moniker for keelboatmen as "half horse and half alligator" was a grudging admiration for his abilities in navigating the river. Merchants entrusted the transport of their goods to the keelboatmen and knowledge of the river was critical. Accounts of storms on the river and boats losing all of their goods were common. In one incident, a passenger going downstream near St. Louis recounts the ferocity of thunder-gusts that "twisted the cotton trees in all directions, as though they had been rushes." He goes on to say that while he and his family survived, two other boats became unlashed and one was "dashed in pieces" while the other sunk. Both boats were carrying "four or five hundred barrels of flour, porter and whiskey," all lost.[15]

While the river appealed to young men, disillusioned with the demands of farm work, experienced raftsmen knew the serene, slow-moving river portrayed by Bingham could easily be interrupted by a snag or sandbar and claim the lives of those unprepared for the "Wicked River's" unpredictability. Fink's reputation and that of other keelboatmen, advertised through venues such as "The Crockett Almanacs," and specialty books published throughout the nineteenth century derived from this relationship with the river and the other traits, bordering on lawlessness, were in large part a product of a riverine environment. Again similar associations were made with the Volga and the barge haulers, who were often depicted in Russian prose, poetry, and song as freedom-loving, lawless men living on the margins of Russian society. The Volga, in turn, allowed for this lifestyle.[16]

Mark Twain echoed the same themes as his writings further immortalized characters such as Fink. Through Twain's writings, these men became mythological figures known for their skill in navigating, their rootlessness, love of the river, and of course their tendency for "brawling." Again, the folklore—oral and written—was similar to the myths surrounding the burlaki. In the following passage from *Life on the Mississippi*, Twain illustrates the necessary skill of the river pilot in navigating a river known for its fluctuating depths: "You've got to have good fair marks from one end of the river to the other, that will help the bank tell you when there is enough water in each of these countless places—like that stump, you know. When the river first begins to rise, you can run half a dozen of the deepest of them; when it rises a foot more you can run another dozen, the next foot will add a couple of dozen, and so on: so you see you have to know your banks and marks to a dead moral certainty."[17]

Skilled river pilots were also needed because of the river's volatility and savagery in creating new channels. In the following passage, Twain evoked the river's constant movement: "The Mississippi is remarkable in still another way—its disposition to make prodigious jumps by cutting through narrow necks of land, and thus straightening and shortening itself. More than once it has shortened itself thirty miles at a single jump! These cutoffs have had curious effects: they have thrown several river towns out into the rural districts, and built up sand bars and forests in front of them."[18]

Foreign visitors in the first half of the nineteenth century frequently mentioned an ongoing theme—the river's ability to surprise with its unpredictable twists and turns. Two of the most well-known visitors, Alexis de Tocqueville and Charles Dickens, remarked upon these impressive features. In Tocqueville's 1839 visit, he observed that "the Mississippi itself sometimes seems in doubt which way it is to go; it twists backward several times, and only after slowing down in lakes and marshes seems finally to make up its mind and meander toward the south." But Tocqueville also recognized the river's role in the emerging nation when he predicted a prosperous future for the United States, including "the inexhaustible valley of the Mississippi" as one of the contributing sources.[19]

In many ways, a less flattering portrait—Dickens referred to the Mississippi as "this foul stream"—he nevertheless registered a sense of wonder at the river's physical strength. Dickens begins his assessment:

> But what words shall describe the Mississippi, great father of rivers, who (praise be to Heaven) has no young children like him! An enormous ditch, sometimes two or three miles wide, running liquid mud, six miles an hour: its strong and frothy current choked and obstructed by huge logs and whole forest trees: now twining themselves together in great rafts, from the interstices of which a sedgy lazy foam works up, to float upon the water's top; now rolling past like monstrous bodies, their tangled roots showing like matted hair; now glancing singly by like giant leeches; and now writhing round in the vortex of some small whirlpool, like wounded snakes.

The power, precariousness, and explosive nature of the Mississippi were staples of the river's folklore. Unlike the Volga, where the dominant imagery is its calmness despite the challenge of shoals and sandbars when traveling the river's course, the Mississippi's volatility becomes one of its trademarks.[20]

The river's precariousness, however, did not preclude the growth of river traffic and as Twain indicated with the arrival of the steamboat; a new actor emerged in the landscape. (The same would be true for the Volga.) Now many of the riverscapes of the Mississippi included images of steamboats docking or a steamboat surrounded by a riverine landscape. The steamboat also prompted tours of the river, and public figures, such as Henry David Thoreau, traveled up the river. In 1854 the Upper Mississippi River was celebrated through the Grand Excursion, a public relations campaign concocted by two railroad financiers who built the Rock Island Railroad. This tour up the river, beginning at Rock Island, included 1,200 guests with many well-known names such as former president Millard Fillmore and Charles A. Dana of the *New York Tribune*. Praise for the scenery came from several of the passengers, and one compared the Upper Mississippi to the Rhine River. But the most glowing description came from a *New York Times* reporter when he wrote: "Perhaps you have beheld such sublimity in dreams, but surely never in daylight waking elsewhere in this wonderful world. Over one hundred and fifty miles of unimaginable fairyland, genie-land, and world of visions, have we passed during the last twenty-four hours… Throw away your guide books; heed not the statement of travelers; deal not with seekers after and retailers of the picturesque; believe no man, but see for your-self [*sic*] the Mississippi River above Dubuque."[21]

The Grand Excursion was the beginning of "boom times in the Upper Mississippi Valley" as other celebrities traveled up the river with similar praise, such as Rufus King who in the following year proclaimed, "The 'Father of Waters' has no peer among all the mighty rivers which furrow the surface of the globe." The period was short lived, however, as railroads began to dominate the transportation industry in the Midwest by the late nineteenth century. With the advent of the railroads and the decline of logging in the Upper Mississippi River Valley, the Mississippi was "deserted by the end of the nineteenth century except for the occasional excursion boat" sparking a new dialogue about the role of the river. But regardless of its diminished role as transportation artery, the Mississippi River, through art, prose, and poetry, was firmly entrenched in the historical memory.[22]

In turning to the Volga River, Russia entered the nineteenth century with a longer history on the river than their American counterparts on the Mississippi. Burlaki labor, although comparable to the keelboatmen, was well established by the 1800s and trade on the river under the Russian tsars dated back to Ivan's time in the mid-1500s. The commonality, however, between both rivers was the role each played in shaping the emergent national narrative. Further, in developing a national identity both Russia and the United States drew upon European vistas for comparisons and found in their own respective landscapes an exceptionalism, exemplified in part by the Mississippi and Volga rivers. In forging an identity, however, Russia also labored under the Enlightenment-constructed idea of Eastern Europe where the Volga often served as the marker between a European and Asian Russia. Similar to the Mississippi and its defining line between the civilized East and frontier West, the Volga represented the division between a developing Europe and the barbaric East. But for Russia, events in the nineteenth century radically changed perceptions of the sprawling empire. Externally, events such as the successful outcome of the Napoleonic Wars juxtaposed with the crushing Crimean War defeat and internally the push for reform all contributed to a Russia in the midst of substantial change. Entering the century as the sleeping giant, Russia's greatness was reaffirmed with Napoleon's defeat and humiliating retreat from Moscow. But less than a half-century later the Crimean War exposed the fragility of the image as Russia suffered a devastating blow to its pride, witnessed by the European powers. Yet at the same time Russia experienced change internally as a growing educated class clamored for reform. Tsar Alexander II responded to the demand for reform through the abolition of serfdom, and throughout the century a gradual economic liberalization occurred resulting in a middle class that had the means to travel and offer new impressions about Russian identity. Still, the call for reform dominated the latter half of the century and Russian intellectuals, including artists, poets, and musicians, played a significant role in this dynamic.[23]

Coinciding with the call for reform was an emergent national conversation regarding Russian identity similar to discussions throughout Europe. For the Russian community the discourse regarding identity was divided as intellectuals pondered whether Russia was a product of Eastern or Western influences. A number of nineteenth-century scholars weighed in on the subject, ranging from Pyotr Chaadaev, who questioned whether Russia possessed any cultural legacy, to those rising number of Slavophiles who prided themselves on Russia's Slavic past and sought to distance Russia from an identity that duplicated Europe. The tension persisted up into the early twentieth century as intellectual Velimir Khlebnikov asked: "And will we remain deaf to the land as it cries 'A voice! Give me a voice!' Will we forever remain mockingbirds, imitating Western songs?" In reviewing the profuse literature of this era, contemporary scholars, such as Sara Dickinson, contend that Russian ties to a Western European identity were reinforced after Russia gained control of the Crimea in 1783. At this juncture, combined with a visit by Catherine the Great in 1787, Russian literature emphasized the "Orientalism" of the territory distinguishing the area and culture from a Russian Western European identity. Still another scholar, Olga Maiorova, suggests that the problem with Russian identity was the blurred distinction between empire and nation. Others credit the multiethnic aspects of Russia, together with its immense geographical reach, from overshadowing any one, single identity. Because of its size which includes so many diverse landscapes, the question was posed: "What is or can be 'symbol' of the Russian landscape? Is it a birch forest? The Siberian tiaga? The vast rivers of the Don and the Volga? The frozen North?" Complementing these inquiries has been recent scholarship into nineteenth-century travel and guide books. Moving beyond the question of identity being rooted in an Orthodox, Slavic, or European past, contemporary Russian scholars are looking at the formation of identity, in part through representations of space.[24]

Returning, however, to the nineteenth century, Russians had mixed views regarding their landscapes. Prior to the century, Russians associated a landscape aesthetic with Western European vistas, especially Italy and the Alps. Even the one area in Russia considered scenic—the Crimea—was referred to as the "Russian Italy." Mentioned earlier, this was not unique to Russia as landscape art in many European countries began with a celebration of the Italian landscape through the works of Claude Lorrain but by the nineteenth century, Britain, France, and Germany had begun to tout their own geographies. Although Russian artists initially ignored their own landscapes, the genre of landscape painting allowed another lens for the portrayal of water and rivers. Up until the nineteenth century, Russians considered their own landscapes, such as the peaceful Volga River winding through the bleak, unbroken steppe country, as inferior.[25]

Others, outside of Russia shared the sentiment, as an 1839 travel account by the Marquis de Custine illustrated. In summarizing his trip to Russia, Custine lamented: "In this country, different from all others, Nature herself has become the accomplice of the caprices of the man who has killed liberty in order to deify unity. Nature too is everywhere the same: two types of trees, blighted and thinly scattered farther than the eye can reach in the boggy or sandy plains—the birch and the pine—make up the entire natural vegetation of northern Russia, that is to say in the vicinity of Petersburg and the surrounding provinces which include a vast expanse of territory." Even Custine's description of Moscow evokes a bleak, unremitting landscape when he writes, "You have before you a sad landscape, but vast like the ocean, and to animate the emptiness, a poetic city whose architecture has no name, just as it has no model."[26]

During this period, the English traveler Robert Bremner visited the same area with an even more damming critique. Bremner begins his account: "Russia is the largest and the ugliest country in the world. Nature seems to have lavished all her deformity on this one empire, which, without question, covers the least beautiful portion of the whole habitable globe." Still Bremner surprises the reader when he recounts his first impression of the Volga in which he also draws upon the imagery of calmness when describing the river. Bremner observes: "The demeanor of this river sovereign is worthy of a king. Leaving less powerful rivals to raise themselves into importance by fuming and brawling—

secure in his might and uncontested dignity—he moves calmly but restlessly on. There is no noise, no surge—the glassy tide lies as peaceful as a lake, and, on the first glance, from its great breadth, bears some resemblance to one."[27]

Still, as late as 1874, visitors offered less-than-flattering descriptions. An 1874 travel booklet, *A Trip Up the Volga to the Fair of Nijni-Novgorod,* comments upon the diversity of the Russian population, which the author, a British tourist, calls "picturesque," in contrast to the landscape. In the author's words, "Russia is in this respect the most picturesque of countries—picturesque not certainly in its natural scenery, which consists for the most part of monotonous and endless plains, but in the races which people them." The supposed lack of a landscape aesthetic paralleled the absence of a nationalism that was emerging throughout Western Europe. European intellectuals iterated this view while other critics prompted Russians artists to examine their own surroundings so that art in Russia "becomes more of a national culture."[27]

But perceptions were evolving—at least internally—and two of the first Russians to recognize and popularize the beauty of the Volga landscape were the Chernetsov brothers, Grigory and Nikanor. In 1838, they traveled down the Volga and similar to the 1840s artists of the Mississippi, Banvard and Henry Lewis, produced a panorama of the river, comprised of seven parts. Another similarity was the challenge of river travel as the brothers commented upon the numerous shoals, sandbars, and strong winds. Like early-nineteenth-century travelers on the Mississippi, they recognized the skill of the riverboat pilot in reaching their destination. In writing about their experiences, they reinforced the Volga's historic role, when they observed that "the Volga is the fertile vein of Russian lands and deserves the name, Matushka." But their most important contribution might have been that "[t]hey raised the undescribed beauty of the Russian land toward the level of classical beauty of West and East."[29]

Still other changes were affecting Russian perceptions of their environment. In the Russian Imperial Academy of Arts in St. Petersburg, the premier institution for established and budding artists, a revolt was staged when a small group of art students left the Academy in the early 1860s and formed their own group called the Society of Wandering Exhibitions. Members of the group were called the Peredvizhniki or the Wanderers. Known for their emphasis on Russian life, "they [the Wanderers] intended to reconnect their art with their homeland" through portrayals of the Russian people, Russian landscapes, and Russian history. The Wanderers, however, were only the beginning as Russian intellectuals and artists throughout the late nineteenth century debated the place of art in an emergent national culture. Many, such as Ivan Kramskoy and Vladimir Stasov urged artists to serve the larger society. The Volga was part of the national awakening as artists that were products of the break with the Imperial Academy, such as Isaak Levitan and Ilya Repin, portrayed the river in scenes that illustrated Russian everyday life. Levitan, a contemporary of Anton Chekhov, is considered by many Russians to be the greatest landscape artist of his time. To Chekhov, his work showed a spiritual response to the natural world. During Soviet Union times, critics were divided over Levitan's legacy. Some, such as Fedorov-Davydov, upheld Levitan's landscapes for their "lyricism and boundless love for one's native land," while others during Stalin's era dismissed the imagery in his art as "nationalistic trifles." But whether a critic or fan, both recognized the nationalist element in his art.[30]

Levitan contributed to the evolving culture of national landscape painting with his Volga paintings, drawn in the 1880s while he summered on the banks of the Volga in the village of Plyoss. In one of his works, *Golden Evening* (1889), Levitan portrays the village of Plyoss with the symbolic onion-shaped dome of the Russian Orthodox Church overseeing a terrain of trees broken by bush vegetation, all on the banks of the Volga. The river is the main actor in the painting as it conveys a sense of boundlessness and immense space; a spaciousness that would be associated with a unique Russian identity. The placement of the Russian Orthodox Church in the painting, perched above the Volga, succeeds in capturing two national icons and in this work, Levitan evokes the spiritual response that Chekhov recognized. Complementing the spiritual response is a sense of timelessness and the quietude associated with village life, prompting one critic to remark: "Do not the slow, tranquil flow of the big river and the sunset haze of a summer day conjure up another image, the image of a country blessed with peace, happiness and plenty?"[31]

But Levitan did more than master the pastoral idyll as he was also a master at unifying what were often conflicting themes as seen in his 1889 work *After the Rain*. In this painting, he again shows the sleepy village of Plyoss on the banks of the Volga but this time with fishing boats and a distant steamship on the river. While Levitan continues to display a spaciousness, the Volga in this painting is a working river; its utilitarian value whether through transportation or as a resource provider is the predominant theme. The Volga as highway is even more pronounced in his 1891 painting *Fresh Wind Volga,* in which barge ships are centrally represented. As one scholar noted, "the Volga is shown in its role as the mighty and important thoroughfare it represents for Russia."[32] In most of Levitan's paintings, however, the balance between the river's aesthetics and utilitarian use is more even. For example, in *Evening on the Volga* (1888) three fishing boats are visible on the shore but they are dwarfed by the river's grandeur, illustrated through its width in conjunction with an endless sky and the steppes that are seen on the other side. The colors in combination with a peaceful evening setting all contribute to an image that is serene and peaceful; an association with the Russian village and countryside.

Another well-known Russian artist who painted scenes of Russian village life and the Volga is Alexei Savrasov. Claimed by many to be Russia's greatest land-

Figure 2.4. I. Levitan, *After the Rain,* 1889, oil on canvas. *Source:* The State Tretyakov Gallery, Moscow.

scape painter, Savrasov is best known for his work *The Rooks Have Returned* (1871). Savrasov's mastery at capturing the everyday in Russian life without diminishing its significance is evident as he places the rooks in detail in the forefront with images of a Russian village in the background. In his painting *End of Summer on the Volga River,* Savrasov presents an agricultural scene with threshed piles of grain dotting a farm field. The Volga and an immense sky are off in the distance. The painting offers a sense of space alongside a rural setting that taken together provide a coherent image of the Russian landscape while the Volga serves as the unifying theme in this national narrative. The agricultural idyll that Savrasov depicts will be celebrated again in Socialist Realist art.

All of the Russian artwork discussed thus far was produced during the last half of the nineteenth century. Contributing to a coherent image of the Russian landscape, these landscape portraits were always part of the narrative regarding identity and one of the unifying themes within this narrative was the Volga River. In the works of Levitan and Savrasov, the Volga's role is two-fold. The river as highway contributes to commerce while its beauty and immensity offer sustenance for the Russian soul. In a departure from the celebratory and traditional riverscapes, however, is another Russian painting where the Volga is a major actor but in a very different sense. Through the provocative work of Ilya Repin in his painting *The Volga Barge Haulers* (1873), the Volga is part oppressor. Interestingly, this work was painted in a very different landscape in the Lower Volga Basin near the village of Shiriaev Burak with the closest city being

Figure 2.5. I. Levitan, *Evening on the Volga*, 1888, oil on canvas. *Source:* The State Tretyakov Gallery.

Stavropol. Considered a classic in the pantheon of Russian art, the painting is one of the leading works of the Peredvizhniki and is credited by many as the inaugural work of the realist school in Russia. Claimed by many as one of their own, ranging from those promoting art's role to serve the nation in the 1880s to the Soviets in the 1930s, Repin tried to remain outside the debates as he saw himself as an artist and not allied to any one political or social trend. (In later Soviet reviews of his work, critics said that Repin, like the "advanced Russian intelligentsia … had a feeling of personal responsibility for the fate of ordinary people and for the historical destiny of the country.")[33]

In this specific painting, *"The Volga Barge Haulers,"* studied primarily for its realist theme of nineteenth-century Russian life, the river is seen as an oppressor in the lives of the eleven burlaki who with leather harnesses strapped across their chests struggle to pull a barge, full of goods, up the river. Largely a social and political statement, as the burlaki were often depicted in a different light, the painting conveys the oppression and despair of the burlaki. This group of laborers, already known in Russian folklore, assumed further status with Repin's portrayal. Repin took two years to complete the masterpiece in which critics often comment upon the quiet dignity of the men's faces despite the appearance of a barely subsistence existence. In his reminiscences of the painting, Repin writes about one of the burlaki in particular, Kanin, who "with a rag on his head, with clothing patched together by his own hand and worn through again, was a man who inspired much respect: he was like a saint undergoing an ordeal." In this same passage, Repin compares the burlak to early Greek philosophers sold into slavery after the fall of Hellas.[34]

Repin's portrayal, however, reflected only one nineteenth-century perspective of the laborers. In earlier centuries Russians associated the burlaki with lawlessness from living on the margins of society. They were associated with the river in that the river embodied a freedom of movement and in earlier centuries travel on the river was also associated with danger because of the lack of law. Unlike the land-bound serfs, the burlaki, like the keelboatmen, were perceived as being free of the constraints of conventional society and as a result, often envied. By the nineteenth century, however, the burlakis' economic status had changed. While in earlier centuries they had entered this lifestyle because it allowed more freedom, by the 1800s the choice to be a burlaki revealed the desperate economic situation in the villages. Repin's work illustrates the dire economic circumstances of this laboring class as their numbers on the Volga swelled in the early nineteenth century before the arrival of steam.[35]

But the river is also an actor in Repin's painting. The Volga is immense and Repin's use of light, in which he "caught the broad white light of the Volga region," communicates the spaciousness of the steppe, so the river, steppe, and sky appear as one. As one art historian noted, "Here is the mighty river that flows through Russia's past and lands; here are the people that have labored for centuries along its banks." While the vista in the painting is never-ending, the portrayal of the burlaki gives the work a bleakness, which is also overlaid on the landscape. The river, or nature, is viewed as overpowering and later depictions of Russian resources in the Soviet era revisit the theme of nature's power but with the Soviet goal of taming and "bridling" their river. Soviet reviewers project this vision of man versus nature into Repin's work; one critic said Repin

Figure 2.6. Ilya Repin, *Bargemen on the Volga*, 1873, oil on canvas. *Source:* State Russian Museum, Saint Petersburg.

chose the subject because of "the courage of the barge haulers in the battle with the elemental force of the river." But during the Soviet era, the worker's face is depicted as contented as he is "joyful" in his labor. One of the first posters to present the worker in this light resulted from work on the Dnieper River project with a smiling laborer, with arm raised standing in front of the river and dam—a stark contrast to the wretched lives of the burlaki. Still the Soviets, with their own school of Socialist Realist art often emulated nineteenth-century landscape art in their efforts to tout the Soviet state. The difference, however, is that the country's resources, such as the Volga, were ultimately subdued in the Soviet success story and the landscapes had an ideological purpose.[36]

Paralleling the art work of the mid to late nineteenth century, were folk songs and literary works memorializing the Russian landscape and the Volga River. The classic folk song, "Volga Boatman," reached a larger audience after Mily Balakirev's trip down the Volga River. (Balakinev was one of several Russian musicians seeking to learn more about Russian folk music.) Folklore about the burlaki was popular and often presented a different imagery than Repin's portrait. Similar to Mike Fink on the Mississippi, the Volga barge haulers had their own celebrities. One, known as Nikituska Lomov, was memorialized for his ability to do the work of four men as well as stories of his protecting those less fortunate. Another famous tale, "The Barge Hauler's Contest with the Frost," shows the barge hauler's strength and endurance in the face of cold. While the nobleman has to wear a fur coat to protect him from the elements, the barge hauler wears only a short peasant's coat and no hat or gloves. But another similarity they share with Fink is a reputation for alcohol consumption and lawlessness. Often depicted as bandits and robbers, their lives were grist for popular folk lyrics in which one has the burlaki cutting off the head of the governor of Astrakhan and throwing it into the "Mother Volga." In another folk lyric, robbers are on the "Mother Volga; along the wide expanse," when they spot a boat with a well-dressed captain who they intend to rob. Still another folk song follows the story of an orphan who "was nursed and fed by Mother Volga," and went on to become a robber from the land of Astraxan.[37]

But the burlaki also immortalized the Volga through their work songs, sung in sync with the rhythms of pulling the barge and its heavy load up the river. In these folk lyrics, the work is exacting with singular heavy movements required of the barge hauler. The river, itself, is an oppressor as the demands of pulling the barge upstream take a deadly toll on the burlaki. In these lyrics, the burlaki are working against the river, much like the keelboatmen did with the Mississippi. Through the words, the sense of constant pulling against the river's current is expressed and the tedious motions of their work:

Eh, uxnem! Eh, uxnem!
Once more, once again!

Eh uxnem! Eh, uxnem!
Once more, once again
We will swing the birch!
We will toss the curly birch!
Aj-da, da, aj-da, aj-da, da, aj-da,
We will toss the curly birch!

This song, known as "Dubinuska" became very famous and its refrain was associated politically as a revolutionary song during the 1905 Revolution.[38]

The well-known Russian writer, Maxim Gorky, also had a special interest in the lives of the barge haulers as his grandfather told him stories about his life pulling a barge by himself up the Volga. In his grandfather's words: "The barge was there, in the water, and I was on the bank pulling it, barefoot, over the sharp stones. I kept at it from dawn to dusk with the sun broiling the back of my neck and my head bubbling as if it were a pot of melted iron. The torments piled on me. I had an ache in every little bone till I could hardly see straight, but I had to hang on; and the tears ran and I cried my heart out." Gorky's grandfather also recalled the songs the barge haulers sang at the end of the day while preparing their meal. Songs, that in his words were "heartbreaking" and would "send a shiver through you to hear it, and you'd feel the Volga current was like a racing horse and that it was heading up to the clouds; and then troubles didn't matter any more than specks in the wind."[39]

Still, the lives of the barge haulers represented freedom and a sense of lawlessness to many. In one folk song, the governor of Astrakhan pleads: "Oh, you're barge haulers, free people. Take all the golden treasure you need" In response the barge haulers told the governor it was not his riches they were interested in but instead his head and so:

They cut off the governor's wild head,
They threw the head into the Mother Volga,
The young men laughed at him:
"You well know, governor, you have been harsh toward us,
You beat us, you destroyed us, sent us into exile,
Shot our wives and children at the gates!"[40]

An 1862 report on the lives of the barge haulers reveals how the land-bound peasants saw barge hauler life as representing freedom. Recent scholarship, however, shows the freedom was often fleeting. According to one source, as Russia's economy grew so did the labor force of burlaki so by 1815, there were 400,000 burlaki on the Volga. Because of the nature of their work, the mortality rate was high (with an annual rate of 7,000) and of those who survived, many were in broken health.[41] In recalling their harsh lives, one well-known poet, N.A. Nekrasov, who grew up in a village near the Volga, lamented:

> Go out to the bank of the Volga: whose moan
> Is heard above the greatest Russian river?
> This groan we call a 'song'
> Barge-haulers go by tow-path!
> Oh Volga, Volga! Even in full-watered spring
> You water the field not as much as
> Great national grief overfilled our land.
> Where there's a nation—there is a groan.

But Nekrasov also remembers the Volga in another light as he wrote:

> Oh, Volga! ... My cradle!
> I wonder if anybody loved you as much as I do.
> Alone, at early dawn,
> When everything in this world was sleeping
> And scarlet shine was gliding on the dark-blue wavers,
> I ran away to the native river.

To Nekrasov, the Volga is nurturing, sustaining the imagery of "Mother Volga," but also part of the tyranny associated with Imperial Russia. (Although Repin was not familiar with Nekrasov's work, his painting of the burlaki complements the poet's emotional rendering of life for the burlaki.) Whether nurturer or tyrant, pastoral or utilitarian, the river remained integral to an emergent national consciousness.[42]

Adding to the newfound appreciation of the Russian landscape, the Volga River was giving rise to another activity—tourism. By the 1870s, around 500 steamboats, many a Mississippi model, traveled up and down the river and the steamships that provided cargo were also beginning to serve tourists. Earlier perceptions of the river as being unsafe and a haven for bandits changed as river travel had become more common by the mid nineteenth century. Excursions on the river offered a respite from city life for many of Russia's nobility, and similar to excursions on rivers such as the Mississippi, the experience cultivated a growing national identity. In travel brochures promoting Volga River cruises, comparisons were made with other major rivers of the world, such as the Rhine, Nile, and Jordan. This phenomenon was not unique to the Volga as numerous travel brochures on the Mississippi and Rhine, in particular, celebrated the uniqueness of their rivers, evincing a national pride. The Rhine River, however, was often the standard by which Russian promoters compared their respective rivers. But in the Volga travel brochures, often written by French authors, the Volga was pronounced more serene than their German counterpart.[43]

Complementing the travel literature was the work of Vasily Rozanov, a Russian critic in the second half of the nineteenth century who referred to the Volga as the "Russian Nile." In describing his trip down the Volga, he writes: "I want to call our Volga, the Russian Nile. But what is the Nile, not in a geographical or physical sense but in a different, deeper sense which was given to it by humans who were living on its banks?" He continues to compare the greatness and divinity of the Nile with its life-giving properties—seen through its annual inundation leaving behind a rich layer of silt—to the Volga. In ascertaining the essence of both rivers, he perceives a similarity as the Volga, like the Nile, has nurtured those living along its banks since ancient times. It is in this role, the Volga earned the epithets, "Kormilitsa-Volga" and later "Matushka Volga." In further arguing the Volga's revered place in Russian consciousness, Rozanov observes that through the river the Russian people realize their insignificance and mortality, prompting the saying, "we are born and die as flies and Matushka Volga keeps flowing." According to Rozanov, the connection to the river is such that the Russian people believe Russia is where the Volga is and it's not truly Russia without the Volga. Popular literature in the nineteenth century supported Rozanov's claim with works such as Volgin's *Vasil Chumak* in which the Volga is presented as "the greatest river in the Russian Empire."[44]

Further adding to the work of philosophers were writers such as Ivan Bunin who immortalized the Volga in his 1916 short story "The Riverside Tavern," when he describes the Russian provinces. One of his characters observes: "[T]he Russian provinces are pretty much the same everywhere. There's only one thing in them that's quite unique, and that's the Volga itself. From the early spring right up to winter it is always and everywhere extraordinary, in all weathers and whether its day or night. At night you can sit ... and look out of the windows ... and when they are open to the air on a summer night you look straight into the darkness, into the blackness of the night, and somehow you sense especially keenly all the wild magnificence of the water wastes outside."[45]

Thus when Russia entered the twentieth century, the Volga, as part of the larger Russian landscape, contributed to an emergent national narrative that established Russia as unique and distinct as other nations; possessing a charm that was at least equal to Russia's European neighbors. Paralleling the Mississippi's role in shaping identity, the Volga was firmly entrenched as part of the national identity. Much more than transportation routes, the rivers were part of a larger national discourse that celebrated each country's exceptionalism while simultaneously promising economic potential. Similar to the Nile and Ganges, the rivers were personified and served multiple purposes with the culture.

Inherent in the valorization of each river, however, and their subsequent shaping of a national identity, lie all the contradictions at the heart of the national and cultural identities of Russia and the United States. While the Mississippi and Volga Rivers offered freedom, both rivers also contributed to the oppression and exploitation of labor. While both rivers afforded numerous vistas, ranging from scenic bluffs on the Mississippi to sweeping steppes on the Volga, both were also havens for disease, particularly with repercussions for populations that had already been marginalized. While both gave rise to a national pride that rested, in part on the uniqueness of each river, this pride was often riddled by the need for comparisons. Finally, while each river was celebrated for its beauty coupled with a nineteenth-century idealization of each, the long history of despoiling the riverine environment with human debris persisted, intensifying throughout the century. These dualities continued into the twentieth and twenty-first centuries with a discourse always bent on reconciling the scenic and useful, the aesthetic and disease-ridden, and liberation and oppression. As a result, multiple narratives evolved as different populations experienced the river differently. All of these contradictions mirror the broader histories of Russia and the United States.

But the twentieth century introduced a more strident rhetoric with a heightened faith in modernization infusing the political regimes of the United States and the recently created Soviet Union. Consequently, the rivers' histories took another turn and by the 1930s both rivers underwent major construction projects that subdued the natural flow and outwardly transformed both into predominantly navigation routes with a series of locks and dams. Yet, the nineteenth-century rhetoric that valorized the rivers persisted. When undertaking large-scale projects in the race toward hydro-modernization, the state appropriated the cultural symbolism of the rivers. As a result, the construction of the Moscow-Volga Canal was not merely a series of locks and dams but a project that "constrained 'Mother Volga.'" With the advent of modernity, the symbolic representations of the Volga and Mississippi remained but the message was conflicted. Serving a nationalist agenda, the rivers fell victim to the abstract realm that touted nature as nationalist conceit while harnessing the river's energy for commerce, whether through transportation or hydropower. Art and literature have faithfully captured all of these uses and representations.

Notes

1. Denis Cosgrove, *Social Formation and Symbolic Landscape* (1984; repr., Madison: University of Wisconsin Press, 1998); Martin Warnke, *Political Landscape: The Art History of Nature* (London: Reaktion Books, 1994); Kenneth Robert Olwig, *Landscape Nature and the Body Politic: From Britain's Renaissance to America's New World* (Madison: University of Wisconsin Press, 2002); Simon Schama, *Landscape and Memory* (New

York: Alfred A. Knopf, 1995). The scholarship in this field is rich and provocative with contributions from a number of scholars. A useful synthesis of many of the ideas regarding representation can be found in John R. Gold and George Revill, *Representing the Environment* (London: Routledge, 2004).

2. One of the most well-known scholars to publish on landscape and identity in Russia is Christopher Ely in *This Meager Nature: Landscape and National Identity in Imperial Russia* (DeKalb: Northern Illinois University Press, 2002). Other scholars include Orlando Figes, *Natasha's Dance: A Cultural History of Russia* (New York: Henry Holt and Co., 2002); and George Heard Hamilton, *The Art and Architecture of Russia*, 3rd ed. (New Haven: Yale University Press, 1992). For a discussion on the Mississippi and American landscapes in the nineteenth century, see Ron Tyler, *Visions of America: Pioneer Artists in a New Land* (New York: Thames and Hudson, 1983); Jason T. Busch, Christopher Monkhouse, and Janet L. Whitmore, *Currents of Change: Art and Life Along the Mississippi River, 1850–1861* (Minneapolis: University of Minnesota Press, 2004); and Elizabeth Johns et al. *New Worlds from Old: 19ᵗʰ Century Australian and American Landscapes* (Canberra: National Gallery of Australia and Wadsworth Atheneum, 1998).

3. Gina Crandell, *Nature Pictorialized: "The View" in Landscape History* (Baltimore: The Johns Hopkins University Press, 1993), 4, 9.

4. Ibid., 67, 83.

5. Claude Lorrain's pioneering work is cited in Klaus Reichold and Bernhard Graf, *Paintings that Changed the World: From Lascaux to Picasso* (Munich: Prestel, 2003), 102–103.

6. Robert Boyle, *The Hudson River: A Natural and Unnatural History* (New York: W. W. Norton & Co., 1969), 60–61; *Kindred Spirits: Asher B. Durand and the American Landscape*, ed. Linda Ferber (Brooklyn: Brooklyn Museum, 2007), 129. For a comparative study of the Rhine River, see Mark Cioc, *The Rhine: An Eco-Biography, 1815–2000* (Seattle: University of Washington Press, 2002).

7. Timothy Flint, *The History and Geography of the Mississippi Valley*, vol. 1, 2nd ed. (Cincinnati: E.H. Flint and L.R. Lincoln, 1832), 129.

8. Stephen Eisenman, *Nineteenth-Century Art: A Critical History* (London: Thames and Hudson, 1994), 120; *A Treasury of Mississippi Folklore: Stories, Ballads and Traditions of the Mid- American River Country*, ed. B.A. Botkin (New York: American Legacy Press, 1955), 117. Further commentaries about the Mississippi panoramas can be found in Bernard Comment, *The Painted Panorama* (New York: Harry N. Abrams, Inc., Publishers, 2000); Busch, Monkhouse, and Whitmore, *Currents of Change*; Walter Havighurst, *Voices on the River: The Story of the Mississippi Waterways* (Minneapolis: University of Minnesota Press, 1964).

9. Christopher Monkhouse, "Henry Wadsworth Longfellow and the Mississippi River: Forging a National Identity Through the Arts," in *Currents of Change*, 140–179.

10. Carol Troyen, "Retreat to Arcadia: American Landscape and the American Art-Union," *American Art Journal* 23, no. 1 (1991): 20–37; Proceedings of the American Art-Union, 1844 Report (Part of the Transactions of the American Art-Union), 3–24. (these are now online, http://archive.org/stream/jstor-20568401/20568401_djvu.txt)

11. Proceedings of the American Art-Union, 1849, 21–65, p. 28; *Bulletin of the American Art-Union* 2, no. 5 (August 1849): 10–12, http://www.jstor.org/stable/20646629/; *Bulletin of the American Art-Union*, no. 9 (December 1851): 137–139.

12. Janet L. Whitmore, "A Panorama of Unequaled Yet Ever-Varying Beauty," in *Currents of Change*, 12–62. Other works that discuss Bingham's place in nineteenth-century American history include Angela Miller, "The Mechanisms of the Market and the Inventions of Western Regionalism: The Example of George Caleb Bingham," in *American Iconology*, ed. David C. Miller (New Haven: Yale University Press, 1993); John Francis McDermott, *George Caleb Bingham: River Portraitist* (Norman: University of Oklahoma Press, 1959).

13. *Half Horse, Half Alligator: The Growth of the Mike Fink Legend*, ed. Walter Blair and Franklin J. Meine (Lincoln: University of Nebraska Press, 1956), 53.

14. Ibid., 10.

15. Timothy Flint, *Recollections of the Last Ten Years in the Valley of the Mississippi*, ed. George R. Brooks (Carbondale: Southern Illinois University Press, 1968), 158.

16. Blair and Meine, *Half Horse, Half Alligator*, 17.

17. Mark Twain, *Life on the Mississippi* (1883; repr., New York: Signet Classic, 1961), 59. In addition to Twain's remembrances, there are numerous early accounts describing the Mississippi River by explorers such as Zebulon Pike, James Duane Doty, and Stephen Long.

18. Ibid., 2.

19. Alexis de Tocqueville, *Democracy in America*, vol. 1–2 (1848; repr., Garden City: Doubleday & Company, Inc., 1966), 24, 30.

20. Charles Dickens, "Boz's Description of the Mississippi," in *Parley's Magazine*, vol. 10 (New York: C.S. Francis and Co., 1842), 390.

21. Quoted here from Nancy and Robert Goodman, *Paddlewheels on the Upper Mississippi, 1823–1854* (Stillwater: University of Minnesota Printing Services, 2003), 2–3, 6–10. One of the best collections of steamboat photos can be found at the Special Collections Room and Area Research Center, Murphy Library, University of Wisconsin–La Crosse. This collection is part of the University of Wisconsin Archives.

22. Busch, Monkhouse, and Whitmore, *Currents of Change*, 12; Goodman, *Paddlewheels on the Upper Mississippi*, 327.

23. For a discussion of Enlightenment thought and the "idea" of Eastern Europe, see Larry Wolff, *Inventing Eastern Europe: The Map of Civilization on the Mind of the Enlightenment* (Stanford: Stanford University Press, 1994). Numerous scholars and writers have considered the construction of an American frontier mentality and the arbitrary one-hundredth meridian as being the division between a cultured East and the "Wild West." The classic text to introduce this idea is Henry Nash Smith, *Virgin Land: The American West as Symbol and Myth* (New York: Vintage Books, 1950).

24. In discussing the contributions of Pyotr Chaadaev to the discourse on national identity, see Robin Aizlewood, "Revisiting Russian National Identity in Russian Thought: From Chaadaev to the Early Twentieth Century," *The Slavonic and East European Review* 78, no. 1, (January 2000): 20–43; Susanna Rabow-Edling, *Slavophile Thought and the Politics of Cultural Nationalism* (Albany: SUNY Press, 2006); *Collected Works of Velimir Khlebnikov*, vol. 1, *Letters and Theoretical Writings*, ed. Charlotte Douglas (Cambridge: Harvard University Press, 1987), 234; Sara Dickinson, "Russia's First 'Orient': Characterizing the Crimea in 1787," *Kritika: Explorations in Russian and Eurasian History* 3, no. 1 (Winter 2002): 3–25; ibid, *Breaking New Ground: Travel and National Culture from Peter I to the Era of Pushkin* (Amsterdam: Rodopi, 2006); Olga Maiorova,

From the Shadow of Empire: Defining the Russian Nation through Cultural Mythology, 1855–1870 (Madison: University of Wisconsin Press, 2010); *National Identity in Russian Culture,* ed. Simon Franklin and Emma Widdis (Cambridge: Cambridge University Press, 2004), 39. Further proof of Russia's focus on forging a national identity can be found in Katia Dianina, "Displaying the Nation and Modernity in Russia: Directions in Museum Studies—Museum and Society in Imperial Russia: An Introduction," *Slavic Review* 67, no. 4 (2008): 907. Dianina convincingly argued how widespread the discussion for a national museum was, going from initial proposals in the 1820s to an exhibition boom in the 1870s. Ibid. For an interesting discussion of the historiography of Russian national identity, see Stephen M. Norris, *A War of Images: Russian Popular Prints, Wartime Culture, and National Identity, 1812–1945* (Dekalb: Northern Illinois University Press, 2006).

25. Robert Bremner, *Excursions in the Interior of Russia,* vol. 2 (1839; repr., London: Elibron Classics, 2005), 11.

26. *Journey for Our Time: The Journals of the Marquis de Custine,* ed. Phyllis Penn Kohler (London: Phoenix Press, 2001), 228, 170. A more flattering view of Russia can be found in August von Haxthausen's *Studies on the Interior of Russia,* ed. Frederick Starr (Chicago: University of Chicago Press, 1972). After Custine's critical assessment, Haxthausen was invited by Tsar Nicholas I to visit Russia in 1842 in the hope that Haxthausen would see Russia in a more positive light, which he did.

27. Bremner, *Excursions in the Interior,* 11, 217.

28. Henry Alexander Munro-Butler-Johnstone, *A Trip Up the Volga to the Fair of Nijni-Novgorod* (Philadelphia: Porter & Coates, 1875), 14. According to the prominent Russian historian, Geoffrey Hosking, "neither the imperial state nor Orthodox Church had succeeded in projecting an image of Russianness or generating a narrative of Russia's history and traditions which was capable of appealing to Russians across a wide spectrum." *Russia and the Russians: A History* (Cambridge: Belknap Press, 2001), 344. Elizabeth Kridl Valkenier, *Ilya Repin and the World of Russian Art* (New York: Columbia University Press, 1990), 103.

29. A. Korobochko, V. Liubovnyi, *Chernetsovy G.G. i.N.G. Puteshestvie po volge* (M., Mysl', 1970), 10.

30. Elena Duzs, "Russian Art in Search of Identity," in *Russia and Western Civilization: Cultural and Historical Encounters* (Armonk: M.E. Sharpe, 2003), 182; Valkenier, *Ilya Repin and the World of Russian Art,* 33; Mastera iskusstv ob iskusstve, vol. 7, (Moscow, 1970) as quoted in *Levitan* (Leningrad: Aurora Art Publishers, 1981); Mark Bassin, "I Object to Rain That is Cheerless: Landscape Art and the Stalinist Aesthetic Imagination," *Ecumene* (2000): 7, 313–336, 331. One Russian critic, however, did not see a true "Russianness" in Levitan's work. According to Georges Nivat, Vasily Rozanov questioned Levitan's work because of his Jewish background. See Nivat, "The Russian Landscape as Myth," *Russian Studies in Literature* 39, no. 2 (Spring 2003): 53. For a general discussion of Russian art, I consulted George Heard Hamilton, *The Art and Architecture of Russia,* 3rd ed. (1954; repr., New Haven: Yale University Press,1983); Orlando Figes, *Natasha's Dance*; Rosalind P. Blakesley and Susan E. Reid, eds., *Russian Art and the West: A Century of Dialogue in Painting, Architecture and the Decorative Arts* (DeKalb: Northern Illinois University Press, 2007). In addition, several visits were made to many Russian art galleries and museums including the State Tretyakov Gal-

lery in Moscow, and the Hermitage and the Russian Museum in St. Petersburg. All three include works by Levitan, Savrasov, and Repin.

31. The literature on the characterization of space in Russian landscape painting is rich as an increasing number of scholars recognize its place in Russian national identity. A few noteworthy studies include: Jeremy Smith, ed., *Beyond the Limits: The Concept of Space in Russian History and Culture* (Helsinki: Studia Historica, 1999); Katarina Hansen Love, *The Evolution of Space in Russian Literature: A Spatial Reading of 19th and 20th Century Narrative Literature* (Amsterdam: Rodopi, 1994); Evengy Dobrenko and Eric Naiman, eds., *The Landscape of Stalinism: The Art and Ideology of Soviet Space* (Seattle: University of Washington Press, 2003); and Jane Burbank, ed., *Russian Empire: Space, People, Power, 1700–1930* (Bloomington: Indiana University Press, 2007). In Emma Widdis's exploration of space and identity, she contends that space, itself, becomes a virtue in Russian consciousness. See Franklin and Widdis, *National Identity*, 139–140. *Levitan*, 13.

32. Averil King, *Isaak Levitan: Lyrical Landscape* (London: Philip Wilson Publishers, 2004), 42.

33. Grigory Sternin, Maria Karpenko, Yelena Kirillina and Sheila Marnie, *Ilya Repin: Painting Graphic Arts* (Leningrad: Aurora Art Publishers, 1985), 9.

34. Valkenier, *Ilya Repin and the World of Russian Art*, 43.

35. Jerome Blum, *Lord and Peasant in Russia: From the Ninth to the Nineteenth Century* (Princeton: Princeton University Press, 1961), 283. Foreign visitors also noted the dire circumstances for the burlaki as Baron Von Haxthausen observed the following in his 1856 visit, "A Burlak, when fortunate, can perform the journey between Samara and Ribinsk three times in the course of a summer; he has then perhaps £3 left; but if, through adverse circumstances, he only makes the trip twice, he generally consumes all he earns." Haxthausen, *The Russian Empire: Its People, Institutions, and Resources* (London: Chapman and Hall, 1856), 146.

36. Valkenier, *Ilya Repin and the World of Russian Art*, 39; Sternin, *Ilya Repin*, 9. For an excellent discussion of landscape art in Socialist Realist art, see Mark Bassin, "The Greening of Utopia: Nature, Social Vision, and Landscape Art in Stalinist Russia," in *Architectures of Russian Identity: 1500 to the Present*, James Cracraft and Daniel Rowland, eds. (Ithaca: Cornell University Press, 2003), 150–172. Hamilton, *Art and Architecture of Russia*, 383; For a discussion of Soviet portrayals of workers and the Dnieper River project poster, see Victoria E. Bonnell, *Iconography of Power: Soviet Political Posters under Lenin and Stalin* (Berkeley: University of California Press, 1997), Plate I.14.

37. Y.M. Sokolov, *Russian Folklore* (Hartboro, Pa: Folklore Associates, 1966), 489; *Down Along the Mother Volga*, ed. Roberta Reeder (Philadelphia: University of Pennsylvania Press, 1975), 200.

38. Reeder, *Down Along the Mother Volga*, 194. A parallel to the burlaki and their work songs can be found in John Randolph's work, "The Singing Coachmen or, The Road and Russia's Ethnographic Invention in Early Modern Times," *Journal of Early Modern History* 11, no. 1–2 (2007): 33–61. Randolph's thesis also reinforces the arguments regarding the importance of the Volga as a transportation route, as his work reveals the significance of Russia's roads or iams "in shaping the first ethnographic conceptions of Russia as a land united by a common set of customs and manners." Ibid., 37.

39. Maxim Gorky, *My Childhood* in *The Autobiography of Maxim Gorky* (Secaucus, New Jersey: Citadel Press, 1949), 20–21.

40. Reeder, *Down Along the Mother Volga*, 198.

41. Blum, *Lord and Peasant in Russia*, 283.

42. Nikolai Nekrasov, *Lyric Poetry* (Moscow: Detskaja Literature, 1976), 81–89.

43. Thomas W. Knox, *The Boy Travellers in the Russian Empire* (New York: Harper & Brothers, 1887), 284; Guido Hausmann, "Historic Memory and Culture in the Russian Empire and Soviet Union," International Colloquium, 25–28 June 2007; Christopher Ely, "The Origins of Russian Scenery: Volga River Tourism and Russian Landscape Aesthetics," *Slavic Review* 62 (2003): 666–682. For a good discussion of earlier perceptions of folk songs regarding robbers on the river, see Reeder, *Down Along the Mother Volga*.

44. Vasily Rozanov, *Ruskii Nil* (M:V. Volgin, *Ataman Kuz'ma Roshchin* (Moscow, 1901), 3, as cited in Jeffrey Brooks, *When Russia Learned to Read: Literacy and Popular Literature, 1861–1917* (1985; repr., Evanston: Northwestern University Press, 2003), 242. Brooks's work shows how Russia's growing national identity and pride in the nineteenth century were invested, in large part, to Russian ideals of their landscape.

45. Ivan Bunin, "The Riverside Tavern" in *The Gentleman From San Francisco and Other Stories* (1916; repr., New York: Penguin Books, 1987), 216.

CHAPTER 3

Rivers and Modernization

With the advent of the twentieth century, the creed of modernization became more pronounced as engineers, scientists, and political leaders joined forces to build what was perceived as a better world. Emboldened by the success of large-scale projects, like the Panama Canal, American political leaders and engineers were confident about the ability of science and technology to transform nature. After the Bolshevik Revolution, Soviet political leaders, such as Lenin and Trotsky, longstanding believers in the transformative potential of science and technology, added their voices to the twentieth-century call to modernize and ultimately conquer nature. Rivers, already prized for their roles as highways and potential power sources, fell victim to the self-assurance that landscapes could and should be remade. For the Volga and Mississippi Rivers, modernization evoked words such as rerouting, rechanneling, harnessing, bridling, and ultimately subduing. Both rivers, already established as major transportation arteries and integral to each nation's identity, were "improved" in the 1930s for navigation and later served as sources for hydropower. A discussion, however, of the historical context where the discourse of modernization—in which large-scale initiatives subsumed political and ideological differences—is critical to an understanding of each river's role in the nation-building that characterized the early twentieth century. At this juncture, the Volga and Mississippi with their untapped economic value, whether realized through navigation or hydropower, were indispensable to modernization. As a result, both were drafted into development discourse with two major consequences. First, despite different political ideologies and regimes, modernization superseded the distinctions as the Volga and Mississippi became engineered rivers. Second, past glories of the rivers were still invoked as "the mighty waters of the Volga are constrained" or the "Father of Waters" is celebrated as the river is dammed. Again, the rivers were appropriated for a rhetoric that touted national achievement, only in this instance the harnessing and subjugation of these national icons gave cause for the celebratory rhetoric. But the Mississippi and Volga were but two examples of this shift as rivers around the world were drawn into service in the name of progress.

For the Soviet Union, the promise of inland waterways such as the Volga, had historical roots dating back to Peter the Great. Looking for ways to enhance navigation and outlets to the West, under Peter's rule a number of canals were started including the Volga-Don Canal. Beginning in the nineteenth century, these efforts were resumed in earnest with proposals ranging from inundating the Caspian Sea Basin through diversion of water from the Black Sea to initial construction of the Moscow-Volga Canal. The lack of resources, however, always plagued the tsars' ambitions. The nineteenth century in the United States was also a period of intense canal building in the early years followed by reclamation works in the latter part of the century. Throughout this time, the Army Corps of Engineers sought to control the Mississippi by building levees to address flooding and enhance navigation in the upper stretches. Despite these historical antecedents, the issue of scale distinguished nineteenth-century projects from the radical transformations of the Volga and Mississippi Rivers in the twentieth century. Improved technology allowed for a grandiosity unknown in earlier generations as rivers were dammed, reservoirs built, and the Volga and Mississippi emerged as barge superhighways by the 1940s.[1]

But the belief in technology alone was not enough either to justify or promote this radicalization of nature. A political imperative accompanied the harnessing and rerouting of rivers. Major New Deal projects such as the Tennessee Valley Authority (TVA)—a project that that combined navigation, flood control, and most important, power to rural populations—were not simply engineering feats and beacons for large-scale planning but examples of democracy's superiority. David Lilienthal, who worked with President Franklin Delano Roosevelt in leading the TVA, became one of the best spokesmen for the project. On numerous occasions, he cited the project's democratic underpinnings in passages such as the following: "A great Plan, a moral and indeed a religious purpose, deep and fundamental, is democracy's answer both to our homegrown would-be dictators and foreign democracy alike. In the unified development of resources, there is such a Great Plan: the Unity of Nature and Mankind. Under such a plan in our valley [TVA] we move forward. ... But we assume responsibility ... [for] the material well-being of all men and the opportunity for them to build for themselves spiritual strength."[2] The TVA, therefore, was a development project aimed not just at providing jobs or providing power, but also one that served as a beacon of the positive power brought forth by the dual ideologies of modernization and democracy.

Yet the United States and its approach to nature in the first half of the twentieth century was not unique. The Soviet Union shared these sentiments toward nature. Leon Trotsky, a founder of the Soviet state, in his 1924 work *Literature and Revolution,* discussed the place of art during the revolutionary period and what he perceived as the changed relation between art and nature. According to Trotsky, "nature will become more 'artificial.'" He predicted a world where: "Man will occupy himself with re-registering mountains and rivers, and will earnestly and repeatedly make improvements in nature. In the end, he will have rebuilt the earth. ... Through the machine, man in Socialist society will command nature in its entirety, with its grouse and sturgeons. ... He will change the course of the rivers, and he will lay down rules for the oceans." In his concluding paragraphs, he goes further in his assessment of nature when he speculates, "The effort to conquer poverty, hunger, want in all its forms, that is, to conquer nature, will be the dominant tendency for decades to come."[3] In these writings, Trotsky set the stage for a new perspective on nature and ultimately, rivers, which dominated Soviet thinking.

His ideas influenced others such as Maxim Gorky, a popular novelist, who in a letter to students in Irkutsk reminded them: "We must cultivate our whole land like a garden, drain swamps, bring water to arid deserts, straighten and deepen rivers, lay millions of kilometers of road, and clean out our huge forests, the work is awaiting us, and it demands extensive scientific knowledge."[4] In further support of Trotsky's ideas, Gorky writes in *At the End of the Earth*, "everywhere you see how the cunning hand of man creates order on earth."[5]

Implicit in the writings of Trotsky and Gorky is the role of science and reason in achieving the new order where nature is an actor to be conquered. Prompting the drive to modernize was a blind faith and utopian ideal in the potential of reason and science to improve the world. Although cloaked in the ballast of socialist ideology, their perspective on nature and its role in serving the state was the same as those touting development and democratic values. As a result, the outcome for the Mississippi and Volga Rivers was identical regardless of differing ideologies. Engineers altered the rivers with changes that resulted in a series of slack water ponds, hydropower, ecosystem degradation, and improved navigation. From the perspective of a riverine narrative, political ideologies were inconsequential.

Though the paths to modernization of the United States and Soviet Union were articulated using similar metaphors, their experiences were different as Russia's path to industrialization lagged behind other Western powers. Even before the Bolshevik Revolution in 1917, the Bolsheviks viewed rapid industrialization as a goal and once they came into power, the need to industrialize and modernize assumed an urgency. Both Soviet leaders, Lenin and Stalin, sought to industrialize quickly. But in the 1920s, however, the instability of the Soviet Union's newfound political gains plagued Lenin and deterred implementation. Unlike Stalin, who enjoyed a degree of stability, under Lenin's leadership from 1917 to the early 1920s, the country faced enormous challenges with the devastating aftereffects of World War I, an ongoing Civil War, famine in the Middle and Lower Volga region, and "the great backwardness of Russia." His correspondence during these years reveals his tenuous hold on the country and his fears that the regime was near collapse.[6] Still, Lenin's vision from the beginning was to industrialize in order to bridge the gap between country and city. According to one scholar, part of his motivation for big projects was to appease discontent and avoid a counterrevolution. Regardless of motives, in order to industrialize and level the differences between the country and city, one of Lenin's first priorities was electrification. Once in power Lenin directed the Supreme Economic Council to begin immediately its work with the Academy of Sciences and draft a plan regarding industrialization with "special attention to the electrification of industry and transport and the application of electricity to farming." He also instructed them to look at water power.[7]

Throughout his correspondence, Lenin discusses what the Soviet Union will need to become "electrical" and by 1920 writes that "in 10–20 years we shall make all of the Soviet Union, both industrial and agricultural, *electrical*."[8] In reaching the goal, in 1920 Lenin recommended to the All-Russia Central Executive Committee that the Supreme Economic Council and the Commissariat of Agriculture draft a plan for the electrification of the Soviet Union. He quotes from a Soviet pamphlet the phrase that would later be revised and associated with Lenin and electrification: "The age of steam is the age of the bourgeoisie, the age of electricity is the age of socialism." By the end of the year, the phrase morphed into the famous slogan, "Communism is Soviet power plus the electrification of the whole country." In the same address, Lenin reiterates how electrification will raise the country's technological footing and thereby facilitate its transition to an industrial economy. One of the most important consequences of electrification, however, is the integration of the peasant and the countryside into Soviet society. Lenin stresses how the peasant must be convinced: "[T]hat the organization of industry on the basis of modern, advanced technology, on electrification which will provide a link between town and country, will put an end to the division between town and country, will make it possible to raise the level of culture in the countryside and to overcome even in the most remote corners of the land, backwardness, ignorance, poverty, disease and barbarism."[9]

Electrifying the country became paramount to Lenin as he told audiences that the long-term plan was to "create 30 large regions of electric power stations which would enable us to modernize our industry—in less than ten years." In efforts to realize the plan, Lenin requested that all engineers and electricians who have taken relevant coursework, be recruited to "deliver not less than two (four?) lectures a week, to teach not less than (10–50?) people about electricity. If they fulfill this—a bonus. If they don't—gaol."[10] He would even ask the army for help in "the cause of electrification" as he told one colleague, "We must bind the army to this great cause—ideologically, organizationally and economically—and must work systematically on it."[11] His belief in the expert's influence in modernizing Russia was observed by others.

Finally, an Integrated Economic Plan was drafted by 1921 and the agency responsible for carrying it out was GOELRO (The State Committee for the Electrification of Russia, established in February 1920). The plan was met with fanfare in the Eighth Congress of the Soviets when one party official claimed that electrification will empower Soviet man and "open the road to a new conquest by technology, which will mark the greatest gigantic victory by mankind over the elemental forces of nature."[12] Comprehensive in its goals, the plan included a number of sectors such as electrification, water power, fuel supply, agriculture, and transport. Another mainstay of modernization, namely the belief in planning and data gathering, was evident in the draft Integrated Economic Plan as the authors estimated a timeline of ten years in order to complete the goals, educate the necessary workers, choose electric power station sites, and realize the output of select manufactured goods, to name a few examples.[13] Implicit in the plan was the belief in the expert's influence in modernizing the Soviet Union. A devotee of Taylorism and the ability of science and technology to improve society, Lenin, in the words of Albert Rhys Williams, always "defers to the expert" and stressed their value on many occasions. Williams, a reporter for the *New York Evening Post,* who spent time in Petrograd from 1917 to 1919, also noted how Lenin wanted American engineers and technicians working in the Soviet Union and was willing to pay them well.[14]

Despite his reliance on American expertise, Lenin distinguished his efforts from those of the capitalists as he sought to eliminate the capitalism still rooted in the villages through modernizing strategies, such as electrification.[15] He believed he could separate American technical expertise with its philosophical underpinnings from the Soviet socialist vision. Lenin, like many Soviet and American political leaders, viewed technology as neutral and separate from the political sphere. Yet the outcome of the relationship between technology and nature differed from a political perspective. For example, under capitalism, nature was exploited for private gain while under a socialist system, resources were developed for the greater good. But again, for nature, the use of the resource for the purposes of industrialization remained the same. The goal to industrialize entailed the same level of resource use regardless of political ideologies. As a result, the ramifications for rivers and their environmental health—whether American or Soviet expertise, private or public gain—were similar.[16]

Regardless of Lenin's convictions about technology, party members at times criticized him for the use of American expertise even though the practice had been longstanding. In response, Lenin and other Soviet leaders always contended that their modernization was anti-Western. The argument of whether Soviet modernization efforts differed from Western, and in particular American, modernization persisted into the 1960s when Walt Rostow and other U.S modernization and development theorists compared the two. Rostow, one of the architects of U.S. modernization and development theory, drew sharp distinctions between the Soviet and U.S. development models, although again, the consequences for nature were the same.[17] But during the 1920s and especially the Stalin era of the 1930s, building a modern socialist country rested upon an anti-Western message. In another Stalin signature project, the 1930s construction of the steel complex, Magnitogorsk, even American observers saw in these Socialist schemes an anti-Western, anti-capitalism form of modernization. According to one scholar, "It was from capitalism that socialism derived its identity and against which it constantly measured itself." He goes on, however, to note that the comparison was not sustainable. But in the 1930s, many Americans saw differences between the two and complimented the Soviet experience. However, no observers, either in the 1960s when modernization theorists were most prolific or in the 1930s, recognized that the attitudes displayed by American and Soviet political leaders and the experts toward nature were identical.[18]

Still even after Lenin's death, the Soviet Union under Stalin's leadership looked to American expertise in their attempts to modernize. Large-scale agriculture in the United States, gaining in popularity in the 1920s, and reliant upon a scientific approach to farming, was particularly attractive to the Soviets. As Stalin sought to abolish individual farms and create collectives, American experts visited the Soviet Union. Agriculture in the United States was undergoing its own transformation in the early twentieth century as farming became more businesslike and scientific. In the words of one scholar, what emerged in agriculture was "an industrial logic or ideal."[19] During the first two decades of the century, land-grant colleges, experimental stations, and agricultural agents all contributed to a more rational, systematic approach to farming. Bonanza farms already dotted the landscape in the Great Plains and large-scale wheat production was a staple in American agriculture. The Soviets studied the American success story and between the years 1927 to 1932 (roughly Stalin's first Five-Year Plan), an estimated 1000 to 2000 American technical advisers visited the Soviet Union. Viewing agriculture from the perspective of a business enterprise complemented Soviet ideas about planning and the rational use of the land. Both Soviet and American agricultural experts shared the same attitudes toward nature which prevented them from adapting to cultural differences.[20]

For example, when the well-known agricultural expert Thomas Campbell advised the Soviets on large-scale wheat production, they merely imported American techniques with no allowances for differences in culture. Because of their similar beliefs regarding technology and its blanket ability to transform nature, no one considered that Russian farmers lacked the business acumen that American farmers had developed in building combines and placing thousands of acres under production. In other words, according to one scholar the U.S. experts believed you could deliver "mere technical transfer without cultural grounding." The differences in culture, however, proved significant as farmers in the United States arrived at their modern, technological approach to farming incrementally over the course of several decades. A continuity between the past and present existed for American farmers, but for the Russians so much that the Socialists tried to do in the name of modernization represented a break with a "backward past." While this was often a cause for celebration, especially when major projects such as the Moscow-Volga Canal were completed, for the introduction of new farming methods a history was needed, a cultural link with the past.[21]

American expertise also lent itself to the area of hydropower with major construction works that began under Stalin. (In contrast to Lenin, while Stalin realized the importance of electrification, it was not the centerpiece in his drive to modernize through heavy industry but merely one of its components.) The first major hydrostation to be built in the Soviet Union was on the Dnieper River, located in present-day Ukraine. The project, Dneprostroi, included a hydroelectric station, dam, and factories on the Dnieper River and was completed in 1932 during Stalin's first Five-Year Plan. With the dam, the project also improved navigation, something that various tsars since Catherine the Great had tried unsuccessfully. Many German and American engineers and technicians from companies such as the U.S. firm General Electric assisted in the dam's design and construction and lived at the work site. While American-built generators were being used, Soviet leaders promised that eventually, the project would operate with Soviet-built machines. This was the heyday of American and Soviet scientific and technical exchanges despite rhetoric from political leaders accentuating the differences that persisted between the two countries. Regardless of the reliance upon American expertise, for Stalin the project signaled success. He later referred to it as "the great historical construction," as Dneprostroi was one of the first and largest projects to be attempted in his first Five-Year Plan.

In constructing Dneprostroi, the discourse in Soviet publications became a benchmark for later hydro-projects—a template for the cascading hydro-projects on the Volga—and offered insights to the 1930s mentality regarding nature. Several themes were included in the rhetoric such as the promise of the machine to transform nature as seen in the achievement of electrification, one of Lenin's most cherished goals; the delivery of the historical goal of navigation; and the speed of the undertaking.[22] Leon Trotsky celebrated this Soviet triumph when he wrote: "In the south the Dnieper runs its course through the wealthiest lands; and it is wasting the prodigious weight of its pressure, playing over age-old rapids and waiting until we harness its stream, curb it with dams, and compel it to give lights to cities, to drive factories, and to enrich ploughland. We shall compel it!" Upon completion of the dam, contemporary accounts such as the Soviet Union's promotional publication, *USSR in Construction*, celebrated the achievement by devoting an issue to Dneprostroi in 1934. Within the article, the authors touted the dam by saying, "The waters of the Dnieper have been bridled by a giant dam, amazing in its beauty and magnificence."[23]

Amid the fanfare, however, there were those who questioned the construction. Russian engineers, such as Peter Palchinsky, argued for additional studies before construction. These critics asked the government to look at the social and economic consequences of the project. But the push to industrialize and to do so quickly subsumed criticism. The United States, particularly with several of its reclamation projects, had a similar experience in the early 1900s. The United States Bureau of Reclamation (USBR), the primary dam-building agency in the United States, initially evaluated each proposed project according to engineering criteria. Little attention was given to a project's social and economic features—the settler's lack of agricultural experience, the suitability of the soil or crops—and early projects often saw settlers ill-equipped to farm and thus unable to repay federal loans for the project's construction. As a result when Secretary of the Interior Hubert Work appointed D.W. Davis as Commissioner of the USBR, the emphasis shifted to include the social and economic features of proposed projects. The New Deal Commissioner Elwood Mead continued to stress the importance of these features as new projects were proposed throughout the 1930s.[24]

Still the display of engineering prowess and other technological feats, all under the umbrella of Stalin's Five-Year Plans, muted critics. According to one scholar, the "Soviet model became a civilizational mirage." Even if critics dismissed the bloated statistics of the Soviets who claimed production output in some areas reached 157 percent and "river-borne freight" went from 9.3 million tons in 1924 to 69.9 million tons in 1936, the country was industrializing quickly. But regardless of whether Lenin's openness to experiment or Stalin's single-minded Five-Year Plans prevailed, the rhetoric of conquest and struggle governed discussions of nature.[25] Returning to Dneprostroi, more kudos for the Soviet model came from American photographer Margaret Bourke-White, who after visiting the project in 1931 praised the achievements of modern-day engineering. In her classic work, *Eyes on Russia*, she comments: "The granite banks of the Dnieper are the scene of a mighty struggle between man and the majestic passage to the sea. Even in the low-water period the angry turbulence of the river is prophetic of the raging torrents which burst out in time of flood, and a constant warning to the engineers who seek to harness the gigantic force of the waters." Bourke-White, however, also noted that in the initial stages of the project the Russian laborers did not even know how to use the cranes, necessitating foreign technical expertise. The shortcomings of Soviet technology and practice was a recurring theme throughout the 1930s as engineers learned new technology while mastering large-scale projects such as the Moscow-Volga Canal.[26]

Dependence on American expertise, however, was not permanent as the 1920s and 1930s saw the growth of the engineering profession and the budget for sciences in the Soviet Union increased dramatically. Between 1917 and the outbreak of World War II, engineers with higher education increased from 15,000 to over 225,000.[27] As one contemporary American observer remarked in 1938, science had become "the new national religion." (Despite the outward appearances, however, of a state-supported technocracy, many engineers and scientists trained before the Revolution did clash with Stalin's perceptions of the role of the engineer and state power. As a result, many of these were either imprisoned or as in the case of Peter Palchinsky, lost their lives.) Along with the increase in spending for science, the expectations for the Soviet Union's transition to a modern state also rose. Political leaders set targets for large-scale projects such as Dneprostroi that were often unrealistic but invited the image of the "revolutionary heroic" that became associated with the era. In the race to industrialize and produce a modernized Soviet society, nature was always one of the forces to conquer and often the improvements assumed the guise of a military campaign as workers and farmers became "veterans" in their efforts to reshape nature. The United States applied the same analogy when FDR told TVA workers they will someday be known as "veterans."[28]

The construction of major projects, whether hydropower or collective farms, was also supported by the constitution of the Soviet Union, specifically Article Six that stated: "The land, mineral deposits, waters, forests, mills, factories, mines, railways, water and air transport, ... are state property, that is, the property of the whole people." Russia's natural resources became an intrinsic part of the new socialist order as the notion of communalism extended outward. The idea of communal ownership of the country's natural resources was a radical departure from the imperial government. In a 1937 issue of *USSR in Construction,* commemorating the twenty-year anniversary of the Soviet Union, the articles discuss the success of scientific socialism including numerous references to the country's abundant natural resources. In one section entitled "Waters of the USSR," the article boasts of the country's vast river resources with "twice the length of navigable riverways in the U.S." and goes on to cite the Moscow-Volga Canal when informing readers that the Soviets "are covering our immense country by a network of new roads and canals." Accompanying the self-congratulatory text are pictures and statistics about the new canals with claims to have doubled the length of navigable routes and in the familiar military references are statements that the government has "tamed and peopled the wide stretches of their country." Harnessing the waterways, under the auspices of Article Six, had facilitated Stalin's declaration that the "country has been transformed from an agrarian into an industrial country." From another perspective, the country's rich natural resource base, in which navigable and power-generating rivers were a large part, was another source of national pride. Communal ownership of the resources ensured that all shared this sense of pride.[29]

For the American engineers and scientists who were often in the position of assisting the Soviet Union with their initial projects, many envied the ability of Soviet leaders to centrally plan these large-scale projects. Since Theodore Roosevelt's presidency, at the beginning of the twentieth century, experts had called for more central planning yet to many decentralization was seen as being "American." A host of obstacles prevented centralized planning in the United States, not the least being competing agency and regional interests for resources. For example, when the Reclamation Act was passed in 1902, establishing a means for the federal government to build and invest in large-scale reclamation projects in the arid West, heated opposition to the legislation came from constituencies in the Midwest and East. Midwestern farmers, in particular, worried that federal support for irrigated crops would undercut their markets. Further, internal politics such as competing federal agencies interested in overseeing the new program discouraged centralized planning. By the 1930s, the unparalleled success of Soviet projects especially compared with the dire economic conditions in the United States added to the conviction shared by experts that central planning represented the preferred development model. The contrast between the economic conditions of both countries furthered positive perceptions of the Soviet model. As a result, Soviet and American political leaders and scientists, alike, saw the advantages to a strong central planning model without the necessary cumbersome approvals at the state and local level.[30] American supporters of central planning, such as Morris Cooke, the chair of the Mississippi Valley Committee, went to great lengths to convince Americans that large-scale planning could be done within a democratic system. In Cooke's words: "It is hardly necessary to point out at this stage that the general planning of the use and control of water resources must rest with the Federal Government as being the nearest we can come to an expression and reconciliation of the various purposes and desires of all our people and all our governmental agencies. In adapting an industrial technique of planning to the needs of the nation we would not be violating the principles of democracy and local self-government; we would merely be giving them a new tool."[31] In the same report, Cooke, in his advocacy of large-scale, integrated planning and development, recommended eventually building 500 dams on the Mississippi River.

The supporters, however, of central planning did not convince the American public of the merits of large-scale planning. The only project that remotely resembled the scale of central planning that was commonplace in the Soviet Union was the Tennessee Valley Authority (TVA). One of the major criticisms of the TVA and any other similar proposed undertakings was what many conceived to be the socialist aspects of this type of planning. For example, in Rexford Tugwell's biography of FDR, he mentions the "creeping socialism" criticism from members of the Republican Party in the 1930s. And director of the TVA, David Lilienthal, recounts a dinner party conversation where one of the guests introduced him with the following jab: "Fifty years from now, when this country is completely Socialist, people will say that the first great administrator of a Socialist venture in this country, who broke the ice and made all the other developments possible was David Lilienthal; or they will be cussing your name plenty."[32]

Both FDR and his successor Harry Truman wanted more TVA-type projects, such as a Columbia Valley Authority but were unable to gain enough support. At one point, FDR suggested establishing seven regional authorities or agencies. For those adherents of a central planning model, the advantages included efficiency and conservation. The predominant thinking being that under the federal government, a stewardship of a nation's resources resulted and guided development. Thus, from a resource management view, there was the belief that state ownership of resources coupled with a command economy were better for conservation. This opinion was later challenged but regardless of the outcome, state ownership and a centralized economy allowed the Soviet government to undertake large-scale projects such as Dneprostroi and later the Moscow-Volga Canal. It was not until the early 1970s that the environmental costs of central planning by the state were revealed to the larger public.[33]

Regardless of differing strategies, for both Soviet and American leaders, the impulse to industrialize and ultimately modernize their nations embodied a Western tradition with roots in the Enlightenment.[34] Although political leaders from both countries stressed how their efforts to modernize differed from the other in that their use of the same technologies and the same changes in nature were considered politically neutral, for nature, particularly rivers, the outcome was the same. For both countries, their efforts to modernize rested upon a "fight against nature" and making nature a servant for humanity. Political leaders such as FDR and Lenin possessed a utopian vision for humankind, which prompted their commitment to modernize. But integral to the transformation of nature was the belief that nature needed improvement as Lilienthal remarked after completion of the TVA. "The river now is changed. It does its work." Before the TVA, Lilienthal characterized the Tennessee River as "an idle giant and a destructive one." But Morris Cooke said it best when he wrote, "The ideal river, which would have a uniform flow, does not exist in nature." One of the most extreme examples of the 1930s urge to improve upon nature is the suggestion that a mechanism be employed to turn on and off the water falls at Yosemite Falls in order to better serve tourist traffic.

But mere improvements were not enough as FDR and others stressed how the nation's water must be fully utilized. In a 1936 speech in Kansas, FDR told the crowd: "I am confirmed in the opinion I formed years ago—that in the watersheds out here in the West we have to aim ultimately at making use of every single drop of water that comes out of the heavens, as it comes through all the States between the Rocky Mountains and the Mississippi River." But using rivers was recognized as a longstanding tradition as the New Deal Secretary of the Interior Harold Ickes commented that, "In modern American life, streams probably play a more important part in developing electric power than they do in their ancient role as highways."[35]

Yet throughout the modernizing process in both countries, a dual image of the rivers persisted. While political leaders admonished engineers to reshape rivers and maximize their use for hydropower, navigation, or irrigation, an iconic status of the rivers was still invoked whether in Soviet songs touting Mother Volga or Hollywood films with the Mississippi as one of the mainstays. Artwork of the twentieth century prolonged the historical memory of each river as artists produced idyllic, pastoral images of both suggesting earlier times before navigation locks and dams. The competing images were longstanding, as improvements to the Volga and Mississippi Rivers were centuries-old (Peter the Great in the eighteenth century sought to connect the Volga to Moscow and build a canal connecting the Don to the Volga). In the case of the Mississippi, business leaders and farmers pushed for deeper channels beginning in the mid nineteenth century. But a difference exists between earlier efforts and twentieth-century changes, given the technology and the ability to radically transform a river. Paralleling the technological advances were ideological shifts as the goal for the modern nation state was to industrialize and ultimately, modernize. One of the major symbols of modernization was electrification and the Volga, in particular, was drafted into this dialogue. Both the Soviet Union and the United States saw nature and their rich natural resources as a means to progress—the Volga and Mississippi Rivers played prominent roles in achieving it.

Despite the absence of central planning on the scale of the Soviets, U.S. engineers still built a number of public works projects throughout the Depression-era 1930s. Unlike the Soviet Union, however, there had been a broader movement in water politics and culture to manipulate and transform water resources for multiple projects going back to the nineteenth century. Further, for those living along parts of the Mississippi such as the Mississippi-Yazoo Delta, major floods like the one experienced in 1927 prompted calls for federal resources to control the unpredictable river. After the failure of the levee system in 1927, new engineering approaches were implemented to avoid future flooding. In other water projects, such as the Columbia River Project, a multiple-purpose approach was pursued. Inherent in multiple-purpose projects was the need for planning and integrating a number of uses; another aspect of modernization that distinguished large scale twentieth-century projects from those in previous centuries. By the early twentieth century in the United States, numerous reclamation projects were increasingly multiple-purpose and contributed to a culture shaped by the language of development.

One of the first projects to embody the multiple-purpose concept of dam building was the Boulder Canyon Project that resulted in the construction of Hoover Dam. With the authorization of this federal project, multiple-purpose planning became the standard as projects were conceived that combined power, flood control, irrigation, and other potential benefits, such as navigation. FDR touted the benefits of integrated planning in his 1937 "Message to Congress on National Planning and Development of Natural Resources," in which he discussed the work of the TVA, the Columbia Valley Authority, and the Mississippi River Commission "in developing integrated plans to conserve and safeguard the prudent use of waters, water-power, soils, forests and other resources of the areas entrusted to their charge." But the best example of the shift to large-scale projects was the TVA. Although the process of developing water resources often differed from the Soviet Union with its reliance on Gulag labor and Stalin's occasional dismissal of the views of the engineering community, projects such as the TVA and the proposed Columbia Valley Authority had similar goals to those promoted in Soviet projects.[36]

In the United States, throughout the 1930s, the engineering community— whether through the bureaucracy of the Public Works Administration, USBR, or the Army Corps of Engineers—dominated water projects. For Americans and Soviets alike, this was the age of the expert and political leaders giving the scientist and engineer latitude in natural resource planning. To well-known engineers, such as Elwood Mead, head of the USBR in the 1930s, rivers were resources waiting to be developed. In many instances the engineering profession and politics combined, such as in the presidency of Herbert Hoover, the president who oversaw Hoover Dam. Hoover, in his acceptance speech for the presidency in 1928, typified the thinking of many engineers when he said: "[T]he time has arrived when we must undertake a larger visioned development of our water resources. Every drop which runs to the sea without yielding its full economic service is a waste."[37]

Franklin Delano Roosevelt (FDR) shared Hoover's ideas. Under FDR, however, the transformation of nature in the 1930s was accompanied by a broader social agenda. His New Deal program, created to address the devastating Depression of the 1930s, intertwined resource development, economic planning, and social welfare. New Deal projects that often combined navigation, flood control, hydropower, and irrigation became symbols of modernization as locks and dams, hydropower stations, and irrigation works dotted the American landscape. The project that perhaps best characterized New Deal thought was the Tennessee Valley Authority. While many associate the TVA with its engineering accomplishments and supply of power, FDR often cited the social aspects.[38] In a 1934 press conference, he reiterated what the TVA meant to him:

> Power is really a secondary matter. What we are doing there is taking a water-shed with about three and a half million people in it, almost all of them rural, and we are trying to make a different type of citizen out of them from what they would be under their present conditions. Now, that applies not only to the mountaineers—we all know about them—but it applies to the people around Muscle Shoals. Do you remember that drive over to Wheeler Dam the other day? You went through a county of Alabama where the standards of education are lower than almost any other county in the United States, and yet that is within twenty miles of the Muscle Shoals Dam. They have never had a chance. All you had to do was to look at the houses in which they lived. Heavens, this section around here is 1,000 percent compared with that section we went through. The homes through here are infinitely better. So T.V.A. is primarily intended to change and to improve the standards of living of the people of that valley. Power is, as I said, a secondary consideration. Of course it is an important one because, if you can get cheap power to those people, you hasten the process of raising the standard of living.[39]

In fact, this aspect of the project was so paramount to FDR that as late as 1940 he remarked to David Lilienthal, the director of the TVA, that he wanted a pamphlet that showed the improvements to people's lives in the area and was unhappy with a recent article that showed the dams and structures. Lilienthal echoed FDR's comments regarding the power of the TVA to be an agent of social change. Sharing the Soviet Union's high regard for the benefits of electrification, Lilienthal remarked: "There is somehow a magic about TVA kilowatts. We have really stirred public imagination about electricity and I am more heartened about the project at this moment than I have been in a long time, because while lower rates and saving on electric bills means a good deal, to have electricity apparently open up a new world for people and to have the form of organization whereby electricity is brought to them through the beginning of cooperative activity in which they participate is really an accomplishment."[40]

Still, the planning aspects coupled with the expertise of the engineers were hallmarks of the project. In considering the planning and expertise that was required for the TVA, Lilienthal touted its benefits and how in the TVA, there was an "emerging kind of skill, a modern knack of organization and execution." And with this skill, engineers could put "yokes upon the streams" and allevi-ate poverty. Thus Roosevelt and his New Deal supporters saw large projects, such as the TVA and its promise to deliver electricity to a rural population, the promise of a better life for America's rural poor. In addition, electricity would integrate the city and country, mirroring the goals of Lenin and other Soviet leaders. The 1930s ushered in an age where the language of development and its visual representations had broad, far-reaching social ramifications that persist today. To the champions of industrialization in the United States and the Soviet Union, modernization promised more than technological improvements and as early as the turn of the century, scientists and boosters alike viewed technology, whether for irrigation, flood control, hydropower, or navigation, as a means to improve the human condition.[41]

Roosevelt and Lilienthal were not the only ones to view the TVA as an exemplar of American planning and expertise. In 1937, Odette Keun, a French journalist, visited the project and heralded the construction in her work, *A Foreigner Looks at the TVA*. Keun portrayed the TVA as an example of how American liberalism works. To her, the project represented a middle road between the excesses of capitalism. In her words: "It seems to me that the TVA represents an effort... to establish an equilibrium, within the limits of the capitalist economy, between inimical but not completely irreconcilable forces; an effort, that is, to adjust capitalism to the present realities and the actual trends of thought."[42] To Keun, it was important to study the TVA as she saw in the project a uniqueness, or in her words, "There is nothing quite like it on the planet." Arguing many of the same points as Lilienthal, she saw in the project an alternative to socialism and communism but in her definition of liberalism, which included private ownership and a spirit of individual enterprise, she also allowed that natural resources would fall under the protective arm of the national government. Thus in her appraisal of 1930s political philosophies, for nature and particularly, rivers, the outcome remained the same. In her book, she also included photographs further emphasizing the effects on nature and how a river is subdued for the purposes of navigation and hydropower.[43]

Another commonality with contemporary Soviet projects was Keun's flattering portrayal of the construction sites and the communities provided for the workers. Both Keun and Lilienthal emphasize the "planned villages" built by the TVA that included libraries, swimming pools, schools, and electricity, to name a few amenities. Mirroring the Soviet projects that boasted of the educational, recreational, and cultural opportunities afforded the workers, Keun praises the TVA camps and their "facilities for the physical and mental development of a modern community." The utopian vision of remaking humans and their landscapes was ever present in her appraisal. In her conclusion, she writes that the TVA "is the noblest, the most intelligent, and the best attempt made in this country or in any other democratic country, to economize, marshal and integrate the actual assets of a region, plan its development and future, ameliorate its standards of living, establish it in a more enduring security, and render available to the people the benefits of the wealth of their district, and the results of science, discovery, invention, and disinterested forethought."[44]

Still, the similarities between the two countries outweigh the perceived differences. By the 1930s, the campaign to modernize, reached an all-time high as the "good life"—whether through Socialist man or everyday American—translated into a cacophony of symbols. At the top was electrification for Stalin, electrification facilitated heavy industry. For FDR, public power was often coupled with improvements for the common man. Both leaders saw in their efforts to modernize a utopian vision to uplift humanity.[45] For Stalin, industrialization meant a break with a Russian past that had resulted in defeat at the hands of developed nations. In his words: "All beat her [Russia]—because of her backwardness, because of her military backwardness, cultural backwardness, political backwardness, industrial backwardness, agricultural backwardness. ... We are fifty or a hundred years behind the advanced countries. We must make good this distance in ten years. Either we do it or we shall go under."[46] Returning to FDR's social and political agenda, improving the material well-being of Americans through public power had been a priority from his early years in politics. Not limited, however, to public power issues, by the time he was serving his first term as president he told reporters in a press conference, "what we are after primarily is to improve the standard of living for the country as a whole." Like Lenin, FDR faced a crisis of epic proportions in his first term, as the year 1933 saw more people out of work in the United States than in any other nation.[47]

But Americans also worried about falling behind. In his support for Cooke's Mississippi Valley Committee Plan, Secretary of the Interior Harold Ickes argued for electricity for Mississippi River Valley farmers by reminding readers, "[I]f Ireland, Bavaria, Alsace-Lorraine, Norway and Ontario can take cheap electric current to the farms, then the farmers of the United States can have these modern conveniences too." FDR employed a similar argument about electrification when he says: "[W]e are most certainly backward in the use of electricity in our American homes and farms. In Canada the average home uses twice as much electric power per family as we do in the United States." Finally, in arguments for the nine-foot channel on the Upper Mississippi River, advocates stressed the importance of not falling behind and staying competitive with an international grain market. From a broader perspective, proponents of New Deal projects touted the benefits of modernity (especially in the form of public power) for the rural poor in places such as Appalachia. As a result, massive undertakings such as the two discussed on the Volga and Mississippi Rivers severed a break with a rural, backwards past whether in the transformation of rural villages along the Volga or modernized homes and an expanding market in the Upper Mississippi River Valley. Yet though these projects showed remarkable similarities in terms of the purposes of the governments touting them, they were also very different in that they were harnessed for different economies and rationalized using different political ideologies.

But underlying the motivations, that is to modernize with the accompanying vision of improving lives and bridging the gap between urban and rural, were the same attitudes toward nature with similar rhetoric and environmental consequences.[48]

Coinciding with the obvious physical transformation of the Volga and Mississippi Rivers were other more nuanced shifts in the collective memory. When Russia entered the twentieth century, the river contributed to a national narrative that established Russia as unique and distinct from other nations. The aesthetics of a Volga landscape evoked national pride, admiration, and awe. This emerging national narrative and its inherent assumptions remained in place throughout the twentieth century despite a language shift that reflected the communist preoccupation with struggle and conquest instead of awe. Instead, the awe resulted from conquest. (Later Socialist Realist portraits of the landscape revisited the themes of Russian pastoralism.) Once entrenched, the Bolsheviks through Trotsky, Lenin, Gorky, Lunacharsky, and others saw Russian nature and its conquest as a continuation of that narrative. Conquest was achieved through the Soviet construction of massive hydroelectric and navigation projects, collective farms, transpolar flights, and eventually, space programs. But before the conquest occurred, Trotsky and others articulated this new relationship with nature as the machine, and the subsequent modernization of Russia would replace the "backwardness" abhorred by the Communist leaders. Complementing the narrative of conquest and inspiring a sense of pride, the Soviets further demonstrated superiority by successfully undertaking projects only contemplated by the tsars such as the construction of the Moscow-Volga Canal and the Volga-Don Canal. Both projects were products and examples of this new national narrative.

For the Mississippi River and other major U.S. rivers, the narrative of conquest also dominated discussion. For example, when Grand Coulee Dam was built on the Columbia River, during construction it was billed as the "Eighth Wonder in the World" and one 1937 article tagged the project as "The Biggest Thing on Earth." Immortalized in song by Woody Guthrie, who was paid to tour the Pacific Northwest and visit the dam site in order to write celebratory lyrics, the dam was part of Roosevelt's New Deal. In commemorating the dam, Guthrie sang:

> Now the world holds seven wonders that the travelers always tell
> Some gardens and some towers, I guess you know them well.
> But now the greatest wonder is in Uncle Sam's fair land
> It's the big Columbia River and the big Grand Coulee Dam.[49]

But accolades for the Columbia paled in comparison to FDR's remarks on the construction of the Fort Peck Dam on the Missouri River. In comparing Fort

Peck Dam with the Gatun Dam in the Panama Canal Zone, FDR calls the Gatun one of the "wonders of the world" and says he did not think a bigger dam
could be built. After seeing Fort Peck Dam, however, the Gatun is a "pigmy"
in comparison.[50]

Yet accompanying the language of conquest and development, both the
Volga and Mississippi Rivers occupied an iconic place in their respective cultures. During a visit to the Midwest, FDR, in a speech about the improved Upper Mississippi River, spoke of a return to the "Father of Waters." Likewise for
the Volga where numerous references to "Mother Volga" were employed when
discussing the river's future as a supplier of hydropower or shipping lane. Visual culture in the United States and the Soviet Union sustained nineteenth-
century images of the rivers, as artists persisted in depicting pastoral unspoiled
rivers untainted by the gains of industrialization. For the Mississippi, scenes
of steamboat paddlewheels lazily traveling the river remain part of a popular
visual culture along with steamboat tours. For the Volga, artists never cease
to depict the river and surrounding vegetation and cruises down the river are
popular among Russians and tourists.[51]

Still by the end of the 1930s, the dominant narrative for both rivers was
conquest through industrialization resulting in the modern nation-state. Ending the decade, prior to the onset of World War II, was the World's Fair in New
York City. The theme of the fair was the "World of Tomorrow" and perhaps
this event, more than any other in the first half of the twentieth century captured Russia's transformation into the modern Soviet state. In witnessing the
transformation, however, American observers also revealed their admiration
for the Soviet success story and more importantly, their shared beliefs regarding nature's role in the conversion. The Soviet exhibits were the most popular
at the fair. In creating their exhibits, Soviets' objectives included the emphasis
on "modernization, technology, social programs, the conquest of nature, and
the ostensibly democratic character of the Stalin constitution." The theme of
nature's submission was present even before the fair began as several of the
nation's dignitaries were to arrive in New York City via a nonstop transpolar
flight over the Arctic. If successful—the flight had to land in Canada—the
flight would have set a new record. One of the Soviet exhibits included the
Arctic with depictions of how the Soviets had subdued this forbidding terrain.
Of course, science and technology accounted for their triumphs and in one
exhibit, there were fifty-square-meter mechanized models showing engineering plans for the Dnieper and Volga Rivers. The plans outlined the hydropower
stations that had been built and were in the planning stages. Electrification and
dam building, along with other outward signs of industrialization were often
depicted in the exhibits as the recent past through the Five-Year Plans and
future were celebrated. To accomplish these goals, nature had to be tamed and
in the words of one Soviet captain who crossed the Arctic to bring materials

for the fair, "nature serves Soviets"—to many another break from a "backward past."[52]

The American exhibits, although not as popular, also contributed to the shrine of technology and science. While their exhibits emphasized the consumer aspects of an industrialized society, their message mirrored the Soviets in that technology and planning signaled success for society. The American exhibits, however, also emphasized ideology and despite the similarities between the two with their reverence for technology and planning, both saw the future in ideological terms. For nature, the distinctions were irrelevant. By 1940, the Soviets chose not to participate in the fair as the threat of war became more real and according to one scholar, the tone of the fair changed to one of nostalgia. The optimism of the 1930s, realized through industrializing strategies to improve the human condition, began to dim as world leaders failed to prevent another cataclysmic war.[53]

Notes

1. Henry C. Spalding, "The Black Sea and the Caspian," *Van Nostrand's Engineering Magazine* 15, no. 92 (August 1876): 122–127; R.A. French, "Canals in Pre-revolutionary Russia," in *Studies in Russian Historical Geography* (London: Academic Press, 1983), 451–481; John Anfinson, *The River We Have Wrought: A History of the Upper Mississippi* (Minneapolis: University of Minnesota Press, 2003); Donald J. Pisani, *Water and American Government: The Reclamation Bureau, National Water Policy, and the West, 1902–1935* (Berkeley: University of California Press, 2002).

2. David E. Lilienthal, *TVA: Democracy on the March* (New York: Harper and Row, 1944), 212.

3. Leon Trotsky, *Literature and Revolution* (1924; repr., New York: Russell and Russell, 1957), 251–252, 253.

4. *USSR in Construction*, no. 4 (1937): n.p.

5. As quoted in *USSR in Construction*, no. 4 (1937): n.p.

6. "The Impending Catastrophe and How to Combat It," *Pribol* (October 1917) in V.I. Lenin, *On the Development of Heavy Industry* (Moscow: Progress Publishers, 1972), 16. Lenin's sense of impending disaster is evident in his correspondence in 1921. In one letter he asks fishermen on the Aral Sea to send some of their catch to help the seven million starving children and the eight million workers. See "Bugun Fishermen's and Workers' Soviet of the Northern Coast, Aral Sea," 7 October 1921, in *V.I. Lenin Collected Works*, vol. 45 (Moscow: Progress Publishers, 1970), 326. Several general histories of the Soviets' early efforts to industrialize and modernize include Sheila Fitzpatrick, *The Russian Revolution*, 2nd ed. (Oxford: Oxford University Press, 1994); Moshe Lewin, *The Soviet Century* (London: Verso, 2005); Stephen Kotkin, *Magnetic Mountain: Stalinism as a Civilization* (Berkeley: University of California Press, 1995).

7. Rosalind Williams, "The Political and Feminist Dimensions of Technological Determinism," in *Does Technology Drive History? The Dilemma of Technological Determinism*, ed. Merritt Roe Smith and Leo Marx (Cambridge: MIT Press, 1995), 227; Lenin,

"Draft Plan of Scientific and Technical Work," first written between 18–25 April 1918, *Pravda* (4 March 1924) in Lenin, *On the Development of Heavy Industry*, 39. For an excellent discussion of Lenin's and later, Stalin's ideas about electrification and industrialization, see Kendall E. Bailes, *Technology and Society Under Lenin and Stalin: Origins of the Soviet Technical Intelligentsia, 1917–1941* (Princeton: Princeton University Press, 1978).

8.   Lenin to G.M. Krzhizhanovsky, 23 January 1920, *Ekonomisheskaya Zhin*, no. 18 (22 January 1925) in *On the Development of Heavy Industry*, 49. In correspondence with E.M. Skljanskij, Lenin predicted, "The electrification plan, which is calculated on ten years (first phase of the work), requires 370 million working days. Per year per man in the army this amounts to $(37:1.6) = 24$ working days, i.e. *two days a month*." See Lenin to Comrade Skljanskij, in *The Trotsky Papers, 1917–1922*, ed. Jan M. Meijer (The Hague: Mouton, 1971), 461.

9.   Lenin, "Report on the Work of the All-Russia Central Executive Committee and the Council of People's Commissars Delivered at the First Session of the All-Russia Central Executive Committee, Seventh Convocation," 2 February 1920, *Pravda* (3 February 1920) in *On the Development of Heavy Industry*, 51–52.

10.   Lenin, "From Our Foreign and Domestic Position and the Tasks of the Party," 21 November 1920 in *On the Development of Heavy Industry*, 78; Lenin to G.M. Krzhizhanovsky, late December 1920 in *On the Development of Heavy Industry*, 80.

11.   Lenin to Comrade Skljanskij, n.d. in *The Trotsky Papers, 1917–1922* ed. Jan M. Meijer (The Hague: Mouton, 1971), 461.

12.   Jonathan Coopersmith, *The Electrification of Russia, 1880–1926* (Ithaca: Cornell University Press, 1992), 177.

13.   Lenin, "Integrated Economic Plan," 21 February 1921, *Pravda* (21 February 1921) in *On the Development of Heavy Industry*, 95. In a conversation with Bertrand Russell in 1920, Lenin discussed the importance of providing electricity for industry, which he estimated would take ten years. See Bertrand Russell, *The Practice and Theory of Bolshevism* (New York: Simon and Schuster, 1921), 32–36.

14.   Albert Rhys Williams, *Lenin: The Man and His Works* (New York: Scott and Seltzer, 1919), 102–103, in *Lenin*, ed. Saul N. Silverman (Englewood Cliffs: Prentice-Hall, 1972), 165–166. Lenin's admiration for the Taylor system was well known and when speaking of wedding Soviet socialism with the organizational strengths of the capitalist model, he remarks "We must organize in Russia the study and teaching of the Taylor system and systematically try it out and adapt it to our own ends." See Lenin, "The Immediate Tasks of the Soviet Government, " 30 April–3 May 1918 in *Selected Works*, II, 714–717. An excellent discussion of Lenin's views on technology and realizing his ideal state can be found in Richard Stites, *Revolutionary Dreams: Utopian Vision and Experimental Life in the Russian Revolution* (New York: Oxford University Press, 1989).

15.   Lenin, "Report of the All-Russia Central Executive Committee and the Council of People's Commissars on the Home and Foreign Policy," 22 December 1920 in *On the Development of Heavy Industry*, 84.

16.   Susan Buck-Morss, *Dreamworld and Catastrophe: The Passing of Mass Utopia in East and West* (Cambridge: MIT Press, 2002), 118. This is not to say that the scale of resource use does not matter only that once industrialization becomes the objective,

rivers are engineered in similar ways, such as dams, levees, rerouting, to support the shift to an industrial economy.

17. Alexander Chubarov, *Russia's Bitter Path to Modernity: A History of the Soviet and Post-Soviet Eras* (New York: Continuum, 2001), 8; Bailes, *Technology and Society*, 408. See chapter 6 for an expanded discussion on modernization theorists, such as Walt Rostow.

18. Kotkin, *Magnetic Mountain*, 360; Chubarov, *Russia's Bitter Path*. Marshall I. Goldman's book, *The Spoils of Progress: Environmental Pollution in the Soviet Union* (Cambridge: MIT Press, 1972), seriously challenged the belief that strong central planning benefitted the environment. He states on page 5 that "Industrialization and urbanization have been at least as demanding on the environment in the USSR as they have been elsewhere in the developed world, and the result is virtually the same." See concluding chapter for additional modernization theories from scholars Paul Josephson and James C. Scott.

19. Deborah Fitzgerald, *Every Farm a Factory: The Industrial Ideal in American Agriculture* (New Haven: Yale University Press, 2003), 3.

20. Ibid., 157.

21. Ibid., 187.

22. Coopersmith, *The Electrification of Russia*, 254; *USSR in Construction*, no. 3 (1934): n.p. For a complete history of Dneprostroi, see Anne D. Rassweiler, *The Generation of Power: The History of Dneprostroi* (New York: Oxford University Press, 1988). One of the best works to discuss Soviet and American collaboration is Norman E. Saul, *Friends or Foes? The United States and Russia, 1921–1941* (Lawrence: University of Kansas Press, 2006). There are also several general works that discuss Dneprostroi including Paul R. Josephson, *Industrialized Nature: Brute Force Technology and the Transformation of the Natural World* (Washington: Island Press, 2002). Interestingly, at first Stalin did not support Dneprostroi. According to Trotsky, "Stalin remarked that the planned power-station would be of no more use to Russia than a gramophone was to a muzhik who did not possess even a cow." Central Committee, April 1926 as quoted in Issac Deutscher, *The Prophet Unarmed: Trotsky, 1921–1929* (London: Oxford University Press, 1959), 211.

23. Leon Trotsky, *Sochinenya*, vol. 21, 437, as quoted in Deutscher, *The Prophet Unarmed*, 211; *USSR in Construction*, no. 3 (1934): n.p.

24. Loren R. Graham, *The Ghost of the Executed Engineer: Technology and the Fall of the Soviet Union* (Cambridge: Harvard University Press, 1993), 51–55. For a more thorough discussion of this period in the history of the USBR see Dorothy Lampen, *Economic and Social Aspects of Federal Reclamation* (Baltimore: Johns Hopkins Press, 1930). Most historians still accept Lampen's interpretation of the bureau's engineering emphasis before the arrival of Commissioner D.W. Davis. Before 1923, the USBR was called the U.S. Reclamation Service.

25. Alexander Chubarov, *Russia's Bitter Path*, 103; Johann P. Arnason, "Communism and Modernity," in *Multiple Modernities*, Shmuel N. Eisenstadt, ed. (New Brunswick: Transaction Publishers, 2002), 81; *USSR in Construction*, no. 9 (1937): n.p.; Fitzpatrick, *The Russian Revolution*, 151. For an in-depth discussion on the favorable views Americans held regarding Russian industrialization in the 1930s, see David C. Engerman, "Modernization from the Other Shore: American Observers and the Costs of

Soviet Economic Development," *American Historical Review* 105, no. 2 (April 2000): 383–416.

26. Margaret Bourke-White, *Eyes on Russia* (New York: Simon and Schuster, 1931), 85. During the construction, however, of major projects in the 1930s the use of manual labor was still very common. At Magnitogorsk, one estimate states that in the mid-1930s over half of the earth-moving work was still being done by hand. See Kotkin, *Magnetic Mountain*, 420.

27. Bailes, *Technology and Society*, 4. The expertise of other Western countries, particularly Germany, was also relied upon for these early projects.

28. Dean Burk, "A Scientist in Moscow," *The Scientific Monthly* 47, no. 3 (September 1938): 227–241; Graham, *Ghost of the Executed Engineer*; Bailes, *Technology and Society*, 274; Franklin Delano Roosevelt in "Extemporaneous Remarks at Clinch River Below the Norris Dam," 16 November 1934 in *The Public Papers of Franklin D. Roosevelt*, vol. 3 (New York: Random House, 1938).

29. *USSR in Construction*, no. 9 (1937). FDR's platform on public versus private power rests in part upon FDR's conviction that "The water power of the State should belong to all the people. The title to this power must rest forever in the people." See FDR, "Campaign Address in Portland, Oregon on Public Utilities and Development of Hydro-Electric Power," 21 September 1932 in *The American Presidency Project*.

30. Donald J. Pisani, *Water and American Government*, 241. Pisani offers one of the most comprehensive studies of the evolution of U.S. water policy in the early twentieth century and the engineering community that promoted it.

31. *Report of the Mississippi Valley Committee of the Public Works Administration* (Washington, D.C.: U.S. Government Printing Office, 1934), 15; Graham, *Ghost of the Executed Engineer*, 50. For a good discussion of Cooke's ideas, see Jean Christie, "New Deal Resources Planning: The Proposals of Morris L. Cooke," *Agricultural History* 53, no. 3 (July 1979): 590–606. By this time Americans had experienced major flooding along the Mississippi prompting numerous pleas for greater federal intervention in controlling the river. See John M. Barry, *Rising Tide: The Great Mississippi Flood of 1927 and How It Changed America* (New York: Simon & Schuster, 1997); Christopher Morris, *The Big Muddy: An Environmental History of the Mississippi and Its Peoples From Hernando De Soto to Hurricane Katrina* (New York: Oxford University Press, 2012).

32. Rexford G. Tugwell, *The Democratic Roosevelt: A Biography of Franklin D. Roosevelt* (Baltimore: Penguin Books, Inc., 1957), 288; *The Journals of David E. Lilienthal, The TVA Years, 1939–1945*, vol. 1 (New York: Harper and Row, 1964), 160. Further illustrations of 1930s criticisms of the New Deal can be found in Neil Maher's impressive work *Nature's New Deal: The Civilian Conservation Corps and the Roots of the American Environmental Movement* (New York: Oxford University Press, 2008). In one example (page 108), Maher cites critics "branded the Corps [CCC] as a Bolshevik threat to the American political system."

33. For the seven regional authorities, FDR recommended "one on the Atlantic Seaboard; a second for the Great Lakes and Ohio Valley; a third for the drainage basin of the Tennessee and Cumberland Rivers; a fourth embracing the drainage basins of the Missouri and the Red River of the north; a fifth embracing the drainage basins of the Arkansas, Red, and Rio Grande Rivers; a sixth for the basins of the Colorado River and

rivers flowing into the Pacific south of the California-Oregon line; and a seventh for the Columbia River Basin." The Mississippi River Commission would have remained intact. See FDR, "Message to Congress on National Planning and Development of Natural Resources," 3 June 1937 in *The American Presidency Project*.

34. Buck-Morss, *Dreamworld and Catastrophe*. In this provocative work, Buck-Morss explores the western origins of socialism's drive to modernize.

35. Lilienthal, *TVA: Democracy on the March*, 26, 2; *Report of the Mississippi Valley Committee*, n.p.; Stephen R. Fox, *The American Conservation Movement: John Muir and His Legacy* (Madison: University of Wisconsin Press, 1986), 189; Harold L. Ickes, "Saving the Good Earth: The Mississippi Valley Committee and Its Plan," Survey Graphic in the Thirties (February 1934).

36. Pisani, *Water and American Government*; David P. Billington and Donald C. Jackson, *Big Dams of the New Deal Era: A Confluence of Engineering and Politics* (Norman: University of Oklahoma Press, 2006). FDR, "Message to Congress on National Planning and Development of Natural Resources," 3 June 1937, in *The American Presidency Project*, http://www.presidency.ucsb.edu/ws/index.php?pid=15415. According to one federal publication, "Hoover Dam was perhaps the most striking American public works project of the twentieth century. It was the first large Federal conservation undertaking based on multiple-based objectives." See Michael C. Robinson, *Water for the West: The Bureau of Reclamation, 1902–1977* (Chicago: Public Works Historical Society, 1979), 51. An interesting discussion on the TVA and FDR's commitment to modernize and electrify American homes can be found in Ronald C. Tobey's *Technology as Freedom: The New Deal and the Electrical Modernization of the American Home* (Berkeley: University of California Press, 1996). For additional insights to Stalin's treatment of Soviet engineers, see Graham, *Ghost of the Executed Engineer*.

37. Cong. Rec., vol. 72, 71st Cong., 2nd Sess. (25 April 1930). For an excellent biography of Elwood Mead that shows the evolution of his thinking regarding irrigation and reclamation and the institutions that guide water development, see James Kluger, *Turning on Water With a Shovel: The Career of Elwood Mead* (Albuquerque: University of New Mexico Press, 1992).

38. For a thorough account of New Deal attitudes toward natural resources and the motivations behind 1930s conservation policies, see Sarah T. Phillips, *This Land, This Nation: Conservation, Rural America, and the New Deal* (Cambridge: Cambridge University Press, 2007).

39. FDR, "The One Hundred and Sixtieth Press Conference," 23 November 1934 in *The Public Papers and Addresses of Franklin D. Roosevelt*, vol. 3, 467.

40. *The Journals of David Lilienthal, The TVA Years 1939–1945*, 141, 53.

41. Lilienthal, *TVA: Democracy on the March*, 3; For a general discussion of the political goals of electrification in the U.S. and Soviet Union see Tobey, *Technology as Freedom*, and Pisani, *Water and American Government*, 219.

42. Odette Keun, *A Foreigner Looks at the TVA* (New York: Longmans, Green and Co., 1937), 3. In David Ekbladh's impressive work, *The Great American Mission: Modernization and the Construction of an American World Order* (Princeton: Princeton University Press, 2010), he argues for the singularity of American modernization and uses text such as Keun's as evidence.

43. Keun, *A Foreigner Looks at the TVA*, 5.

44. Ibid., 13, 88.

45. For general discussions on the utopian ideals guiding modernizing efforts in the Soviet Union and the United States, Tobey, *Technology as Freedom,* and Stites, *Revolutionary Dreams.*

46. Joseph Stalin, quoted here from Fitzpatrick, *The Russian Revolution,* 130.

47. FDR, "The Fourth 'Fireside Chat'—We Are on Our Way, and We Are Headed in the Right Direction," 22 October 1933 in *The Public Papers and Addresses of Franklin D. Roosevelt,* vol. 2, 420. In this address, FDR tells listeners "there were about ten millions of our citizens who earnestly, and in many cases hungrily, were seeking work and could not get it." Ibid., 421.

48. Ickes, "Saving the Good Earth"; FDR, "Campaign Address in Portland, Oregon on Public Utilities and Development of Hydro-Electric Power" 21 September 1932 in *The American Presidency Project;*" Dorothy Zeisler-Vralsted, "The Cultural and Hydrological Development of the Mississippi and Volga Rivers," in *Rivers in History: Perspectives on Waterways in Europe and North America,* ed. Christof Mauch and Thomas Zeller (University of Pittsburgh Press, 2008), 63–77.

49. Paul C. Pitzer, *Grand Coulee: Harnessing a Dream* (Pullman: Washington State University, 1994), 264–265; Richard L. Neuberger, "The biggest thing on earth: Grand Coulee Dam," *Harper's* (February 1937): 247–342. "The Grand Coulee Dam," Woody Guthrie, 1944.

50. FDR, "Extemporaneous Remarks at Fort Peck Dam, Montana," August 6, 1934 in *The Public Papers and Addresses of Franklin D. Roosevelt,* vol. 3, 363.

51. Dorothy Zeisler-Vralsted, "Cultural and Hydrological Development," in *Rivers in History,* 63–77; In Dietrich's work on the Columbia River, he draws an interesting comparison between the Columbia and Mississippi Rivers in that he suggests "The Mississippi … will always remain in the American imagination a nineteenth-century river. It will forever be the place of Tom and Huck, of sternwheeler and flatboat, of the siege of Vicksburg and the Battle of New Orleans. The Columbia, in contrast, is our twentieth-century river." See William Dietrich, *Northwest Passage: The Great Columbia River* (New York: Simon and Schuster, 1995), 46.

52. Anthony Swift, "The Soviet World of Tomorrow at the New York World's Fair, 1939" *Russian Review* 57, no. 3 (July 1998): 367; 364–379.

53. Marco Duranti, "Utopia, Nostalgia and World War at the 1939–40 New York World's Fair" *Journal of Contemporary History* 41, no. 4 (October 2006): 663–683.

 CHAPTER 4

Moscow

A Port to Five Seas

Returning to the early 1930s—and a background heralding the promise and advances of technology with engineering coups such as Dneprostroi or the Tennessee Valley Authority (TVA)—the construction of the Moscow-Volga Canal and the Mississippi River Channel Project commenced. Both projects, regardless of political ideology, were born out of a faith in modernity and a need to industrialize that prompted Trotsky to say that he could transform landscapes and U.S. engineers to promise they could make the American West "blossom like the rose." Veering on the messianic, the belief in technology's potential and modernization's unequivocal blessings, the perceived success of projects like Dneprostroi or Hoover Dam emboldened political leaders and engineers to do more. The fanfare that greeted each project during construction and completion boosted confidence about the merits of rerouting and damming each nation's rivers. As a result, in serving the mandates of an industrialized nation-state, the Mississippi and Volga Rivers were redesigned, rerouted, and in the Russian context, "bridled." Yet during the construction of each, with descriptions rife with superlatives, historical images of the rivers were often invoked. Accompanying this recognition of each river's largesse, the projects represented unprecedented feats, reflecting a mastery over nature seized upon by engineers and politicians alike.

For the Moscow-Volga Canal, plans for its construction were included in Stalin's second Five-Year Plan, from 1933 to 1937. The canal—a longstanding dream of past tsars—had been considered since Peter the Great's reign when he wanted to connect Moscow to the Volga through a waterway allowing shipping from Moscow to the mouth of the Volga River. After Peter's death, although smaller projects to improve navigation were started under Nicholas I, the initial plan was not raised again until the late 1920s under Joseph Stalin. Under Stalin, the canal served two purposes: to supply domestic and industrial water to a growing Moscow population, and to accommodate shipping from Moscow to the Volga. But more importantly, the canal, along with other signature projects such as the Moscow metro system, became another symbol of Soviet ambition and promise. Marked by a frenetic pace to catch up with the West, these years saw nature and landscapes transformed as projects such as the White Sea–Baltic Sea Canal (Belomorkanal), Magnitogorsk, and of course Dneprostroi ushered the Soviet Union into modernity. But the historical memory of nature's greatness was always invoked, as when upon completion of the canal, journalists boasted they had "constrained Mother Volga." So even when being subdued, Mother Volga as national icon—capturing centuries of mythology, folklore, prose, and song—was being celebrated, endowing the triumph over river channels, banks, and untapped flow with that much more meaning.[1]

By the 1930s, the need to supply drinking water to Moscow's burgeoning population was critical. The available sources for drinking water were limited and yet during the first Five-Year Plan, the Moscow region population increased by three and a half million. A dire situation, one Soviet source claimed that only 42 percent of the houses in Moscow were connected to running water. Along with the need for drinking water was the growing demand for water to supply factories in the Moscow region. Underlying these obvious reasons, however, were other considerations. In discussions during the plenary meeting of the Central Committee of the Communist Party in January 1931, party leaders cited the necessity to serve the population in accordance with Socialist ideas of development. Drawing comparisons between the capitalistic city and its lack of planning that resulted in squalid conditions for the worker, Soviet leaders touted the Socialist city—a planned city with an adequate water supply. Similar to David Lilienthal's penchant for planning, Central Committee members, when considering Moscow's growth, demanded "more organization to develop a serious and scientifically proven plan for the enlargement and construction in Moscow." Holistic planners, guided by their vision of a Socialist future, they also emphasized the importance of parks and adequate roads within the growing city. During the same meeting, the Central Committee charged Moscow organizers to start the design of the canal at once as the immediate goal was for Moscow residents to have twice the amount of water available for consumption by 1935. This was in keeping with plans for Moscow's continued growth and an expanded water supply was paramount for factories as well as the residents.[2]

But the Moscow-Volga Canal also addressed a problem that became more evident during the first Five-Year Plan. As the Soviet planners sought to industrialize, they identified infrastructure weaknesses with the need for additional transportation routes becoming more pronounced. Upon completion of the Moscow-Volga Canal, Moscow would become a port with access to the Caspian, Baltic, and White Seas. Unlike the United States, where navigation on the Mississippi River was improved to challenge the railroad's monopoly on freight, the Soviet state did not have sufficient rail capacity to meet the needs of what would become a major industrialized nation. Although at first glance a disadvantage, when Soviet planners considered railroad development they touted the advantages of Socialist planning in addressing the state's transportation needs. As one observer remarked "unlike other states, the various forms of transport do not compete with each other, but supplement one another, constituting a single socialist system." Thus in 1932 when Stalin began construction of the Moscow-Volga Canal, it was built to supplement the railroads and also provide a cheaper form of transportation.[3]

But the Moscow-Volga Canal did more than increase Moscow's water supply and improve transportation, as the canal fed Stalin's ambition for grandiosity. Prior to the Moscow-Volga project, Stalin's first major water project was the Belomorkanal which connected the White Sea to Baltic ports. To Stalin and other leaders of the industrialized world, damming rivers and building canals spoke well of his leadership and ability. For the Soviet Union, the achievement was even more significant when the projects were ones where the tsars had failed. According to one source, the canal was an opportunity for Stalin to promote himself and demonstrate there "was nothing that communism could not do." Canals in general interested Stalin as they "seized his imagination ... and it sometimes seemed as if he wanted to dig them almost indiscriminately."[4] But canals were also part of the Stalinist landscape with its monumentalist structures often interspersed with neo-classic architecture. Breaking with the tradition of functional design, the Moscow-Volga Canal would later boast of locks and dams that "were so architecturally designed as to serve as a fitting monument that would tell future generations of the heroic work of the tens of thousands of workers engaged in its construction." At this time, architecture, in keeping with the utopian Socialist vision, was to deliver Stalin's promise of a "svetloe budushchee" or radiant future. For example, one lock has a replica of one of Columbus's ships, the Caravel, while another is modeled after the design of a diesel ship. In the case of the Caravel, the reproduction symbolized the Soviet entry into a new world, similar to Columbus's journey five centuries earlier. Other statues line the canal with names such as "ship and human body" or "water and health." Complementing the canal construction, waterfront space in Moscow and along the Volga was improved and later Soviet promotional brochures show beaches, excursions, and other recreational activities in this space—realizing the ambitions of the 1931 plenary meeting. In a further tribute to the Socialist zeal that prompted the project, two colossal statutes of Stalin and Lenin were built and placed on the banks of the Sea of Moscow where the canal begins. The statues were reported to be the third largest in the Soviet Union although today only Lenin's statue remains. (Under Khrushchev's tenure, Stalin's statue was removed.) These innovations—canal aesthetics and recreational opportunities—coupled with the actual work of re-routing the river, all lent an unprecedented scale and complexity to the project, which in the words of one scholar, "received even more accolades if they seemed to flout nature." The ability to manipulate the river, which was the core of the project, became especially significant given the earlier doomed efforts by the imperial government.[5]

In tandem with the monumentalism seen in the built environment, new ways to describe the undertaking were expressed. Similar to Dneprostroi (as well as U.S. projects in the 1930s) military references were drafted into use to underline the project's enormity. For example, one party official described hydraulic success by saying: "The water does not want to go into the Moskva River, so we have to force it to go. As we know, there are no fortresses Bolsheviks cannot storm." The overseer of the project Genrikh Yagoda, who was also head of the People's Commissariat of Internal Affairs (NKVD), remarked that "an engineer on the construction is a commander who holds full responsibility for his front." Statistical measurements also dominated published accounts about the canal. For example, in a 1938 issue of *USSR in Construction* devoted to the Moscow-Volga Canal, one page quantified the project with descriptors that cited the use of "37 times the amount of concrete required at the Dnieper hydroelectric plant for a project that included 11 locks, 3 concrete dams, 8 earth dams, 7 spillways, 6 bottom outlets, 5 pumping stations, 8 hydroelectric stations, 7 railway bridges, 12 viaducts or in all 240 magnificent engineering works." One Soviet engineer in his account of the project said that "In order to make the waters of the Volga flow into the Moscow River, it was necessary to excavate approximately 262,000,000 cu. yards of earth and pour about 7,000,000 tons of concrete. " In his litany of statistics, he even cited the number of railroad cars, tractors, trucks, steam shovels, and telephone and telegraph lines that were used. Another testimony to the project's accomplishments, and a shared similarity with Dneprostroi was the speed in which the canal was built. Numerous publications emphasized the completion of a project of this magnitude in record time. The herculean task of industrializing Russia and overcoming the remnants of a "backward" nation could not happen quickly enough.[6]

Thus in response to the need for an improved domestic and industrial water supply and transportation for goods from the Caspian Sea to Moscow, the construction of the Moscow-Volga Canal commenced in 1932. The canal was to extend from Moscow to Dubna for 128 kilometers. To place the canal in the larger context of Soviet society during this period, Soviet planners, working closely with Stalin, were beginning the Moscow metro system—another "national" achievement in Stalin's Five-Year Plans—and planning the never completed Palace of Soviets. Again, all three initiatives illustrate the times when projects, such as these, seemed out of proportion to everyday life. The goals of industrialization and subsequent modernization were occurring at an accelerated pace, heightening the sense of achievement. In Nikita Khrushchev's memoirs, he recalls: "It was a period of feverish activity, and stupendous progress was made in short time. A hundred important projects seemed to be

Figure 4.1. Moscow-Volga Canal view with Stalin. *USSR in Construction*, no. 2, 1938. *Source:* University of Saskatchewan Archives and Special Collections.

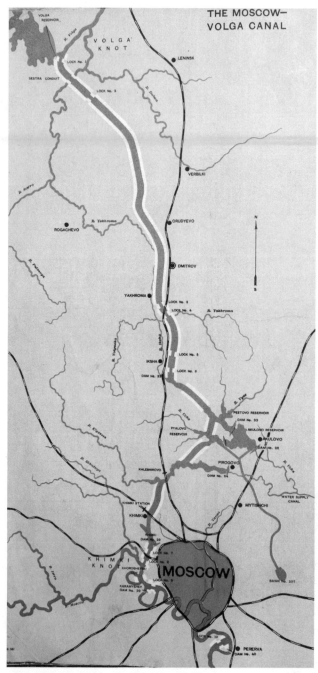

Figure 4.2. Moscow-Volga Canal map. *USSR in Construction*, no. 2, 1938. *Source:* University of Saskatchewan Archives and Special Collections.

Figure 4.3. Moscow-Volga Canal Village of Ivanovo power station. *USSR in Construction,* no. 2, 1938. *Source:* University of Saskatchewan Archives and Special Collections.

proceeding all at once: the construction of a ball-bearing factory, the enlargement of the Dux Number One aviation factory, the installation of oil, gas and electricity plants, the excavation of the Moscow-Volga Canal, to name just a few." Or in the words of one Russian novelist: "Moscow, highly strung in every respect, to the extent of convulsions, even as all of U.S.S.R., kept up a soldier's pace in the military march to socialism, in order to conquer. History in those years was not flowing, but was being constructed, even as Russia was being constructed." In the midst of all this activity, rivers and their reconstruction were some of the most noteworthy projects. For example, in a primer for children recounting the first Five-Year Plan, the author entitled one section "War with the River" in which he admonished young readers, "Man must fight for the river, as the animal-tamer fights with beasts." Novelists also joined the fray with works such as *The Volga Falls to the Caspian Sea.* Under the tutelage of Maxim Gorky, authors produced a "waterworks library" valorizing this chapter in Soviet history. The Moscow-Volga Canal, once again drafting the Volga into service, exemplified this spirit.[7]

In planning the Moscow-Volga Canal, contemporary accounts reveal that engineers initially considered several routes, and when the earlier mentioned plenary session of the Central Committee resolved to build the canal on 15 June 1931, the route had still not been determined. After deciding upon a route in 1932, Stalin and his advisers relied upon the labor of thousands of prisoners to build the canal. The prisoners were housed in Dmitlag, a camp located in Dmitrov, an old Russian provincial city partway between Moscow and present-day

Figure 4.4. Moscow-Volga Canal lock and pumping station. *USSR in Construction*, no. 2, 1938. *Source:* University of Saskatchewan Archives and Special Collections.

Figure 4.5. Moscow-Volga Canal famous lock no. 3 with decoration. *USSR in Construction,* no. 2, 1938. *Source:* University of Saskatchewan Archives and Special Collections.

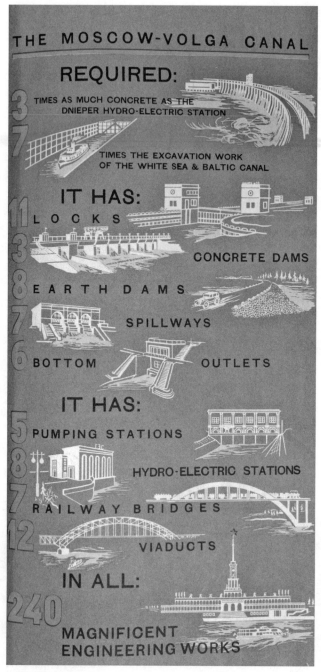

Figure 4.6. Moscow-Volga Canal diagram with statistics. *USSR in Construction*, no. 2, 1938. *Source:* University of Saskatchewan Archives and Special Collections.

Dubna. Depending upon prison labor was not new; prisoners constructed the Belomorkanal Canal under the oversight of many of the same Soviet leaders. In both instances the official goal was "reforging" (*perekovka*) or "remaking" the convicts with the end result a new Soviet citizen or *sozidayustchee chelovek*. Not all the labor, however, drew from the prison population. In the memoirs of Sergei Golitsyn, when remembering his first unsuccessful application for work on the canal, there was a "whole line of people, newly arrived from the train" waiting to apply. In Golitsyn's recollections, those waiting included graduates who despite their skills were rejected.[8]

But the prison population constituted the majority of workers, reaching 146,920 in 1937. (The camp work force at its height was around 200,000.) For these workers, their everyday lives, revealed in archival sources, endured countless abuses. The stories surrounding the construction of the Moscow-Volga Canal, which officially began in 1932, are legend to many Russians as the prisoners who actually built the canal were oftentimes imprisoned for minor "political crimes" such as the telling of an anecdote. The majority of prisoners were men and women who committed minor crimes, particularly what was known as the law of 7 August 1932. In the words of one who lived during these times, this law punished "anyone caught taking any state property at all, whether a handful of hay, or a few ears of wheat, or some youths shaking an apple tree on a collective farm.... If the 'criminal' was over twelve years of age, the sentence was ten years. The camps were full of such youngsters." Nevertheless, these prisoners worked at breakneck speed to finish the canal, often with wheelbarrows and shovels, and completed it in four years and eight months. When retelling this part of the history of the canal—despite Soviet efforts to distinguish the two—workers resembled Repin's burlaki whereby the river is the oppressor. One famous story recounts workers being ordered to take wheelbarrows filled with dirt into the icy waters of the Volga as one of the coffer dams broke; not surprisingly none of the workers survived. According to a worker, most of the canal was dug by hand as prisoners could be seen "laboriously hauling their maryusas up the slopes as fast as they could in their pairs, desperate to fulfill their quotas and so earn a remission in their sentence."[9] Given such conditions, the high mortality rates are not surprising as contemporary records indicate 23,000 to 28,000 workers lost their lives over the course of the canal construction. Yet, more laborers always seemed to be available and in a 1934 letter, the NKVD head Genrikh Yagoda, requested 15,000 to 20,000 prisoners, saying they "were needed urgently in order to finish the Moscow-Volga Canal." In a 1935 account of the project and its labor force, Syemyen Firin, the chief administrator of the Dmitlag prison camp, noted that shovel operators alone included 10,000 former criminals. Despite high mortality rates, with the steady influx of labor the first ships traveled up the canal to Moscow in 1937.[10]

During construction, project leaders produced a dense visual and print culture for internal and external audiences with the two often overlapping. Internally, workers were inundated with posters, newsletters, and in-house cultural events as a means to encourage production and "redeem" labor. Externally the work was publicized through journals, books, and newsletters, to develop a sense of nationalism, all under the auspices of building world socialism. Touting an undertaking this large crystallized the citizenry's sense of belonging to a great experiment, and ultimately, a great nation. In the words of one historian, "In the 1930s, the people of the USSR were engaged in a grand historical endeavor called building socialism." Another scholar contended that by the 1930s the Soviet Union recognized the need to promote a state unity, which "the previous decade's internationalist proletarian ideology had failed to stimulate." Touting large-scale construction projects such as the Moscow-Volga Canal satisfied the 1930s shift to "national Bolshevism." The visual culture also contributed to this sense of belonging. Artists were enlisted to promote the Moscow-Volga Canal, and the many images they produced included representations of the merits of industrialization, portrayals of the nobility and dignity of the worker, and drawings of well-known political figures. The person responsible for most of this was Syemyen Firin, who followed up on Maxim Gorky's discovery of Gleb Kun, who Gorky noticed when the artist worked on the Belomorkanal. According to Firin, Gorky became involved with the construction of the Belomorkanal as he advocated art as being one of the main tools to use in "reforging" man or perekovka. As a result, Kun later became the principal artist of the Moscow-Volga Canal and the head of the Dmitlag Artists' Studio, which existed for three years.[11]

As chief artist, Kun produced many works—in traditional Soviet style—celebrating the Moscow-Volga Canal with sketches of women and men laborers as well as drawings of the dams and actual construction. Indicative of the times, his work personalized and dignified the work of the laborer while recounting moments in the construction of the canal. Further, in 1937 when the first ships went upstream on the canal, all along the banks were Kun's portraits of Soviet leaders. Despite his talent and contributions, Kun and many of his colleagues were executed later that same year while many other workers were released. The official reason for the executions was their role in a proposed plot to assassinate Nikolai Yezhov, the head of the NKVD, succeeding Yagoda, who was also purged during this period. With the end of Yagoda's political career, the chief architect of the canal, Friedland, who was Yagoda's son-in-law, also disappeared and his position was eliminated. For many, the year 1937 was the worst in Soviet history or in the words of one scholar, "'Moscow, 1937' is a historical symbol in Kant's sense, a code word for one of the greatest historical catastrophes of the twentieth century."[12]

Returning to camp life, Firin complemented the artwork of the canal by establishing a professional theater and orchestra. He also organized a committee of talented journalists, writers, and poets. In the area of journalism, the accomplished Roman Tihomirov and several of his colleagues published the journal, *Na SHTURM Trassy,* with Firin as the editor. The publication included photographs and testimonials from visitors to the site. One issue included pictures of the orchestra playing while the men and women are involved in different tasks. The caption says, "The orchestra is helping the workers build fast and joyfully," an ongoing theme in the visual and print culture. Promotion of the heroic laborer, remembered in the image of the Stakhonovite, an extraordinary productive worker commemorated in Soviet propaganda, was another facet in the Five-Year Plan projects with data to support the worker's output. Similar to other project accolades, statistics were employed to illustrate the productivity of individual workers and their units. For example, one bricklayer on the canal laid 40,578 bricks or the equivalent of eight railroad cars of bricks during one shift. In the canal publications, such as *Moskva-Volgastroi,* articles appeared regularly with the quotas exceeded by units in tasks such as laying concrete and excavations. In fact, the incentive for many to exceed their quotas was a reduced prison sentence. Various posters decorated the halls where the workers ate and slept with slogans celebrating work and individual work productivity. For example at Dmitlag, one poster with a picture of Stalin has his arm upraised, exhorting, "By Stalin's Glue—the Life has Become More Joyful and When you Live with Joy the Work is Quicker and Easier." Below this banner, the worker is prompted "Stalinska—like the Stakhonovite workers let's widen the front of the Stakhonovite Movement." The imagery of heroic worker fused with military references gave the sense of waging a war in the cause of Socialism. According to one worker, the imagery of "canal soldier" did not "catch on." Other posters referred to work as the "ticket out," a common Soviet expression in the 1930s.[13]

One particularly interesting example of canal promotion that integrates several Soviet goals can be found in three publicized songs about the Volga written by non-native workers on the canal. The laborers are from Central Asia and along with lyrics celebrating the Five-Year Plan, one song specifically glorifies the Volga. While the songs were publicized to demonstrate the Soviet Union's success and the universality of socialism with the inclusion of Central Asian labor, the predominant Volga River theme in the songs revealed again the significance of the Volga in Russian history. The Volga, as nationalist symbol, collapsed and transcended differences based upon ethnicity and former state status. Drawing upon Russian attitudes toward the Volga, one song begins with the following:

> For centuries the celebrated Volga
> Rough beauty of mine
> In a blue dress, her path is long

While still another song honors Stalin's plan and uses a military analogy to describe their work on the Volga. His lyrics include: "We are fighting on track in favor of the plan / Reborn in the work order."[14]

The dignity of labor, whether Russian or Central Asian, enlisted in the cause of socialism was a constant refrain, particularly in contrast to the miserable, harsh lives of earlier laborers such as the burlaki. Under the Soviet system, labor was promoted not only as a means of reeducating political prisoners at the camp but as a contribution to a greater cause that benefitted all, while under the tsar labor only benefitted one class. Literary works, the products of Gorky's "waterworks library," spoke to the purity of the Soviet laborer, contrasting the Socialist era with Imperial Russia. In one novel in which the engineer is rerouting the Oka River, he muses on the effects this work will have on the laborers, in which he believes: "Human labor, reconstructing rivers by sheer force of will, washing away with these rivers the refuse of serfdom, was building up new labor relations. History like the river will be the glacier become limpid waters, destined to wash away the overcrowding of the military camps, the weariness of dissatisfaction and time; for human longevity is created not only by the academicians … but also by emancipated labor, which emancipates man from itself—for meditations, for the training of intelligence, and for leisure."[15]

While the reality was far different than these ideological claims, as everyday life in the camps was brutal and the workers saw reduced rations if the day's work quota was not filled, there were those reportedly heartened by the promise of hard work. Further for those whose output was greater than their quotas required, they were celebrated and rewarded. Still the cost in human lives cannot be ignored as post-Soviet scholarship revealed an inhumane labor system. Along with academic exposés are the memoirs of canal workers such as Sergei Golitsyn who described harsh living conditions for him and his family while working on the canal or the memoirs of those recounting how so many lost their lives while trying to complete the project.[16]

Yet according to the camp journal, *Na SHTURM Trassy*, work at Dmitlag also had other advantages as it gave the workers exposure to a Soviet education; another opportunity to overcome a backward past, in this instance the illiterate Russian village. Numerous publications boasted of the educational opportunities afforded to the canal laborers. One work, entitled, "Ot prestupleniia k truda," a propaganda piece by camp commander Yagoda's wife, I.L. Avarbach, touts the camp's secondary agenda in turning people into useful citizens. She mentions that the majority of laborers are criminals convicted under Article 35 for minor crimes like stealing or mugging. Once they arrive at the camp, they are given the chance to learn to read and write. Unlike other works promoting the Soviet's emphasis on education, Avarbach provides data and admits to difficulties. For example, in her words women were more difficult to teach. But in an overview of all the laborers arriving in Dmitlag in 1933,

2200 were illiterate and only 1500 were interested in school. Out of the 1500, only 251 completed their schooling and while she cites a possible loss of interest or poor teachers for the low success rate, a number of additional reasons beginning with ill health or fatigue are feasible given the camp's work conditions. Similar to other contemporary journals, she remarks upon the cultural life afforded the laborers with radio and a number of journals. Newspapers such as *Pravda,* published by the Central Committee of the Communist Party, were also available with one copy for 25 people. All of the cultural initiatives, however, were a means to raising the level of the worker, which in turn raises productivity. Avarbach gives an example of how in 1934, a Soviet party propaganda group visited the camp and gave a concert during the lunch hour. After the concert, the mood changed and the people worked harder. Numerous camp posters reiterated this theme as work would set the laborers free or in Russian slang work was the "ticket" out. Various clubs, whether sports, music, or reading also contributed to an improved cultural environment at the camp. Even nature is drafted into the transformation as she remarks later in the text: "In our camps, the deepest thesis of Marxist-Leninist philosophy has come true. Man remaking nature remakes himself."[17]

At the end of their experience at the camp, many left with new professions. According to one propaganda item produced specifically for the Moscow-Volga Canal, out of 25 groups, 296 women were taught and became qualified as librarians, hairdressers, dressmakers, and draftsmen. In another instance, Firin boasted how 10,000 criminals became shovel operators. In other accounts, training courses were offered at Dmitlag so the technical work could be undertaken. As a result by the time engineers completed the canal, one source claimed camp instruction produced "specialists in 43 professions—section chiefs, technicians, foremen, concrete and soil analysts, excavator operators and stokers, fitters, electricians, mechanics, motor men, motor drivers, electric welders, etc." But it was not only the worker that was transformed. Soviet art also promoted the canal by projecting the image of sleepy rural villages being changed by industrialization. For example, Gleb Kun's *Dva Dmitrova* depicts two images of the town: the old church with its surrounding kremlin juxtaposed to an image of a young man driving a truck with a steam shovel in the background. Since the town of Dmitrov was an old Russian provincial town located on the canal route, the visual representation of progress and modernity illustrates the bright future for Dmitrov upon completion of the canal. During Stalinist Russia, the "liquidation of backwardness," particularly the Russian village, pervaded Russian society, and the Moscow-Volga Canal and all the activities associated with it were another means to modernization. (The idea that Stalin's Five-Year Plan transformed rural Russia was not only supported in the 1930s and 1940s but still has believers today as contemporary historians indicate.)[18]

Thus construction of the canal was multifaceted as the canal itself helped the Soviet Union in its war to industrialize quickly, while workers, called soldiers of the canal army, waged their own battles over a backward past. In a special issue of *Na SHTURM Trassy*, testimonials from foreign observers supported the canal with glowing praise, such as, "Built with Soviet made equipment and labor refutes the old capitalist lies of the proletariat being incapable of doing anything," while others wrote of the great success of socialism. References to Soviet-made equipment were another persistent theme in recounting Five-Year Plan projects.[19] Other issues of the journal included poems and songs that portrayed an endeavor that united the workers with the historical dreams of past and present governments as one song illustrated:

> We unloaded trucks,
> That had brought us concrete, and then pressed it
> To make a dream that had appeared long ago true.
> And the town [Moscow]—majestic as a mountain,
> Beckoned us to the wonderful far.
> And the song, and the love [to the Motherland], and the flag
> United us in friendship and we were pushing tons of concrete and ground
> To bury at the canal bottom all the evil we had had before.[20]

In addition to Firin's promotional activities, news about the canal came from other printed materials such as the journal *Technics of the Youth,* and radio programs. As scientists were often unwillingly drafted into service, their technical works about the project appeared. An example of one well-known professional working on the canal is the case of soil scientist Valery Krutizovsky, who had been sent to prison for refusing to follow an order for an early sowing of crops. For this crime—translated into an act of treason and sabotage—he was initially sentenced to death in 1933. Due to the efforts of his colleagues and family the sentence was reduced to prison time, which is how he became a laborer on the canal. Once Firin learned of his profession, he assigned him the problem of stopping the erosion of the canal banks. Unlike Kun, Krutizovsky was allowed to continue his work as a scientist after the canal was completed. Thus journals devoted to canal building, such as *Belomorstroi*, discussed the evolution of technology or in contemporary language "science." For example, when engineers built the first gate of the canal, they used wheelbarrows, but by the end of construction, they used machines. Another example cited was the practice of pouring concrete and how that became perfected over the four-year period. Although technological advances undoubtedly did occur, other accounts emphasize that "mechanization came in very late." Though more technologically advanced from the outset, the Mississippi River Channel Project experienced a similar evolution with technology in that while building the Upper Mississippi locks and dams, engineers remarked upon how one technology even became obsolete by the end of the project's construction.[21]

After completion in 1937 in record-breaking time and amidst great fanfare, the Moscow-Volga Canal became one of the signature projects of Stalin's second Five-Year Plan. In a 1937 *Pravda* article, the canal was referred to as "the pride of Stalin's Second Five-Year Plan." In a tribute to socialism, the article emphasized how the canal provided drinking water to seven million people in Moscow and how construction of the canal contrasted with capitalism's treatment of its citizens. According to the article, Soviet man did not accept squalor and poverty. The canal became a symbol of Moscow's success as a socialist city and not just a success because of the technology or expertise required. Instead, the canal was a symbol of the virtues of central planning in the service of a nation's citizens. The article went so far as to give an example of an irrigation project on the Platte River in Nebraska being stopped; something that would not have happened in the Soviet Union with its ability to plan centrally and overrule special interests. Yet in 1937, President Roosevelt and many of his cabinet members saw improvements such as these as keeping with the goals of a democracy. Projects such as the locks and dams on the Upper Mississippi River, the TVA, and the proposed Columbia Valley Authority reflect the same attitudes toward nature and modernization. Despite the rhetoric of political leaders, the similarities between the two countries outweighed the differences.[22]

But the Moscow-Volga Canal also represented Stalin's attempts in the 1930s to not only industrialize the Soviet Union but to leave his imprint—harnessing the Volga River testified to the success of this new government. In one account, Stalin's "persistence" in building the canal was praised as it will benefit the Soviet people for thousands of years as the "Volga's water flowed obediently to Moscow." The imagery here is one of conquest and testifies to the strength of Stalin's regime. Aware of the historical significance of the canal, Soviet journalists when publicizing the project's completion boasted: "[T]he Bolsheviks nevertheless constrained Mother Volga to change her course. In four years they dammed up the Volga, created an enormous reservoir known as the Moscow Sea and built a canal joining the Volga with the R. Moscow. The ancient walls of the Kremlin are now washed by the waters of the Volga." In the same commemorative issue devoted to the canal, journalists reiterated earlier efforts by the tsars to accomplish what Stalin did in less than five years. Again, the memory of earlier attempts to constrain the Volga was ever-present—elevating the accomplishment.[23]

Although Five-Year Plan projects such as the metro in Moscow came to overshadow the Moscow-Volga Canal, in the mid-1930s the canal was touted as "the greatest construction of the Stalin Epoch." One later scholar noted that the canal and the Moscow metro system, both signature projects of the second

Five-Year Plan, "sustained a new mood of optimism after the trauma of collec-
tivization and dekulakization and offered the hope for a more stable course of
future development." To Soviet journalists, the canal even deserved a place on
the world stage as it overshadowed all other canals—such as the well-known
Suez—with the exception of the Panama Canal. So many elements converged
in the construction of the canal and its importance was such that Soviet youth
were told to learn its history and the lessons it imparted. These included the
Bolshevik remaking of people, Soviet achievements in technology, the acquisi-
tion of complex modern machinery, and perhaps most important, the canal as
an example of the subordination of nature's power to the will of creating man.
In more colorful prose, "the stern hand of the Bolsheviks are turning the Volga
and are making a new route for it." The Volga, always noted for its calm waters,
was now a subdued waterway serving the Bolsheviks.[24]

Completion of the canal was noted outside the Soviet Union as the U.S.
magazine *Time* included an article in July 1937 entitled "Stalin's Mercy." While
the opening of the canal was mentioned, the gist of the article remained Stalin's freeing 55,000 workers that had been "sent to the purgatory of digging
immense canals under the last of Ogpu overseers." In addition to the Moscow-
Volga Canal, many of the workers, or in the language of the article, "sinners,"
had worked on the Belomorkanal. Along with their freedom, the former laborers received "a free ticket to his or her home town, a bonus of between 100
and 400 rubles ... and an honorary badge proclaiming their redemption." The
article failed to mention the many that were arrested as being part of a terrorist
plot against Yezhov, of these many were talented poets, writers, and engineers.
Still, many of the workers went on to the next major Volga project—construction of the Kuibyshev Reservoir under the supervision of one of the Soviet's
most well-known engineers, Sergei I. Zhuk.[25]

Still the environmental and social costs were high as seen in the number
of towns that were inundated. A total of 110 towns were relocated. One of
the better-known lost towns was Korcheva, which was built by Catherine the
Great and is still remembered today with commemorative plates. Still, the
most lasting impressions of the canal are the accounts of the workers and prisoners. In the area around Dubna, there are several commemorative sites and
museums for those who lost their lives building the canal. Noted earlier, an
official Russian count places the number of lives lost over 28,000 prompting
an outpouring of articles and remembrances in towns affected by the canal. In
a series of newspaper articles commemorating the sixtieth anniversary of the
canal's completion, one author ends her piece, recalling those who lost their
lives because of their connection with Firin. She laments:

All the untold sorrow,
Half-forgotten weight of the injury
The water of the canal will rush to the sea

And the sea will not bring them back …

Yet the history of the canal and its consequences has undergone varying interpretations and emphases since Perestroika when Mikhail Gorbachev sought economic and political reforms within the Soviet Union. For example, when first studying the canal in the early 2000s, local newspapers such as *Ploschad Mira* focused on the loss of lives and brutality incurred while constructing the project. In recent years, while not diminishing the human costs, there is an acknowledgement in some quarters of the benefits of the canal. For example, publications from the Muzej Kanala imeni Moskvy and the museum's exhibits include the use of forced labor while also illustrating the canal's contributions. Current scholarship, however, in Russia and the United States continues to uncover what Douglas Wiener called "the darker legacy" of the canal.[26]

While not diminishing the human costs, however, the canal was successful by increasing Moscow's water supply, substantially improving barge traffic, and generating electricity. (Today, the hydroelectric station at Dubna still is a power source for the well-known Joint Institute for Nuclear Research.) Other reasons many supporters deemed the canal a success include the following. First, by establishing a trade route from Moscow to the mouth of the Volga, many Russian villages were remade into bustling trade cities. Second, the canal provided an additional water supply to Moscow's residents, although Soviet claims that after construction Moscow's water supply was greater than any other capital city in the world is suspect. Third, all of the work on the canal was completed by homemade Soviet equipment—a source of pride for many. For example, the pumps that were used at construction sites were built at fifty plants in the biggest cities throughout the Soviet Union while engineers were designing a new type of riverboat and special Soviet-built 150-ton cranes were also used.

For the Soviet Union, the canal was only the beginning of the Volga's transformation. By 1950, the Volga River supported two-thirds of the river traffic throughout the Soviet Union from the times of the Revolution. By the 1950s, the "Great Volga Scheme" began and more activity occurred in the Middle Volga region. One of the largest undertakings was the completion of the Volga-Don Canal in 1952. Although a greater engineering challenge, the Volga-Don Canal still shared similarities with the Moscow-Volga Canal as it was another project with historical antecedents and connections with Imperial Russia. But reflecting the history of the Moscow-Volga Canal, it required the Soviet wherewithal to realize the dream of earlier dynasties. The experts who first saw service in building the Moscow-Volga Canal became well-known names for subsequent hydro-projects, some on the Volga. For example, Petr Ivanovich Vasilenko, who oversaw work on the Moscow-Volga Canal as the Assistant Chief for Work in the Volga Region, went on to supervise the design and construction of the "largest hydroelectric plants in the Soviet Union." Sergei I. Zhuk, a hydrologist, also a supervisor at the canal, went on to oversee the

Zhiguli Reservoir on the Volga, the largest reservoir in Europe. In the transformation of the Volga River, a new dynamic between humans and nature was evolving. Empowered with their initial successes, engineers and political leaders saw the appropriation of nature, and in this instance, the Volga, as an entrée into a new world that freed labor from the burdens of the past while raising the standard of living for all. The reverse was true, the appropriation of the Volga only served to increase the brutality of labor and despoil a resource. Or in the words of one scholar, the Moscow-Volga Canal "was an object lesson in which something of essential significance came into view: the interaction of science and terror, specialization and forced labour, the transformation of knowledge about the appropriation of nature into knowledge about how to subjugate human beings."[27]

Nevertheless, the twentieth century ushered in a new era for the Volga River. While paying homage to modernization, the images enlisted in the new wave of nation-building were reminiscent of the past as "Mother Volga" was constrained by the Bolsheviks. Harnessing a river as great as the Volga, however, enhanced the transformation to modern nation. The national narrative in the beginning of the century was laced with words such as struggle, conquest, and bridle. Awe and reverence were still present but resulted from the Socialists' perceived superiority over nature, rival nations, and earlier governments, to name a few. But the Soviet experience was not distinct as the decade of the 1930s was pivotal for the shift in attitudes as large-scale and multipurpose projects became the standard bearers for modernization. This messianic faith in modernization changed the dynamic between nature and humans. Yet, as Simon Schama's thesis points out, the historical memory of nature remains. In the case of the Soviet Union, the beneficence and magnitude of the Volga legitimized Stalin's rhetoric of Soviet greatness realized through the manipulation of the river. It was probably no coincidence that Stalin's favorite movie was the 1937 comedy, *Volga, Volga,* a film that, in illustrating the growth of the country, included a scene with the statues of Lenin and Stalin at the beginning of the Moscow-Volga Canal. The lyrics to the "Song of the Volga" by Vasily Lebedev-Kumach provided further testimony to the Volga's place in Soviet culture as the aesthetics of the Volga also continued to be celebrated as it had in the past. Every Soviet school child knew the lyrics, which praised the Volga as "beautiful, like the sea" and like "the Motherland, free, wide, deep, strong." Immersed in the throes of modernization, the Soviet Union still looked to the Volga River when crafting national identity.[28]

Notes

1. A. Komarovsky, *The Moscow-Volga Canal* (Moscow: Foreign Languages Publishing House, 1939): 6; *USSR in Construction,* no. 2 (1938): n.p.; Richard Stites, *Revolution-*

ary Dreams: Utopian vision and Experimental Life in the Russian Revolution (New York: Oxford University Press, 1989), 244; Chubarov, *Russia's Bitter Path to Modernity,* 104. For general histories of the canal, I have relied upon a number of sources including archival material at the Dmitrov History and Regional Studies Museum, Muzei kanala imeni Moskvy, oral history interviews, newspaper clippings from *Pravda, USSR in Construction, Ploschad Mira,* and *Vyesti Dubnia* and publications that include N. Fedorov, *Byla li tachka u Ministra?* (Dmitrov: SPAS, 1997). For general histories of the Stalin era that include the Moscow-Volga Canal, see Timothy J. Colton, *Moscow: Governing the Socialist Metropolis* (Cambridge: Harvard University Press, 1995); Nobu Shimotomai, *Moscow Under Stalinist Rule, 1931–34* (New York: St. Martin's Press, 1991); Paul R. Josephson, *Industrialized Nature: Brute Force Technology and the Transformation of the Natural World* (Washington, D.C.: Island Press, 2002).

2. *Pravda,* 17 June 1931, 3; Kommunisticheskaia partiia Sovetskogo Soiuza v rezoliutsiiax I resheniiakh c''ezdov, konferentsii I plenymov TsK 1898–1953. Izdanie sed'moe. Chast' II (vtoraia (1825–1953)/Gosudarstvennoe izdatel'stvo politicheskoi leteratury. 1953 (This work includes the Plenum of the Central Committee of Communist Party, 11–15 June 1931, 637–669.) In a 1934 Russian promotional piece, the author cites the Plenum discussions and the Five-Year Plans, in which he contrasts the inadequate water and sewage facilities allowed for the workers under the tsarist system and in discussing the expected improved Moscow water supply, states, "The standard of living in any city can be conveniently measured by the amount of water consumed." M.I. Levidov, *Moscow: Past, Present, Future* (Moscow: Vneshtorgisdat, 1934), 92.

3. Fedorov, *Byla li tachka u Ministra?*; Interview with curator Galina Ivanovna Yurchenko, Muzej Kanala imeni Moskvy, 15 March 2011; *USSR in Construction,* no. 7 (1937): n.p.

4. Anne Applebaum, *Gulag: A History* (New York: Anchor Books, 2003), 55–56.

5. Catherine Cooke, "Beauty as Route to the 'Radiant Future': Responses of Soviet Architecture" *Journal of Design History* 10, no. 2, *Design, Stalin and the Thaw* (1997): 137–140, published by Oxford University Press on behalf of *Design History.* In this article, Cooke challenges the prevailing critical view of Soviet architects by many U.S. academics. She challenges Colton and others by looking past the judgment of "superficial and dismissive historians" and studying the periodicals of the time. Her criticism of these scholars includes their lack of knowledge of architecture. In contrast with Cooke's assessment, American journalist W.L. White, who during World War II was allowed to travel down the canal described the construction as "pretentious" and "over-ornamental." See White, *Report on the Russians* (London: Eyre & Spottiswoode, 1945), 60. Yoshira Ikeda, "Reconstruction of Moscow by Stalin and Waterfront Spaces," Research Meeting of City Core and Bay Area Renovation project & Oversea Research Project," Hosei University, 18 July 2007; A. Komarovsky, *The Moscow-Volga Canal,* 18; Colton, *Moscow,* 326. Another discussion of the canal architecture can be found in Karl Schlogel, *Moscow, 1937* (Cambridge: Polity Press, 2012). (This is the English edition). An excellent discussion of Belomorkanal can be found in Cynthia Ruder, *Making History for Stalin: The Story of the Belomor Canal* (Gainesville: University Press of Florida, 1998).

6. Colton, *Moscow,* 326–327; Yagoda, *Na SHTURM Trassy,* n.p., Dmitrov History and Regional Studies Museum; *USSR in Construction,* no. 2 (1938): n.p.; Komarovsky, *The Moscow-Volga Canal,* 11–14.

7. Chubarov, *Russia's Bitter Path to Modernity,* 106. *Khrushchev Remembers,* 60; M. Ilin, *New Russia's primer: The Story of the Five-Year Plan* (Boston: Houghton Mifflin Co., 1931), 35; Boris Pilnyak, *The Volga Falls to the Caspian Sea* (New York: Cosmopolitan Book Corporation, 1931), 21; Frank Westerman, *Engineers of the Soul: The Grandiose Propaganda of Stalin's Russia* (New York: The Overlook Press, 2011), 129.

8. Plenum of the Central Committee of Communist Party, 11–15 June 1931, 637–669. Sheila Fitzpatrick in one of her classical works makes the argument that some prisoners were actually inspired by the rhetoric of work's potential to redeem the individual although not dismissing the brutishness of the campus. See *Everyday Stalinism, Ordinary Life in Extraordinary times: Soviet Russia in the 1930s* (Oxford: Oxford University Press, 1999), 23, 75–79. In Applebaum's earlier cited work, *Gulag,* she offers a thorough overview of the use of forced labor throughout Stalin's tenure and compares the gulags with the forced labor during the German Nazi regime. Sergei Golitsyn, *Memoirs of a Survivor: The Golitsyn Family in Stalin's Russia* (London: Reportage Press, 2008), 503–504. In his memoir recalling his work on the Moscow-Volga Canal, Golitsyn claimed that Dmitlag was better than other camps because of its proximity to Moscow. See Golitsyn, *Memoirs of a Survivor,* 509.

9. Karl Schlogel, *Moscow, 1937,* 277; Golitsyn, *Memoirs of a Survivor,* 508; Schlogel, *Moscow, 1937,* 284; Golitsyn, *Memoirs of a Survivor,* 509. Wheelbarrows used by the laborers (also known as zeks) are on display at the Muzei kanala imeni Moskvy as are other tools considered obsolete even by 1930s standards. Ironically, anecdotes survive—despite these remembrances—that cast Stalin and the treatment of at least one worker in a different light. One story still circulating recounts a visit by Stalin to the canal during construction, in which Stalin saw one of the workers in boots unfit to wear. In response, Stalin ordered the supervisor to have new boots on the worker within a few hours or the supervisor would lose his job. The story ends with the worker receiving new boots. Oral interview with Galina Yurchenko, curator of Muzei kanala imeni Moskvy, 15 March 2011. Another excellent introduction to the gulag system and its evolution under Stalin's tenure can be found in Moscow's Muzei GULga. The museum hosts an impressive collection of historical maps, political posters, news clippings, camp artifacts, and artwork form camp survivors. American journalists also reported on the issue of forced labor as William Henry Chamberlain, journalist for the *Christian Science Monitor,* commented on how the canal was being built by "class enemies," of which he suspects there will always be plenty as long as canals need building. See Chamberlain, *Russia's Iron Age* (Boston: Little, Brown and Company, 1934), 64.

10. *Belomorstroi,* 1936, Dmitrov History and Regional Studies Museum; Schlogel, *Moscow, 1937,* 284.

11. Stephen Kotkin, *Magnetic Mountain: Stalinism as a Civilization* (Berkeley: University of California Press, 1995), 355; D.L. Brandenberger and A.M. Dubrovsky, "'The People Need a Tsar': The Emergence of National Bolshevism as Stalinist Ideology, 1931–41" *Europe-Asia Studies* 50, no. 5 (1998): 875; Gorky expressed many of his views regarding his Belmorkanal experience in *Belomor: An Account of the Construction of the New Canal between the White Sea and the Baltic Sea* (New York, 1935); Federov, *Byla li Tachka u Ministra?,* 43–59.

12. Federov, *Byla li Tachka u Ministra?,* 43–56. While news of the executions was published in a number of venues, the American magazine *Time* also reported on Yagoda's

demise as well as the release of workers on who had labored on the Moscow-Volga Canal and the Baltic–White Sea canal. *Time,* 26 July 1937. Yagoda's fate is recounted by Aleksandr I. Solzhenitsyn in which Yagoda begging Stalin for mercy exclaims: "I appeal to you! For you I built two great canals!" See Solzhenitsyn, *The Gulag Archipelago, 1918–1956* (New York: Harper and Row, 1973), 411. Yagoda's replacement, Nikolai Yezhov, would be also be executed two years later and photographs of him walking with Stalin along the Moscow-Volga Canal erased from history. See David King, *The Falsification of Photography and Art in Stalin's Russia* (New York: Metropolitan Books, 1997), 163. Golitsyn, *Memoirs of a Survivor,* 518; Schlogel, *Moscow, 1937,* 1.

13. *Na SHTURM Trassy* (June 1936): n.p.; Roman Tikhomirov, "Puteshestvie po kanaly," *Texnika-molodyozhi,* no. 11 (1936): 58–65, Dmitrov History and Regional Studies Museum; Federov, *Byla li Tachka u Ministra?*; *Moskva-Volgostroi,* no. 99 (1 September 1936): n.p., Dmitrov History and Regional Studies Museum; *Kanal imeni Moskvy: 70 let* (Moscow: 000Prazdnik, 2007), 50; Golitsyn, *Memoirs of a Survivor,* 509. In the Muzej kanala imeni Moskvy, numerous artifacts from the canal's construction are on display. In addition to posters, curators have kept some of the actual tools, correspondence and photographs. For an excellent general work on Soviet political posters, see Victoria B. Bonnell, *Iconography of Power: Soviet Political Posters Under Lenin and Stalin* (Berkeley: University of California Press, 1997).

14. *Volga,* Muzukal' naia biblioteka "Pevekovki" (December 1936): 7–8, Dmitrov History and Regional Studies Museum. The inclusion of songs by Central Asian workers revealed Soviet attempts to integrate all of those living within the Soviet Union. According to Francine Hirsch, the Soviets wanted to include all Russian and non-Russians. Further Soviet control and actions in areas such as Central Asia were distinguished from imperialism and instead seen as "helping the shift to modernization." See Hirsch, *Empire of Nations: Ethnographic Knowledge and the Making of the Soviet Union* (Ithaca: Cornell University Press, 2005), 5, 8.

15. Pilnyak, *The Volga Falls to the Caspian Sea,* 22.

16. Golitsyn, *Memoirs of a Survivor,* 507–538. Dissent was also voiced during Soviet times although through indirect means. For example, in Boris Pasternak's 1953 translation of Hamlet, he inserted, "Does a canal justify human sacrifices? He is godless, your engineer and what a power did he acquire!" He did something similar in a Faust translation when he asked, "How many poor workingmen were killed by this canal?" Both quotes are cited and discussed in Vladimir Markov, "An Unnoticed Aspect of Pasternak's Translations," *Slavic Review* 20, no. 3, 508.

17. I.L. Avarbach, "Ot prestupleniia k truda," (OGIZ (Ob'edineni gosudarstvennykh knizhno-zhurnal'nykh izdatel'stv: Gosudarstvennoe izdatel'stvo, 1936): 101.

18. *Kanal imeni Moskvy,* 48; *Belomorstroi,* 1936, Dmitrov History and Regional Studies Museum; *USSR in Construction,* 1938, no. 2; Fedorov, *Byla li Tachka u Ministra?*; Fitzpatrick, *Everyday Stalinism,* 9. In interviews with two historians and a number of Russians outside of academics, there is still a tendency by many to view the Stalin years in a positive light. In one interview with Nikolai Prislonov, historian and journalist, he discussed his own personal history, in that his parents were from a village and how their lives were transformed with the opportunities available during Stalin's tenure. Prislonov interview, 23 September 2003; Ivan Yaroslavovich Shimon interview, 5 April 2010.

19. *Na SHTURM Trassy,* June 1936, n.p.; Ibid, June 1935, n.p. Dmitrov History and Regional Studies Museum. The canal is still a source of pride as evidenced while interviewing the curator of the Muzei kanala imeni Moskvy, Galina Yurchenko, who had worked at the museum for 57 years. In the interview, she emphasized on several occasions how the equipment used to build the canal was Soviet-made.

20. *USSR in Construction,* no. 2 (1938): n.p.

21. Fedorov, *Byla li Tachka u Ministra?,* 95–99; *USSR in Construction,* no. 2 (1938): n.p; *Belomorstroi,* 1936, Dmitrov History and Regional Studies Museum; Golitsyn, *Memoirs of a Survivor,* 510.

22. *Pravda,* 14 July 1937.

23. Ibid; *USSR in Construction,* no. 2 (1938): n.p.

24. *Belomorstroi,* 1936; A.Kosarev, Velichaisheie sooruzhenie stalinskoi epokhi," *Texnika-molodyozhi,* no. 11 (1936): 5, Dmitrov History and Regional Studies Museum; E. A. Rees, *Iron Lazar: A Political Biography of Lazar Kaganovich* (London: Anthem Press, 2012), 164. The scale of the undertaking for the Moscow-Volga Canal still impresses Russians as one local Dubna resident informed me that if the amount of earth that was dug was loaded into railroad cars, these cars would circle the globe, via the equator, five and a half times—proving that the volume of work was much larger than needed for the Suez or Panama Canals. Oral history interview with Sergei Pipenko, 23 December 2011.

25. *Time,* 26 July 1937; Lyudmila Pirogova, *Vyesti Dubni,* 15 July 1997; Golitsyn, *Memoirs of a Survivor,* 522.

26. Pirogova, *Vyesti Dubni,* 15 July 1997; Yurchenko oral interview, 15 March 2011; Douglas Wiener, *A Little Corner of Freedom: Russian Nature Protection from Stalin to Gorbachev* (Berkeley: University of California Press, 1999), 355.

27. Holland Hunter, *Soviet Transportation Policy* (Cambridge: Harvard University Press, 1957), 148; David J.M. Hooson, "The Middle Volga: An Emerging Focal Region in the Soviet Union," *The Geographical Journal* 26, no. 2 (June 1960): 181; P.A. Warneck, "The Volga-Don Navigation Canal," *Russian Review* 13, no. 4 (October 1954): 285–290; "Memoir of Petr Ivanovich Vasilenko," *Hydrotechnical Construction* 10, no. 10 (1976): 1053; In Josephson's work, he discusses Zhuk's career, see Paul R. Josephson, *Industrialized Nature: Brute Force Technology and the Transformation of the Natural World* (Washington, D.C.: Island Press, 2002); Schlogel, *Moscow, 1937,* 273.

28. Supposedly after Khrushchev came to power, the scene in *Volga, Volga* showing the statues of Lenin and Stalin overlooking the beginning of the canal was removed from the film. In 2011, a new irreverent version of *Volga, Volga* was staged in Moscow. In this production, Soviet boasts of Moscow as a port to five seas were satirized. See *The Moscow Times,* 10 March 2011.

 CHAPTER 5

Navigating the Mississippi

The 1930s in the United States was a busy decade for engineers in which the Upper Mississippi River 9-Foot Channel Project with its eventual twenty-nine locks and dams was only one of many technological successes. Other well-known hydro-projects that were planned, started, or completed during the decade include Fort Peck Reservoir, which crosses the Missouri and was once the largest earthwork dam in the world; Grand Coulee Dam on the Columbia River, still one of the world's largest concrete dams; and of course, the Tennessee Valley Authority (TVA) with its numerous structures. Complementing and preceding the public works projects of the 1930s, however, was a broader movement in water politics and culture to manipulate and transform water resources for large-scale and multiple purpose projects. Undertakings such as the Panama Canal at the turn of the century and numerous reclamation projects that were increasingly multiple-purpose became the standard-bearers for modernization and contributed to a culture shaped by the language of development. One of the first projects to embody the multiple purpose concept of dam building was the Boulder Canyon Project that resulted in the construction of Hoover Dam. With the authorization of this federal project, multiple purpose planning became the norm as projects were conceived that combined power, flood control, irrigation, and other potential benefits, such as navigation. The best example of the shift to large-scale projects was the TVA, a New Deal Project that integrated navigation, flood control, and most important, power to rural populations. Although the process of developing water resources often differed from the Soviet Union with its reliance on Gulag labor and Stalin's frequent dismissal of the views of the engineering community, U.S. and Soviet projects (such as Dneprostroi, Belomorkanal, and the Moscow-Volga Canal) shared similar goals during this period. More importantly, the outcome for the rivers was the same. For the Mississippi and Volga, each has become the nation's highway with their history of "improvements" testimony to an evolution from free-flowing rivers to "human artifacts."[1]

Thus the rhetoric surrounding the engineering feats echoed that of Soviet leaders and engineers as the rivers were enlisted to serve the needs of a modern society. In a 1934 speech by President Franklin Delano Roosevelt at the Fort Peck Reservoir site, he boasted:

Now people talk about the Fort Peck Dam as the fulfillment of a dream. It is only a small percentage of the whole dream covering all of the important watersheds of the Nation. One of those watersheds is what we call the watershed of the Missouri River, [largest tributary of the Mississippi River] not only the main stem of the Missouri, but countless tributaries that run into it and countless other tributaries that run into those tributaries. Before American men and women get through with this job, we are going to make every ounce and every gallon of water that falls from the Heaven and the hills count before it makes its way down to the Gulf of Mexico.[2]

Included in these larger-than-life visions and the growing list of hydro-projects—reminiscent of Trotsky's call to "change the course of the rivers"—that ultimately transformed many of the nation's rivers was the construction of the Upper Mississippi River locks and dams, also known as the Upper Mississippi River 9-Foot Channel Project. Initially twenty-three locks and dams, using technology that "represent(s) technological breakthroughs in navigation engineering," this large-scale project reshaped the Upper Mississippi River into an intra-continental canal; a commercial highway.[3]

Although not having the stature of Stalin's Moscow-Volga Canal, at least in the American press, the constructed Mississippi River locks and dams were hailed by politicians, engineers, and area promoters as one of the greatest engineering feats of an era known as the "golden age" of American engineering. For American engineers the "aquatic staircase" that linked Minneapolis to St. Louis through a nine-foot canalization project finally allowed for the long hoped-for barge traffic to the flour mills of the Twin Cities. Although there were differences between the two projects, planners for the Moscow-Volga Canal and the Upper Mississippi River 9-Foot Channel Project shared an ambition—oftentimes unrealistic and grandiose—for improved navigation and commerce. As one Soviet brochure touted upon completion of the Moscow-Volga Canal, "Large ships under the Kremlin wall—does this sound improbable?" Likewise, for those living along the Mississippi River, they looked "forward to having foreign vessels tie up at their docks" and anticipated the day when "French and English freighters load and unload." Some predicted the Mississippi channel plan "may in the next century revolutionize the transportation system of a great inland empire." But the comparisons did not end with dreams of improved navigation as the physical attributes of each river were dramatically changed. For the Upper Mississippi—the once-unpredictable channels and main stem with fluctuations in depth at times so great that local residents recalled walking across the river—emerged as a series of slack-water ponds. Now the river, through the final construction of twenty-nine locks and dams, maintained a consistent channel depth of nine feet up to Minneapolis, facilitating barge travel for the temperate seasons. For the Volga, the river itself was extended as the Moscow-Volga Canal gave Moscow access to the Soviet Union's major water transportation artery, allowing for barges to travel up to Moscow for almost six months each year.[4]

A further unity of purpose can be found in the actions and rhetoric of the political leaders, Josef Stalin and Franklin Delano Roosevelt, who were involved and committed to these large-scale endeavors. In the earlier discussion of the Moscow-Volga Canal in chapter 4, Stalin included the project in his second Five-Year Plan. His participation in the canal construction is recorded through a rich repository of print and visual culture. In the case of Roosevelt, he supported the Mississippi River Channel Project from the earliest considerations of congressional funding. (Prior to Roosevelt, in 1927 former president Herbert Hoover, in his earlier position as Secretary of Commerce, advocated a channel depth of six to nine feet for the whole course of the river.) In backing the locks and dams, the president had several goals including an aggressive three-year construction schedule with a completion date of 1936; employment for thousands through his New Deal agency, the Public Works Administration, which oversaw the labor force for the project; and the potential for a twelve-foot channel. In a 1933 meeting with Minnesota Senator Thomas Schall, Roosevelt reiterated "he was deeply interested in the project and intends that it shall be pushed rapidly to completion" but also stressed that "in building the 23 new dams and locks for the upper river provision should be made for a future 12 foot channel." In an article prepared for another presidential visit in 1934, references were again made to the project's potential to deliver "cheap water transportation to the interior of the country."[5]

Another similarity between the two projects was the historical memory that was conjured up and appropriated in the interests of these engineering undertakings. For example, just as Soviet journalists referenced "Mother Volga" when discussing the Moscow-Volga Canal, the author of a retrospective article upon completion of the locks and dams remarked upon earlier steamboat travel upstream on the "Father of Waters." The same author noted how "in the pioneer days, when civilization started to move westward to start new communities and create additional states, the Mississippi River was unhampered by the hand of man as it flowed unrestricted on its way to the Gulf of Mexico." References to "Old Man River" were also used when the river's historical flooding occurred throughout the nineteenth century despite the best efforts of the engineers. The image of an "unhampered river" was forever changed with the completion of the Upper River Channel Project as the river accommodated an increasing amount of tonnage and barge traffic. Still, improved navigation resonated with historic uses of the river as transport. A new use, however, for the rivers occurred with the 1930s projects in that the Mississippi and Volga were not only valued for their navigation, and subsequently, commercial shipping, but recreational aspects of the projects began to be promoted.[6]

Paralleling Soviet literature that underscored the need for recreational opportunities for the new Socialist man, engineers for the Mississippi locks and dams discussed how boating and fishing will be improved upon completion of the channel project. But in the case of the Mississippi undertaking, one engineer representing the Army Corps of Engineers, an agency under the War Department, went even further and told a group of local residents that the slackwater ponds that will result in lieu of the main stem of the river are even more attractive than the river. He observed to a gathering of local residents: "A swift running river is pretty, but does it afford the means for recreation that a lake does? Not when this lake is held at a constant level throughout the year. Fishing and boating will be better. Summer cottages can be located with a certainty as to where the shore will be and good roads will give easy access to them."[7]

A similar remark regarding the improved aesthetics of the Volga after the Volga-Don project was made, with the assumption that these large-scale engineering projects improved the landscape. The notion that natural beauty could be enhanced was shared by engineers and political leaders alike regardless of political loyalties. Yet again, the political rhetoric and ideologies mattered little for the Volga and Mississippi Rivers as the outcome for both rivers was the same after the modernizing schemes of the 1930s.

Adding to the newfound aesthetics of an engineered river, another new use considered for each river was in the area of hydropower. In the initial discussions regarding the Mississippi River locks and dams, one plan included waterpower development. According to an interview with Minnesota governor Floyd B. Olsen in 1933, President Roosevelt told him that the Upper River Channel Project would incorporate plans to generate "all the waterpower the upper valley can use." Sharing the President's desire to supply all American households with electricity, Secretary of the Interior Harold Ickes, in reviewing the work of the Mississippi Valley Committee Report, asserted that streams were probably more important as providers of electricity than in their earlier transportation roles. He also went on to note, "Even a cursory study of the Mississippi Valley discloses the need to bring electricity to the largest possible percentage of its rural population." Despite the backing of Roosevelt and his administration, the plan selected by the Corps of Engineers did not allow for water power development. According to Corps engineers, a power plan would have necessitated "an elaborate wing dam scheme with new reservoirs on tributary rivers such as the Chippewa, Minnesota, Black, and Wisconsin rivers." Still, the rhetoric regarding water power development and electrification embraced the same goals as the Soviets with their equation of electrification and modernization.[8]

The dream, however, of enhanced navigation on the Upper Mississippi was long-standing with calls for a deeper channel in the late nineteenth century. Similar to Russia beginning with the dreams of Peter the Great to connect

Moscow to the Volga, these early efforts on the Mississippi were only concerned with navigation. Since the first steamship, the *Virginia*, plied its way up to Minneapolis in 1823, commercial interests sought to insure a channel depth that would allow for shipping throughout the warm seasons, particularly in the first half of the century. Actual development of the Mississippi River began in the nineteenth century with work that included improvements to insure a channel depth of four and a half feet, the removal of snags and debris, continued dredging, and closing sloughs and constructing wing dams to bolster the main channel. In the years preceding the Civil War, the river served as a major highway for commercial traffic, carrying lead from mines in Illinois and Wisconsin, serving the agricultural sector, and later transporting immigrants to the Upper Midwest. For example in the 1853 season, commercial traffic between Galena, Illinois, and St. Paul, Minnesota, surpassed four hundred thousand dollars in goods. For further comparison purposes, "In the 1840s steamboat tonnage on the Mississippi, even exclusive of New Orleans, was greater than that of all Atlantic ports combined, with some boats already operating with loaded tows." Even after the arrival of the railroads, for several decades the railroads and river traffic were interdependent as newly built rail lines intersected with steamship routes. After the Civil War, production and shipping had increased to the point that many questioned the reliance on one form of transportation. As late as 1880, western waters were still carrying up to twenty million tons of goods but there were signs of its decline although river traffic was still considered viable up to World War I. In support of river trade, additional improvements to enhance navigation in the late nineteenth century included a lock and dam below St. Paul and the construction of six reservoirs on the headwaters of the Mississippi.[9]

Still by the 1870s with the expansion of the railroads and a robust river trade, the need for a greater carrying capacity was not the problem; instead farmers and local businesses were dissatisfied with the high prices the railroads could command. As a result, beginning in the mid-1860s, an alliance comprised of farmers, flour mill operators, and related business interests tried to improve navigation for shipping. Railroads, however, continued to dominate and by the end of the nineteenth century, trade had dwindled to the point that the only major shipping was the log rafts from the northern forests of Minnesota and Wisconsin. The logging industry was a major presence on the river, reaching its zenith in the late nineteenth century. Like other interest groups, loggers expected the government to come to their aid when problems arose with the river. The following early-twentieth-century poem exemplifies their attitudes about the Mississippi and the role of the federal government:

Who Owns the Mississippi?
The river belongs to the nation,

The levee, they say, to the state;
The government runs navigation,
The commonwealth, though, pays the freight.

Prior to the logging industry, the major commodity, in addition to lead, to be shipped on the river was grain (Minneapolis was known for its booming flour mills). So the perceived need for a deeper channel differed from the motives of the Moscow-Volga Canal where there were no competing rail lines and the demand for improved transportation was critical. But regardless of the motives for improved navigation on these rivers, the outcomes were similar—an engineered river serving as the nation's super highway. Further, the reservoirs, locks, and dams needed to create these transportation arteries have incurred significant environmental and social costs.[10]

In responding to the needs of the Minneapolis grain market to find another competitive form of shipping, the Corps of Engineers in 1878 began to build a four-and-a-half-foot channel. (The average depth of the river is three and a half feet.) Soon it became apparent that a deeper channel was necessary and a group of like-minded business interests who lived in river towns in the upper Mississippi Valley formed the Upper Mississippi River Improvement Association. In contrast to the Volga, engineering developments on the Mississippi were prompted by local demand. Each significant project on the Mississippi River was initiated by local organizations, often comprised of businessmen who shipped grain, operated barge lines, or owned the flour mills. Their concern for generating river traffic was well-founded as shipping continued to decline. Between the years 1889–1906, Upper Mississippi River commerce had fallen 85 percent.[11]

But local advocates for improved navigation persisted. As one of the most successful area organizations, the Upper Mississippi River Improvement Association's lobbying resulted in Congressional authorization of a six-foot channel in 1907. The early years of the twentieth century looked promising for the Mississippi River with political leaders such as President Theodore Roosevelt remarking upon the importance of the Mississippi Valley and its central role in America's future. Not everyone, however, supported the work of the association as well-known skeptic Mark Twain criticized Roosevelt's activities with the "Mississippi Improvement conspirators, who for thirty years have been annually sucking the blood of the Treasury and spending it in fantastic attempts to ameliorate the condition of that useless river." But Twain's criticism does not end there as he predicts: "These efforts have never improved the river, the reason that no effort of man can do that. The Mississippi will always have its own way; no engineering skill can persuade it to do otherwise; it has always torn down the petty basketwork of the engineers and poured its giant floods whithersoever it chose, and it will continue to do this. The President's trip is in the interest of another appropriation, and the project will succeed—succeed and furnish an advertisement." Groups such as the Mississippi River Improvement Association were common in the early part of the twentieth century as community chambers of commerce and other local constituencies promoted water projects.[12]

But even with Roosevelt's support, funding for the six-foot channel was limited although campaigns persisted for the channel until the mid-1920s. Again, in sharp contrast to the Moscow-Volga Canal where no alternative commercial transportation was available, even boosters for improved navigation on the Upper Mississippi, such as the Secretary of the War Department, recognized that traffic was limited. He cited a 1926 report from the Corps of Engineers that admitted the "tonnage moved on the Upper Mississippi is small" but added they expected a new barge line to operate between St. Louis and the Twin Cities. The report went on to predict "a potential commerce of some magnitude appears to be available" and that the Upper Mississippi should not "be cut off from connection with the main Mississippi transportation system and unable to realize the economics of traffic movement by water." Still, no funding was forthcoming despite increased attention to the nation's water transportation. By the late 1920s, however, promoters and engineers realized that a six-foot channel would not be sufficient and instead focused on a nine-foot channel.[13]

The push for a nine-foot channel found support among area farmers, local business interests, and the federal government. Area farmers who depended on the sale of grain for their livelihood particularly suffered before the construction of the nine-foot channel, as they were wholly dependent on the railroads for shipping which in turn allowed the railroads to charge exorbitant rates. Part of the reason the railroads charged what were considered by many to be inflated rates, was the opening of the Panama Canal. In the words of Assistant Secretary of War Harry H. Woodring: "[T]he Panama Canal just about ruined the Midwest. It caused discriminations in freight rates which drove industry to the seaboard." By opening up another viable transportation route, farmers and businessmen reasoned, the shipping rates would become more competitive. Supporters also stressed the potential of a greater international market. Not surprisingly, the railroads opposed the project. In a series of moves—including an injunction filed by the Burlington Northern Railroad against the federal government for condemning land for construction of a high dam—the railroads persevered in their opposition. (As recently as 1976, railroads argued that "barge lines using federally improved waterways are unfairly compensated.") Finally in July 1933, President Roosevelt announced his order to the Public Works Board to begin work on the project, temporarily ending the railroads' interference.[14]

But the railroads were not the only detractors of a nine-foot channel; other critics included the Izaak Walton League, a conservation group, and Major

Charles Hall, one of the engineers from the Corps charged with evaluating the proposed project. Further, little interest for the channel was shown initially in the smaller river towns. Among the critics, reasons for opposing the project varied. For the Izaak Walton League, which had successfully established a wildlife refuge in the Upper Mississippi River Valley in 1924, members viewed the proposed nine-foot channel as a threat to the refuge as many conservationists already considered the river polluted. Hall's major criticism was that the cost of the project would outweigh the commercial gains. While there have been environmental consequences, justifying many of the League's concerns, Hall's criticism was unfounded as barge traffic was greater than expected prompting contemporary business interests in the Upper Mississippi Valley to call for a twelve-foot channel in order to remain competitive with other countries. Unlike the earlier requests for improved navigation, today's statistics are compelling as 83 million tons of goods were shipped on the upper river in 2000. The growth is impressive considering that in 1940 only 2.4 million tons of goods were shipped.[15]

Despite the opposition, which in itself was unusual in that earlier navigation projects did not encounter criticism, the channel was authorized in the 1930 Rivers and Harbors Act. The act authorized a number of inland waterway projects and in the words of one of its supporters, "represents in the aggregate a project larger than the Panama Canal." The actual language in the bill, which was the largest in water transportation development at the time, included one provision "for canalization and the preliminary carrying out of a nine foot project for the Upper Mississippi." Approving the bill, Josephus Daniels, Secretary of the Navy, declared: "This country has always had a vision of some great enterprise—as evidence, the Panama Canal and the Alaskan Railroad, which were in keeping with the spirit of our country when we built the great transcontinental railroad. Now the big thing is water transportation." In his enthusiasm for water projects, Daniels discussed a study of inland transportation and how one of the improvements will be "barges down the Mississippi River." Most legislators, however, who endorsed the bill emphasized the cheaper transportation rates that would result in helping farmers "regain a place among the prosperous classes in our Nation." In one congressional speech, cheaper transportation for the movement of agricultural and manufactured goods was said to be "the primary purpose of rivers and harbors improvement."[16]

President Hoover signed the act but did not award full funding. In emphasizing the planning aspect of the project, however, Hoover was quoted from an earlier speech in which he stated: "We cannot develop modernized water transportation by isolated projects. We must develop it as a definite and positive interconnected system of transportation." Despite his early support and a commitment to large-scale planning for the nation's waterways, Hoover's commitment seemed to waver by 1930. According to one observer, he "cooled to the project in the face of railway opposition."[17] Still, the penchant for planning river basins persisted as Hoover's successor, Franklin Roosevelt, formed the Mississippi Valley Committee which under the leadership of engineer Morris L. Cooke, published a report in 1934 emphasizing the planning aspects of Mississippi River development. The work of the committee, according to Secretary of the Interior Harold Ickes, was to "gather together, correlate and interpret existing data, and having thus obtained a picture of the Valley, its assets and liabilities, it will be ready to prepare the blueprint of a long-term scheme, drawn in units of five-year or ten-year orts." The plan would benefit the "twenty-seven states drained by Ol'Man River." But in one of the most compelling passages, Ickes stresses not only planning but the social change that will result:

> I shall have failed in the task I set myself in attempting to show how vital is planning to navigation, flood control, erosion, agriculture, power and forestation, unless I have at the same time shown the larger considerations that called the committee into being and that inspire its own effort and the effort of all the governmental agencies cooperating with it, or working along similar lines in other areas. Here we have the reverse of private industrial planning. Here, within the framework of a democracy, we have a tremendous common effort toward a better distribution of the products of our Machine Age, a striving for social as well as economic dividends, for a better basis of life for the men and women of the Mississippi valley and for their children.[18]

While the legislation, reminiscent of the Soviet predilection for planning, affirmed the importance of large-scale planning, Ickes also promised social change to one of the country's most depressed groups—the farmer. Like the Soviets, planning was linked with the goal of improving social and economic conditions. Despite the lack of funding in 1930, promoters of the project persisted and in 1933 additional funding for the project came from the Public Works Administration, with further funding in 1934 and 1935.

With the advent of the Depression and the new funding source of the Public Works Administration, construction of the nine-foot channel also became a public works project with a mandate to provide jobs. Even in the Congressional discussions of the 1930 Rivers and Harbors Act, passage of the bill was to "provide employment for thousands." Political leaders, particularly President Roosevelt, emphasized this aspect as the project's purpose evolved from strictly a commercial enterprise to social engineering in the cause of the Midwestern farmers to 1930s public works project. In the context of the times—the nation at the height of the Depression—the employment goals became the most important, with Roosevelt claiming in 1933, "In the early spring of this year there were actually and proportionately more people out of work in this country than in any other Nation in the world." Jobs did materialize and by

August 1934, the War Department, which oversaw the Army Corps of Engineers, claimed that 9,396 were employed on the nine-foot channel. In addition to these jobs, the War Department estimated over 12,000 men were employed indirectly through the provision of materials for construction, services for campsites, and other related activities.[19]

Once funding was secured, local newspapers kept residents in towns bordering the Upper Mississippi River abreast of the project's purpose and progress. One of the more thorough articles, entitled "Magic Overalls to Rejuvenate Old Man River Provided in Channel Plan," cited an estimated cost of $124,006,139 for twenty-four dams that would insure a nine-foot depth for 660 miles. The article continued to refer to the river as Old Man River as the author claimed the channel plan will "make a more efficient worker of Old Man River." As the author gushed about the "revolutionary" aspects of the project with predictions of a transformed transportation system for the region, he also revealed insights unnoticed by other journalists. First, he remarked that the channel plan "will completely change the topography of the upper reaches of the American continent." Second, and perhaps the more profound realization was the author's description of the process: "By maps, graphs and charts, this especial undertaking is dissected into units. A living thing like a majestic river has been converted on paper into a group of blue prints as uninviting as the plans of a house, yet an analysis of them discloses and visualizes a systematic program to harness Old Man Mississippi River, a marvel of this age of engineering." In addition to these detailed accounts, local papers posted numerous updates with subheadings such as the one in July 1934 "8,500 men now Employed; 4 locks and dams, 3 locks completed."[20]

Similar to the public face of the Moscow-Volga Canal, fanfare surrounded the Upper River Channel Project which was also consistent with other New Deal projects. Thus the federal agency responsible for the complete construction, the Army Corps of Engineers, documented every phase of the project. Photographs were taken along with film footage for technical and non-technical viewing. All together, Corps personnel shot almost "19,000 feet of film with almost 14,000 feet related to actual dam and lock construction." A monthly journal, *Old Man River,* was published with project updates and safety tips for the workers. Unlike construction of the Moscow-Volga Canal, where Gulag labor was exploited, Corps personnel worried about the safety of so many unskilled workers. (On other parts of the river, however, there are instances where the exploitation of labor is comparable to the Gulag.) But even with the Corps' safety concerns, in one district alone eleven people died due to accidents. Still similarities existed between the two projects as seen through publications such as *Old Man River*—part progress report with an emphasis on the safety record—part promotional copy. In addition to the title, a reminder of the river's place in the historical memory, the journal paralleled the Soviet

Figure 5.1. Cover image adapted from *Old Man River* 4, no. 9, 1937. *Source:* U.S. Army Corps of Engineers, St. Paul District.

literature with its sprinkling of self-help platitudes. For example, in the early editions, one section entitled "The Road to Success and Happiness" included words of advice such as: "We cannot step on an elevator and be whisked up to our goal. The road is steep as a ladder. Exertion of brain and muscle is necessary; we must climb step by step." Other items included the importance of working with others "harmoniously" or the importance of "good temper" and a cheerful disposition. Although this was symbolic of the times, particularly during the Great Depression, the emphasis on self-improvement surely would have resonated with Soviet planners in their efforts to create Socialist man.[21]

Figure 5.2. FDR at Lock and Dam No. 5. *Old Man River,* 1938. *Source:* U.S. Army Corps of Engineers, St. Paul District.

Complementing the drive for self-improvement was a number of community events around the construction sites, resulting in a sense of camaraderie at the sites. While this sense of community mirrored Soviet efforts on the Moscow-Volga Canal, Soviet planners often emphasized cultural opportunities for the workers such as a concert at lunchtime. On the Mississippi project, the social environment was different. For example, in one issue of *Old Man River* an article entitled "The Engineers' Skating Party" reported an all-day event that included skating, singing, and dancing with the employees of the St. Paul District. The article was one of several that presented a sense of community that evolved at the sites, often depicted through a homespun humor such as describing a dance with a "10-piece orchestra with 9 pieces missing." This sense of community also extended to local populations as one issue recounted a Visitor's Day at Lock and Dam Number Six. According to the article, the event had been "well-advertised," and while the number of visitors did reach 650, representing eight states, the Corps staff expected double the number if a rain shower had not intervened. Those who did attend "expressed satisfaction

Figure 5.3. Tainter gate construction. *Old Man River,* 1938. *Source:* U.S. Army Corps of Engineers, St. Paul District.

at being able to see for themselves just what the government was getting for its money."[22]

Despite the boosterism, the technical aspects of the project were never ignored. Reflecting Moscow-Volga Canal publications such as *Na SHTURM Trassy,* the journal, *Old Man River,* always included the engineering facets with the same sense of pride that Soviet issues evoked. For example, one journal article mentioned the "considerable time ... devoted to studies and tests in connection with foundations and foundation materials which has resulted in the design of structures of greater stability." Other journals, such as *The Military Engineer* and *Engineering News-Record,* also reported on the technological features. Yet, the differences between the two countries in technical expertise and infrastructure were striking. Like other public works projects in the 1930s, the Upper Mississippi River locks and dams were products of new engineering technology as the decade is considered the Corps of Engineers' "Golden Age." Oftentimes the technology that was first developed to build the "non-navigable dams that incorporated both roller and Tainter gates" was obsolete by 1940 when the final lock and dam were completed. While the Soviets also expe-

UPPER MISS. RIVER -- DAM NO. 8
E.R.A.- CONT. No. E.R.- W923 ENG. 15
OPERATING MACHINERY--
PIERS NOS. 4 AND 5
8

Figure 5.4. Roller gate construction. *Old Man River,* 1938. *Source:* U.S. Army Corps of Engineers, St. Paul District.

rienced this—for example, their growing expertise with concrete over the course of the canal construction—the Moscow-Volga Canal publications do not reveal the same level of engineering sophistication. But the labor force that both projects depended upon was similar in that many of the workers were unskilled. For the American construction companies contracted to do the work, this was a source of tension resulting in at least one lawsuit with the federal government.[23]

Accompanying the engineering advances were design improvements. For example, modern design can begin to be seen in the architectural and engineering planning for the lock and dam systems to enhance their visual interest. New technologies and design elements at the time were used in the construction of dams and their surrounding industrial infrastructure. Some examples

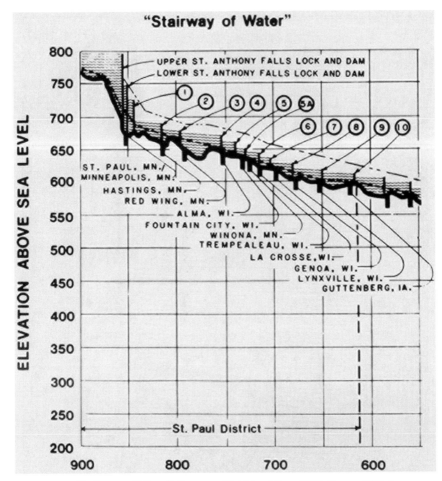

Figure 5.5. "Stairway of Water" diagram. *Old Man River,* 1938. *Source:* U.S. Army Corps of Engineers, St. Paul District.

include the use of curtain walls systems on railway service bridges to "break up the monotony" of their upstream facades, the use of arched girder spans in bridge construction, and the use of new pier types in dam construction to provide sleek curves that express their structural stability. Even the operating houses were designed to provide visual interest through the use of expressionist design features such as height and shadow.[24]

But in a return to the differences between the two projects, the most significant was in the level of infrastructure. For the Upper River Channel Project, the work was a culmination of a century's efforts to increase the depth of the Upper Mississippi River. The bureaucracy and technical expertise had been evolving over the last two centuries without the fits and starts that Russia

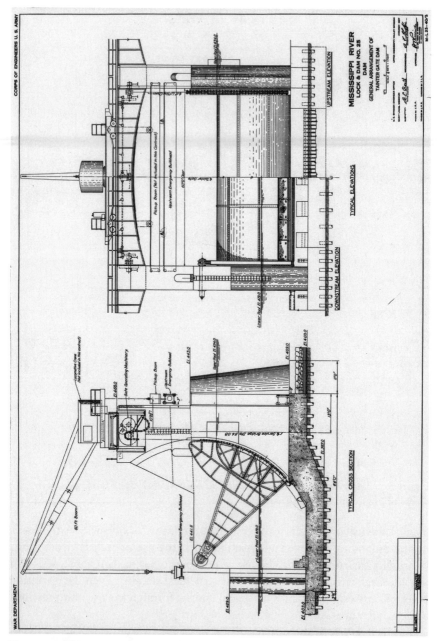

Figure 5.6. "73. Dam—General arraignment of Tainter Gate Dam M-L 25 40/3." Section and elevation technical drawing views of the Upper Mississippi River Nine-Foot Channel Project, Lock & Dam No. 25 in Cap au Gris, Lincoln County, MO. *Source:* Library of Congress (1937). Call number: HAER MO,57-CAG,1–73.

had experienced. In the case of the mass project, Corps engineers already had the plans in place. According to the *Engineering News-Record,* "The Corps of Engineers as a continuing organization plans its work ahead, generally for a number of years." As a result, although the project was celebrated upon completion, it was not cast in the same light as the Soviets' hydro-projects that were further vindication over the tsars' rule. Instead advance planning had become the norm with an infrastructure in place that included large-scale hydro-projects such as Hoover Dam and a number of Bureau of Reclamation projects. Early Soviet leaders such as Leon Trotsky recognized and criticized the Soviet self-congratulatory tone when in a late 1920s speech, he implored Soviet leadership to view their accomplishments in a more realistic light. Instead of benchmarking their successes against earlier regimes, Trotsky advised Soviet leadership to compare their technological advances with those of Western nations. Worthy of note, nevertheless these differences did not affect the similar outcomes for both rivers. Political leaders and engineers, alike, possessed the same utilitarian perspective regarding the rivers, namely as vehicles to enhance commercial traffic, produce hydropower, or provide additional drinking water to a growing urban population.[25]

One characteristic, however, of the U.S. project that differed from the Moscow-Volga Canal with dramatic ramifications for the future was the opposition voiced by conservation groups, such as the Izaak Walton League. In the 1930s, their concerns went unheard but in later years when other projects were considered, these groups had an impact. The same outlets for dissent did not exist in the Soviet Union although post–Soviet era scholars have demonstrated that the Soviet scientific community, dating back to Stalin's tenure, often argued for environmental protection. The scale of opposition, however, would have been less than in the United States with its outpouring of environmental advocacy groups in the 1950s and 1960s.[26]

Still, in the 1930s, criticism went unheeded and the nine-foot channel was completed quickly. By June 1937, 70 percent of the project was finished. In summarizing the project, one of the district engineers, mirroring the promotional language upon completion of the Moscow-Volga Canal, recited a litany of statistics when he noted: "This construction program has involved the placing of about 800,000 cubic yards of concrete, 52,000,000 pounds of steel, the driving of more than 3,000,000 linear feet of timber piling, almost 2,000,000 square feet of permanent steel sheet piling, the removal and placing in embankment dikes of around 8,000,000 cubic yards of material, and has afforded more than 13,000,000 man hours of direct employment exclusive of government personnel."[27] By 1938, the project was near completion and in the words of Corps District Engineer Philip Fleming, they had reached a "mile-stone in the history of the Nine-Foot Channel Project" as now there was "a full nine-foot depth in the St. Paul District." The commercial benefits of the channel were already apparent as barge traffic in the 1938 season looked to exceed the previous season.[28]

The 1930s Mississippi River Channel Project ushered in a new era for the Upper Mississippi Valley as barge traffic increased dramatically prompting calls to double the capacity of twelve locks on the Mississippi and Illinois Rivers. By the late twentieth century, the entire Mississippi River system— including tributaries, and the Ohio, Illinois, and Missouri Rivers—carried more freight than the combined traffic on the Panama Canal, Great Lakes, and Intra-Coastal Canal.[29] Along with barge traffic, the years succeeding the River Channel Project continued to see passenger ships captained by riverboat pilots, who in their reminiscences perpetuated earlier associations and characterizations of life on the Mississippi. For example, one riverboat pilot in a 1979 remembrance described life working on the river in the following: "Well, a riverman is just like a coal man. A riverman starts as a riverman, he's goin' to finish up that way. A coal man starts in the coal digger, he's goin' to finish a coal digger. You can't break him . . . You see some mighty exciting things when you're on the river."[30]

Or in another paean to the power of the river by a long-standing riverboat pilot, "the river was and is one of the fundamentals in making and keeping the United States the home of the individualist."[31] This romanticized view of the river persisted—in the midst of debates calling for a twelve-foot channel— with the 2004 Grand Excursion. Evoking memories of an earlier Upper Mississippi River Valley, the 2004 Grand Excursion was organized to commemorate the 1854 Grand Excursion. The 2004 flotilla traveled upstream from the Quad Cities, Iowa, to the Minnesota Twin Cities, with the largest collection of riverboats and steamboats in more than a century with one million people attending various related events. Further memories of a nineteenth-century Mississippi River traversed by steamboats—or in the words of one brochure, "the world of Mark Twain"—continue through regular tours on the *American Queen* steamship. Similar to the Volga, these historical memories coexist with an industrial waterway.

Notes

1. According to one federal publication: "Hoover Dam was perhaps the most significant American public works project of the twentieth century. It was the first large Federal conservation undertaking based on multiple-based objectives." See Michael C. Robinson, *Water for the West: The Bureau of Reclamation, 1902–1977* (Chicago: Public Works Historical Society, 1979), 51. For a discussion of the development of multiple purpose planning and the evolution of a national water policy that included all facets, see Samuel P. Hays, *Conservation and the Gospel of Efficiency* (Cambridge: Harvard University Press, 1959); Donald C. Swain, *Federal Conservation Policy, 1921–1933* (Berkeley: University of California Press, 1963); Donald J. Pisani, *Water and American*

Government: The Reclamation Bureau, National Water Policy, and the West, 1902–1935 (Berkeley: University of California Press, 2002). In two works on the Upper Mississippi River Valley, the authors stress how the river has become a human design, or, in Phil Scarpino's words, a "human artifact." See Phillip V. Scarpino, *Great River: An Environmental History of the Upper Mississippi, 1850–1950* (Columbia: University of Missouri Press, 1985); John Anfinson, *The River We Have Wrought: A History of the Upper Mississippi* (Minneapolis: University of Minnesota Press, 2003).

2. Franklin Delano Roosevelt in "Extemporaneous Remarks at Fort Peck Dam," 6 August 1934, in *The Public Papers of Franklin D. Roosevelt*, vol. 3 (New York: Random House, 1938).

3. William Patrick O'Brien, et al., Gateways to Commerce: The U.S. Army Corps of Engineers' 9-Foot Channel Project on the Upper Mississippi River (Denver: National Park Service, 1992), 14.

4. O'Brien et al, *Gateways to Commerce*, 15; Richard Hoops, *A River of Grain—The Evolution of Commercial Navigation on the Upper Mississippi River* (Madison: University of Wisconsin–Madison College of Agriculture and Life Sciences Research Report, 1993), 3; M.J. Levidov, *Moscow: Past, Present, Future* (Moscow: Vneshtorgisdat, 1934), 140; Harold L. Ickes, "Saving the Good Earth: The Mississippi Valley Committee and Its Plan" *Survey Graphic: Magazine of Social Interpretation* (February 1934): 33; *Winona Republican-Herald*, 29 February 1932, 21 February 1946.

5. In Donald Pisani's work, he credits Hoover as being "the first president to take a comprehensive view of the nation's waterways." He quotes Hoover from a 1926 speech in which he urged "the coordinated long-view development of each river system to its maximum utilization." See Pisani, *Water and American Government*, 242. *La Crosse Tribune*, 11 September 1933; *Winona Republican-Herald*, 29 July 1933, 17 August 1933, 26 July 1934. Even the use of laborers from the Public Works Administration was contested initially by organized labor as they did not think enough manual labor would be required for a Public Works project. The ever-vigilant Mississippi Valley Association, however, persuaded "organized labor that for each $1,000 expended on river and harbor work and flood control the war department employed an average of 3.7 men per month and for each $1,000 spent on buildings an average of only 2.6 men per month were used." See *Winona Republican-Herald*, 27 November 1933. The twelve-foot channel that Roosevelt suggested would someday be needed has been an ongoing issue in the Upper Mississippi River Valley. While the Army Corps of Engineers has drafted plans for a twelve-foot channel, citing increased traffic, resistance to any enhancements has been strong from area environmental groups. See Nicollet Island Collection, *Big Price—Little Benefit: Proposed Locks on the Upper Mississippi and Illinois Rivers are Not Economically Viable* (February 2010).

6. *Winona Republican-Herald*, 1 July 1938, 6 April 1933. Recounting the Mississippi's historic flooding patterns in an issue of *Old Man River*, a Corps of Engineers' publication, the following report was given "The Father of Waters came true to form once more—flooding the low lands, leaving destruction in his wake." See "Construction Notes," *Old Man River* 1, no. 2 (April 1934), RG 77, St. Paul District, *Old Man River Safety Bulletins*, Box 155, Entry 1626, NAKCB.

7. *Winona Republican-Herald*, 6 April 1933.

8. *Winona Republican-Herald,* 15 May 1933; Ickes, "Saving the Good Earth: The Mississippi Valley Committee and Its Plan," 35. For Ickes's exact words regarding the changing roles of rivers, see chapter 3. By 1925, hydropower had already arrived in the St. Paul area with the Ford Motor Company generating power at Lock 1 and 2. The issue of hydropower on the Upper Mississippi River was a contentious one with the Corps of Engineers initially resisting multiple purpose projects believing that "navigation should supersede" other uses. See John O. Anfinson, "The Secret History of the Earliest Locks and Dams," *Minnesota History* 54, no. 6 (Summer 1995): 254–267.

9. *Old Man River* 5, no. 5 (May 1938): 2, *Old Man River* Safety Bulletins 1938–1940, Box 2, Entry 1626, NAKCB; Spencer Carr, *A Brief Sketch of La Crosse, Wisc'n* (La Crosse: W.C. Rogers, Printer, Democrat Office, 1854), 9.; Jane Curry, *The River's in My Blood: Riverboat Pilots Tell Their Stories* (Lincoln: University of Nebraska Press, 1983), 3.

10. *American Lumberman,* 12 October 1912. For general works of the early history of transportation and the economy in the Upper Mississippi River Valley, see Anfinson, *The River We Have Wrought*; Hoops, *A River of Grain*; and Sam J. Graber, "The Upper Mississippi River Improvement Association," Master's thesis, University of Wisconsin–La Crosse, 1968. A general discussion of the environmental consequences of the 1930s channel project can be found in Nicollet Island Collection, *Big Price—Little Benefit.*

11. Graber, "Upper Mississippi River," 43. In 1940, 2.4 million tons of goods were shipped along the Mississippi; by 2000 that figure had risen to 83 million tons.

12. Graber, "Upper Mississippi River," 62; Mark Twain, *Mark Twain in Eruption,* ed. Bernard De Voto (New York: Grosset & Dunlap, 1922), 18. In Robinson's *Water for the West,* he discusses the impact local interests had upon developing an effective reclamation policy.

13. Graber, "Upper Mississippi River," 62; H.R Doc. 583, 69th Cong., 2nd Sess., 14 December 1926.

14. In his 1927 talk to the Mississippi Valley Association, Secretary of Commerce Herbert Hoover provided statistics on the increased rail rates. For example, Midwest farmers "rail rates to seaboard on wheat … have increased about 8 to 18 cents per bushel" since World War I. He also reiterated the effect the Panama Canal had on Midwest shipping. See Herbert Hoover, "The Improvement of Our Mid-West Waterways," *Annals of the American Academy of Political and Social Science* 135 (January 1928): 17. *Winona Republican-Herald,* 23 November 1931, 29 July 1933; *Winona Daily News,* 21 April 1976.

15. The local press in towns along the Mississippi River reported extensively on opposition to the canal, with articles supporting and opposing the project. For example, see *Winona Republican-Herald,* 3 September 1930, 18 February 1932; Graber, "Upper Mississippi River," 62. Additional accounts on the history of navigation on the Upper Mississippi River can be found in the Oral History Collection at the University of Wisconsin–La Crosse, which has many firsthand accounts by residents who have lived along the river and witnessed its development.

16. Rivers and Harbors Act (3 July 1930), 71st Cong., 2nd Sess., Chapter 847; Cong. Rec., 71st Congress, 2nd Sess., vol. 72, part 2, p. 12645; 7738; 7723.

17. Cong. Rec., 71st Congress, 2nd Sess., vol. 72, part 2, p. 7744; *Winona Republican-Herald,* 29 July 1933. The newspaper's observation might have been accurate as a 1926 Report from the Board of Engineers for Rivers and Harbors noted: "The Twin Cities

of St. Paul and Minneapolis ... are served by 23 railway lines, grouped into 9 systems, including 5 lines to Chicago, 4 to Duluth, 4 to the Pacific coast, and 6 to the South. ... The vast network of railway lines centering in the Twin cities adequately serves all their transportation needs at the present time and will continue to do so for many years to come. An increase in river transportation, therefore, must come from competition with well-organized railway service or from new business with cheaper transportation will bring to this territory." See H.R Doc. 583 at 17, 69th Cong., 2nd Sess. (14 December 1926).

18. Ickes, "Saving the Good Earth: The Mississippi Valley Committee and Its Plan," 9, 5, 42.

19. Cong. Rec., 71st Cong., 2nd Sess., vol. 72, part 2, p. 12645; FDR, "The Fourth 'Fireside Chat'—We Are on Our Way, and We Are Headed in the Right Direction," 22 October 1933 in *The Public Papers and Addresses of Franklin D. Roosevelt*, vol. 2, 420; *Winona Republican-Herald*, 8 August 1934; *Old Man River* 1, no. 5 (September 1934): 2, *Old Man River* Safety Bulletins, Box 155, Entry 1626, NAKCB. In this issue of *Old Man River*, President Roosevelt's August 1934 visit to the project was reviewed in which he was given an accounting of the current expenditures and the number of men employed at each work site.

20. *Winona Republican-Herald*, 29 February 1931; *Winona Republican-Herald*, 26 July 1934. In this news article, the President's visit was announced in which FDR was inspecting "PWA projects in the Columbia River basin, in Fort Peck, Mont., and on the Upper Mississippi River. ... [with] attention focused on some of the outstanding engineering feats that are being accomplished under the public works program."

21. O'Brien, et al, *Gateways to Commerce*, 58; "Road to Success and Happiness," *Old Man River* 1, no. 2 (April 1934), *Old Man River* Safety Bulletins, Box 155, Entry 1626, NAKCB. The film footage and journal *Old Man River* had historical precedents in that water projects in the United States have a long history of visual and print culture, particularly in the arid American West. With the passage of the 1902 Reclamation Act and subsequent creation of the U.S. Reclamation Service, federal employees began the print and visual documentation of numerous water projects. In the case of *Old Man River*, the last issue appeared in 1942 with increasing attention upon safety-related and technical topics. In contrast, during the 1927 Great Mississippi Flood, African Americans were forced, in some instances at gunpoint, to shore up the threatened levees. See John M. Barry, *Rising Tide: The Great Mississippi Flood of 1927 and How It Changed America* (New York: Simon & Schuster, 1997).

22. "The Engineers' Skating Party," *Old Man River* 1, no. 2 (April 1934), "Visitors' Day at Lock and Dam No. 6," *Old Man River*, 2, no. 4 (April 1935) *Old Man River* Safety Bulletins, Box 155, Entry 1626, NAKCB.

23. "4 Years Progress on Improvements in the Saint Paul District," *Old Man River* 4, no. 6 (June 1937) *Old Man River Safety Bulletins*, Box 2, Entry 1626, NAKCB; O'Brien, et al, *Gateways to Commerce*, 15, 56–57.

24. "4 Years Progress on Improvements in the Saint Paul District," *Old Man River* 4, no. 6 (June 1937) *Old Man River Safety Bulletins*, Box 2, Entry 1626, NAKCB.

25. *Engineering News Record*, 19 July 1934; Leon Trotsky, *Sochinenya*, vol. 21, 397–405 as quoted in Isaac Deutscher, *The Prophet Unarmed: Trotsky, 1921–1929* (London: Oxford University Press, 1959), 210. In Deutscher's words, "Trotsky argued that new scales of

comparison were needed and that the progress of recent years should be measured by the standards of the industrial west rather than by those of native backwardness." Ibid.

26. Numerous local publications such as the *Winona Republican-Herald* and the *St. Paul Pioneer Press* comment on the opposition launched by the Izaak Walton League. For a discussion of environmental politics in the Soviet Union, see Douglas Wiener, *A Little Corner of Freedom: Russian Nature Protection from Stalin to Gorbachev* (Berkeley: University of California Press, 1999).

27. "4 Years Progress on Improvements in the Saint Paul District," *Old Man River* 4, no. 6 (June 1937) *Old Man River Safety Bulletins,* Box 2, Entry 1626, NAKCB.

28. "A Nine Foot Depth in the St. Paul District Below St. Anthony Falls," *Old Man River* 5, no. 5 (May 1938) *Old Man River Safety Bulletins,* Box 2, Entry 1626, NAKCB.

29. Curry, *River's in My Blood,* 3.

30. Captain Gale Justice interview with Jane Curry, 1 March 1979, as quoted in Curry, *River's in My Blood,* 231.

31. Captain Donald T. Wright, introduction in Ben Lucien Burman, *Big River to Cross,* as quoted in Curry, *River's in My Blood,* 236.

Epilogue

The 1930s was a pivotal decade as large-scale, multiple purpose projects became the standard bearers for modernization. The role of nature, especially rivers, changed as their manipulation, whether for improved transportation, irrigation, or hydropower was critical Further, with the completion of large-scale projects such as the Moscow-Volga Canal and the Upper Mississippi River 9-Foot Channel Project, the Soviet Union and United States demonstrated to the world that rerouting and reshaping river regimes was free of any ideological imperatives. Despite rhetoric to the contrary, the belief in modernization, oftentimes realized through multiple purpose river basin projects, superseded political distinctions. Instead the motivations that drove the Moscow-Volga Canal, such as overcoming the backwardness of Imperial Russian society and employing technology to societal ills, mirrored U.S. projects as the multifaceted Tennessee Valley Authority (TVA) sought to improve rural life or construction on the Upper Mississippi introduced new technologies to facilitate river commerce. Embraced by the United States and the Soviet Union after World War II and subsequent demise of the old colonial world, modernization became a product for export. Rivers such as the Nile, Jordan, and Ganges were redesigned—with assistance from the industrialized West and Russia—to serve emergent modern nation-states. Building monumental dams became the currency of modernization and in the words of one political leader, they were infected with the "disease of giganticism" as states modernized and subsequently reshaped the environment.[1]

In addition to the complementary views of diverse political leaders, engineers from all political persuasions shared the same beliefs regarding the potential of large-scale water projects to improve cultures. In the case of the Soviet Union and United States, with their long histories of engineering rivers, technocrats from both countries believed their relationship with nature was a model to replicate. To the American and Soviet technocracy in the 1930s, rivers were a resource to be exploited providing symbols of modernization through hydroelectric dams, irrigation works, or improved waterways. Concomitant with their ideas about nature's role was their "shared faith in the ability of technology to change the face of nature for the better." Although each country's expertise and willingness to engineer former colonial river regimes was cloaked in rhetoric touting democratic values or the fairness of socialism, the outcome for the rivers that were dammed, rerouted, and harnessed was the same regardless of whether the state was socialist or democratic. A culture of modernity with its own symbols and ethos superseded political ideology with devastating results for the Mississippi and Volga Rivers.[2]

Still, Russian and American political leaders, in the throes of the Cold War, persisted in emphasizing differences in their respective modernization efforts. When Khrushchev recalled the Soviet Union's assistance in building the Aswan Dam in Egypt, he said, "Our assistance to the Egyptians would demonstrate that the Soviet Union could be counted on to aid needy peoples the world over who were liberating themselves from colonial rule." He also relayed how the Soviet Union took great pains to offer assistance and not act under the auspices of an exploitative contractor and employee relationship. For the Nile River, however, ideology mattered little as Khrushchev described the fateful day when the Nile's course was altered. According to Khrushchev, Egyptian President Abdel Nasser invited him to Egypt for the occasion and together they threw the switch that would "divert the waters of the Nile from their ancient course." In recalling the scene, Khrushchev wrote: "An explosion shook the air, and the water rushed into its new course. There were huge crowds of people attending the ceremony, and I can't express how marvelous it was to see all the faces light up and the eyes sparkle with triumph as the mighty waters of the Nile began to turn the turbines which would give Egypt a new way of life."[3]

Reinforcing Khrushchev's view toward the newly liberated countries in Africa and the Soviet Union's role was the USSR representative to the United Nations, Nikolai Fedorenko, who when addressing a western academic audience in 1964 spoke of a Soviet "policy toward Africa calculated to assist the African countries in attacking and ending backwardness." In bringing the policy to fruition, he said the Aswan Dam was only one example as "The Soviet Union has the same kind of agreements with a number of countries, including Algeria and Kenya." Fedorenko uses examples of Soviet assistance in Soviet Eurasian borderland states to demonstrate how a Socialist state "can do away with backwardness, poverty, disease and ignorance within the lifetime of a generation and rise to the level of economically advanced countries."[4] On a more practical level, Soviet aid to socialist countries wishing to industrialize was quantified in an article by scholar, I. Kapranov. In his research, Kapranov recorded how aid to countries ranging from Bulgaria to China to Cuba was increasing. Of particular interest was the support given to the hydropower industry. The ultimate goal, according to Kapranov, was to "help the socialist countries in the construction of power stations with a total capacity of 18.5 million kw." Soviet aid had already built enough plants to produce 8.2 million kilowatts.[5]

The United States had similar experiences, some realized and some left in the planning stages. One of the leaders of U.S. development efforts abroad was Lilienthal who wrote prolifically about the relationship between river basin planning and inculcating democratic principles. His voice was especially prominent given his oversight of the TVA, which became a model for export to the developing world. In the race to secure allies among the decolonized world, the TVA which transformed one of the United States' poorest areas, and as a result, "completely remade the physical, social and technological terrain of a seven-state region roughly the size of Ohio;" given the opportunity, could duplicate this multiple purpose model in the former colonies. The notion of backwardness and the postcolonial world was also shared by high-ranking U.S. government officials such as Paul Nitze, who along with others in the State Department in 1948 proposed an "Asian Recovery Program," in which they discussed how in less-developed areas, the people "were weighed down by 'backward' cultural and political beliefs."[6] One proposal popular among American political leaders, including President Lyndon Johnson, called for a Mekong Project Authority, similar to the TVA. Although never constructed, plans for the project were widely supported by well-known foundations and companies such as the Ford Foundation and Shell.[7]

Complementing the views of Lilienthal and other politicians was the work of development theorist, Walt Rostow. He, like Lilienthal, built upon earlier pronouncements of nation-builders such as Trotsky, Lenin, and Franklin Roosevelt, who perceived nature as an instrument to realize a nation's wealth. Rostow refined the ideas of Lilienthal and other 1930s thinkers with his modernization theory which provided a framework for U.S. policy makers when determining the fate of the postcolonial world. To Rostow and other modernization theorists, modernism was "not just aesthetics but also a form of social and political practice in which history, society, economy, culture and nature itself were all to be the object of technical transformation." Further, according to Rostow, modernization was a western concept and what was practiced in the Soviet Union was "a pathological form of modernization." The perceived difference was emphasized on numerous occasions as each country sought to forge the destiny of the postcolonial world.[8]

Ironically, one of the major differences that did exist between the two ideologies as it related to natural resources was overlooked at the time. To many, the Soviet Union, with a command economy and ability to oversee resources without divisive competing interests, could rationally develop their resources as opposed to the United States and the whims of corporate interests which often led development efforts. Discussed earlier, several U.S. political leaders envied the Soviet ability to plan projects in their totality, one of the advantages of centralization and a command economy. Not until the 1972 publication of Marshall Goldman's landmark work, *The Spoils of Progress: Environmental Pollution in the Soviet Union,* was this idea dispelled. After the breakup of the Soviet Union, the environmental costs of Soviet modernization were apparent to everyone and as one scholar noted, the Soviet Union's environmental record "seems to prove that communism offered no solution to the environmental destructiveness of a capitalist economy." Instead the Soviets because of their ability to undertake large-scale projects with a minimum of dissent exploited the environment on a monumental scale. According to one critic, during the Soviet Union's tenure: "More land has been flooded by hydroelectric dams than the total area of the Netherlands. More land was lost between 1960 and 1989 through salinization, changes in the water table, and dust and salt storms than the total areas of cultivated land in Ireland and Belgium together." As environmental tragedies such as the shrinking Aral Sea were revealed, the consequences of unchecked development became evident. Although scale made a significant difference, the motivations—and the underlying beliefs regarding the natural world— behind modernization and development were the same.[9]

Post–World War II river basin planning, however, was not only under the auspices of the Soviet Union and the United States. The creed of modernization with its commitment to river basin planning was also a part of the United Nations' agenda as the organization lent aid and support to developing countries. Today, the World Bank is often the lender for water projects despite coming under attack for its environmental record beginning with the critical World Commission on Dams report, published in November 2009. Still, the commitment to modernization, and its concomitant need to redesign nature and rivers, prevails as recent projects such as the Three Gorges Dam demonstrate, as well as a host of projects in developing nations. As a result, rivers such as the Yangtze have been completely transformed in an effort to meet an ever-growing demand for power.[10] But the dam building that began in the postwar years marked more than a transition to modernization as these large-scale undertakings reflected an emergent nationalism in much the same spirit as they did in the United States and Soviet Union in the 1930s. For India, under Prime Minister Jawaharlal Nehru, river basin planning and the construction of dams represented a newfound nationalism, best summarized in his dedication speech at the Bhakra Nangal Dam in 1963: "This dam has been built with the unrelenting toil of man for the benefit of mankind and therefore is worthy of worship. May you call it a temple or a gurdwara or a mosque, it inspires our admiration and reverence." For Nasser—following a similar trajectory to Stalin's monumental hydrostations—completion of the Aswan Dam was a testament to his leadership and ability to provide Egyptians with much-needed power. For China, Three Gorges Dam is proof of its superpower status with an unsated need for power.[11]

In returning to the Volga and Mississippi Rivers, the decades following World War II were a continuation of earlier engineering efforts. The development touted by U.S. and Soviet officials for the decolonized world proceeded internally as well. For the Volga, the Moscow-Volga Canal was only the beginning of the river's transformation. But the emphasis changed in that while navigation continued to be important, focus shifted to the untapped potential for hydropower. Under what was called the Great Volga Scheme, a series of reservoirs were constructed on the river. Today, there are eleven hydropower stations on the Volga and its major tributary, the Kama River. In the broader Volga River Basin, 716 water reservoirs have been built which supply 13 percent of the basins' power facilities. Two of the largest projects are the Rybinsk and Kuibyshev Dams built in the 1950s. As a result of these power sources, 45 percent of Russia's industry and 50 percent of its agriculture are located in the Volga basin.[12]

Still, the Volga was more than a power source as Soviet leaders improved access and transportation. One project that had its antecedents in sixteenth-century Turkey and during the reign of Peter the Great was the Volga-Don Canal. Completed in 1952, with plans dating back to the 1930s, the Volga-Don Canal provided access to the Caspian and Black and Azov basins. (Still heavily used in the twenty-first century, an estimated ten million tons of cargo are shipped annually as ships navigate the thirteen locks in one day.) Now, the Soviet Union could boast of access to five seas; a boon for shipping a number of goods with Donetz coal being among the most important. Throughout the 1960s and 1970s, the Volga was redesigned and engineered to curb flooding and serve irrigation, navigation, and power needs under the dictates of the Great Volga Scheme. The Middle Volga, in particular, experienced further development and became an important economic hub for the Soviet Union. Similar to the Upper Mississippi River, the landscape changed with the river becoming a series of slack water ponds as reservoirs dotted the riverscape.[13]

But the Volga's transformation was symptomatic of other efforts to exploit and reshape the country's natural resources. Under Soviet leaders, projects such as Khrushchev's Virgin Lands Campaign and the proposed Siberian river diversions were considered. (While the first was implemented, the second was only seriously discussed.) Still, a note of caution began to be voiced in Soviet literature. The attitude toward resources was changing, at least in the public sphere. In a 1972 speech, "Fifty Years of Great Achievements of Socialism," Soviet leader Leonid Brezhnev, while acknowledging nature's contributions to Soviet success, also cautioned "how important it is to treasure nature, to protect and augment its wealth. Economical, efficient use of natural resources, concern for the land, forests, rivers and pure air, for the floral and fauna—all this is our vital, communist cause. We must preserve and beautify our land for present and future generations of Soviet people."[14] Adding to these comments, Soviet scientists wrote of the need for resource planning to complement an integrated economic plan, paralleling the approach toward resources in the Western technological and scientific community. Scientists in the Soviet era also contended that resource planning should follow an integrated approach.

Quoting from well-known texts, such as *The Limits to Growth,* one Soviet scholar argued for better planning while conceding that shortages did exist and one was in water. Still, he observed the USSR had enough resources for the "distant future" while not discounting the need to conserve. Not without ideological blinders, he credited the Soviet Union's success to a socialist state. Concerns, however, about Soviet plans for the Volga were also expressed outside the Soviet Union. When hearing about the proposed Siberian rivers diversion plan that would in part supplement a shrinking Volga flow into the Caspian Sea, scholars questioned the international implications of such a scheme.[15]

Despite expressions of caution, large-scale undertakings in the United States and Soviet Union persisted throughout the Cold War era. Yet the belief in modernization, and its ability to improve lives and realize economic wealth for the state, severely hurt the environments of each country. The river systems of both have been degraded through agricultural runoff, toxic dumps, and inadequate sewage treatment, to name a few water quality issues, and both rivers are experiencing the loss of wetlands. There is, however, a difference in scale as numerous accounts chronicle the environmental degradation that occurred under the Soviet system and still plague Russia today. Discussed earlier, the Soviet system allowed for large-scale undertakings with a minimum of dissent although scholars such as Douglas Wiener have demonstrated there was an active community of scientists who prevented some of the most egregious schemes. Still, because of the Soviet ability to implement plans under the auspices of a command economy, environmental tragedies such as the decimation of the Aral Sea occurred. While their goals were often the same as those of U.S. leaders, in this instance increasing agricultural output through a large-scale irrigation project, the enormity of the undertaking is the crucial difference. Not that agriculture in the Central Valley of California with its effects on wetlands, water quality, and climate are not comparable, as the comparison is valid, but the surface area affected is smaller and there are ongoing efforts to address the problems in the United States. Further complicating the environmental record of the Soviet Union, and now Russia, is the dissolution of the USSR and the inability or disinterest of the recently created affected states to address a growing environmental crisis.

For the Volga specifically, threats to the ecosystem include unregulated dumping of industrial waste. For example in a 2003 scientific paper, out of an estimated forty-two million tons of toxic waste annually produced in the Volga Basin, only thirteen tons are managed and treated. Still another source of pollution affecting water quality comes from agricultural byproducts. Without the proper mechanisms to insure water quality, native organisms are under siege as recent findings of fish without fins attest.[16] But the fish population is also threatened by hydropower stations that block their passage to upstream spawning grounds. For many Russians, the loss of a robust sturgeon population is particularly painful. In the words of one Russian fisherman: "The hydroelectric plant [near Volgograd] has done significant damage because it's stopped fish swimming upriver to their spawning grounds. They turn back and start swimming downstream. Now we don't know where they are." Underlying these outcomes to the river regime, however, was the belief that nature and people were commodities to be manipulated in the interests of the state. Of course, the major hydro-projects on the Volga, resulting in a diminished Caspian Sea and loss of sturgeon population, were products of this. Another environmental concern, shared with the Mississippi, is the loss of wetlands. According to a 2006 UNESCO publication, the lack of wetlands preservation is the result of "insufficient understanding of the relevance of the Volga wetlands; the lack of preservation efforts from governmental, private, and public organizations, but also from the local population; deficient training of professional environmentalists, teachers and educators; and the inexistence of joint action and coordination of the activities towards conservation among all these interest groups." Today, the issues persist and the Volga River basin is still highly polluted although there are efforts by fledgling environment groups and UNESCO to bring back a healthy Volga River and wetlands.[17]

Similar to Volga development, the Mississippi River also underwent additional redesigning and engineering as politics and technology converged to create a river that facilitated substantial barge traffic in its upper reaches and stayed outside the levees in its lower reaches. Environmental consequences resulted from both. With robust traffic and bottlenecks during the high shipping season, one of the latest proposals is to double the capacity of twelve locks on the Mississippi and Illinois Rivers. If constructed, the locks could handle 1,200-foot barge tows without breaking them in two to enter the 600-foot channels. (The tows are reconnected after passage through the locks.) Once again, one of the arguments for increasing the capacity is to remain competitive in the international grain market. Debates between environmentalists and developers have been spirited as environmentalists view the barge traffic as a "tax subsidized transformation of the Mississippi into an industrial waterway." In 2012, however, the major concern was a crippling drought that threatened shipping interests. By late summer 2012, nineteen harbors were closed and at least "12 barges ran aground." Under a headline entitled, "Drought hits Mississippi: Ol' Man River just keeps limping along" one river user lamenting the situation, said "We've gone from a superhighway to a little one-lane road."[18]

Paralleling the Volga's history are environmental costs including the growing loss of wetlands as "less than 50 percent of original floodplain fish and wildlife habitat is left." Many key native organisms are also declining in population. Further, with increased shipping on the river has been the arrival of nonindigenous species, which threaten native species. In recent years, the population of zebra mussels, that were first detected around 1990, has grown and could be particularly harmful. Other causes for the river's loss of flora and fauna include ongoing industrial pollution. As a result in spring 2004, American Rivers, a well-known environmental group, placed the Mississippi River on its list of "the nation's endangered rivers."[19]

But upstream responses to the needs of an expanding economy were matched downstream as residents of the growing city of New Orleans expected to remain dry despite an ecosystem where flooding was a natural phenomenon. As one scholar noted, "The residents of New Orleans, like Americans generally, imagine that people and their cities stand apart from the natural world." Their concerns about flood protection were shared by residents living along the river upstream spawning an industry of flood control works under the leadership of the Army Corps of Engineers. But flood control is not the only downstream concern as the Mississippi River is heavily polluted, as numerous articles have documented, the dumping of chemicals from petrochemical companies in the lower valley and agricultural runoff. Toxic waste in the Lower Mississippi River Valley is especially a problem as a recent report by Environment America revealed in 2007. In the report *Wasting Our Waterways: Industrial Toxic Pollution and the Unfulfilled Promise of the Clean Water Act*, one of the most disturbing findings was the following: "ExxonMobil Refining & Supply Baton Rouge Refinery released over 4.2 million pounds of toxic chemical waste into the Mississippi River in Louisiana" and the Ohio River, a tributary of the Mississippi, "topped the nation for toxic chemicals that are cancer causing and chemicals that cause reproductive disorders." For the Upper Mississippi River Valley, while scientists recognize the positive effects of increased regulation for contaminates such as mercury, lead, DDT, and PCBs there is still concern with emerging contaminants and the biological effects that include endocrine disruption.[20]

In the case of the Lower Mississippi River, engineers have disrupted an intricate delta ecosystem where floods and hurricanes are not only expected but help maintain an ecological balance. As a result, these human efforts have left a river without many of its self-regulating functions. While there is consensus that the U.S. government is doing more to clean up the river and is more sensitive to the demands of environmental groups than Vladimir Putin or earlier Russian governments, from the perspective of the health of the Mississippi River, is it a healthier river basin than the Volga? In other words, both rivers have been engineered to serve increasingly industrialized societies and given that the scale of manipulation was greater in some respects in the former Soviet Union, still the engineering expertise that created the false sense of security in New Orleans was just as harmful.

Further, are the differences more in the area of inadequate science on the part of Russia or is the scale of pollution greater? While not diminishing the differences, for the rivers that have been enlisted to serve in nineteenth- and twentieth-century nation-building, other questions take precedence. Contemporary debates over dam building and the manipulation of river regimes are still couched in political terms. For example, beliefs once considered inviolable—under the auspices of modernization theory and its homage to strong central planning—such as the potential of technology and the ability to harness nature to serve industrialized cultures have recently come under attack from those championing a neoliberal economic framework with less state investment and more from the private sector. Still, other critics of modernization theory are those who decry the loss of local knowledge and rural traditions in the wake of large state-supported water projects. Proponents of both have large, vocal followings. For the rivers, however, the most important debates—intersecting with all of the above—reveal the environmental cost of engineered waterways. An overlap, however, exists as dams are still being built but oftentimes with the support of the World Bank. Further, disagreement persists over the fate of cities such as New Orleans. Should technology still be employed and keep New Orleans dry or should a mix of wet and dry conditions be introduced, drawing upon an earlier local knowledge, resulting in a more sustainable community?

Whether sustainable or not, part of the discourse surrounding the Volga and Mississippi Rivers is their central role in each country's history. The rivers—through modernization schemes in navigation, hydropower, or irrigation—have been beacons of modernization and a promising future while the same waterways, through art, prose, poetry, and song are reminders of a pastoral, idyllic past. In the twenty-first century this duality endures as the rivers are still valorized through river boat cruises, songs, poetry, and plays. The historical memory first crafted through folklore and mythology, honed and refined through nineteenth- and twentieth-century nationalist narratives and exploited through the nation-building of the twentieth century is still called into service for a receptive public. In the case of the Mississippi River, cruises aboard the *American Queen* paddle-wheeler are offered throughout the summer months for tourists eager to visit relics of nineteenth-century river life. In addition to the trip on the river, the cruise offers a stop at the Oak Alley Plantation in Louisiana where "two young women in full-gown regalia, including parasols, stand at the plantation entrance." Other stops include well-known river towns such as Vicksburg, and while onboard, passengers can choose from diversions such as a Mark Twain imitator or a presentation on steamboat history. The Mississippi that tourists experience is a river captured in historical memory; far removed from the engineering expertise of succeeding centuries. Similarly, for tourists wishing to experience the Volga, numerous cruises are offered, and tourists on the Volga are reminded of the river's historic past with stops at cities whose fates are tied to the river. In the words of one promotional cruise brochure: "No Russian can hear the word 'Volga' without picturing the river's wide, plangent waters, gracious ships, and hovering ivory gulls. Mother

Volga's place in every Russian heart is assured and is celebrated in the famous song of the Volga boatmen, 'Mighty stream so deep and wide, Volga, Volga, our pride.'" Russian history and culture are staples on the cruises as passengers are reminded of the river's role in uniting East and West.[21]

Nostalgic images of the rivers are also found in almost any town bordering the rivers. For example, in Dubna, Russia, where the Moscow-Volga Canal begins, stores selling photographs and the popular genre of landscape painting portray a Volga that might easily be mistaken for a nineteenth century image. Even those portraits that depict a river populated with twentieth-century barges often include the onion-shaped dome of the Russian Orthodox Church in the background, conveying a historic sense of serenity and sustenance. Visitors to the Mississippi River towns can have the same experience as sentimental images of the Mississippi, found in paintings and drawings, fuel an ongoing tourist industry in Americana. In these images, the Mississippi is often cast in a scene with a nineteenth-century paddle-wheeler, or if a twenty-first-century barge is in the centerpiece, the scenic bluffs loom in the background, recreating the same landscape prized by nineteenth-century American enthusiasts; a landscape untouched by twentieth-century engineering prowess.

But the rivers that are celebrated are far different than the ones etched in the historical memory, lending credence to Schama's argument regarding memory's role. Yet cultures persist in reconciling a nostalgic riverine past with rivers that have been increasingly redesigned, rerouted, and subdued. Will an industry of nostalgia supersede a historical memory that might play a role in each river's future? Or will there continue to be an uneasy reconciliation between each river's past and a modernizing future, making each unrecognizable to the nineteenth-century river boat pilot? Clouding the future of each river are their historical roles as highways for the transformation of each could not have occurred without earlier perceptions of them as the nation's transportation artery. Thus the commodification and manipulation of each river is not recent and the result of longstanding efforts. Other constants include a longstanding ability to reconcile an unhealthy river environment with mythology extolling the virtue of each river. Still, the contemporary environmental costs to both rivers have been significant as the increase in industrialization, which spawned the need for enhanced navigation, hydropower, and irrigation, resulted in deterioration in the health of both ecosystems. For the future ecological integrity of both rivers, humans will have to weigh the needs of commercial and recreation interests against each river's ability to absorb these increasingly numerous demands. Perhaps at this juncture, the role of historical memory, conjuring up images of rivers that offered sustenance and identity will outweigh the drive for further development.

One certainty, however, remains in that the Volga and Mississippi Rivers are essential lenses through which to understand the past and envision the future. Through the rivers, a history unfolds that subsumes the periodization of traditional histories and the priority often given to the narrow lens of political interpretation. Instead, the rivers offer a past rich with the exchange of cultures, sources for cultural and national identity, prompts for technological innovation but also havens for disease, oppressors and liberators of labor, and partners in modernization. By looking at the rivers, a history unfolds that allows movement across time, incorporating a number of disciplines in this rich retelling of the past from a riverine perspective. This perspective poses new questions—such as how do class and race determine different interactions with the resource—and reinforces other historical assumptions including the role of trade in fostering cultural diffusion. Perhaps most importantly, history from the perspective of the Volga and Mississippi Rivers offers a more comprehensive view of the past, infusing the historical record with a potpourri of characters not usually found in one story. Regardless of the more significant contribution, the comparative history of these two rivers reminds us of their pivotal role in the past and present and how both enrich our lives—a legacy humanity should strive to preserve.

Notes

1. J. Nehru, *Irrigation and Power* 16.1 (January 1959): 172; quoted from Patrick McCully, *Silenced Rivers: The Ecology and Politics of Large Dams* (London: Zed Books, 2001), 20. When discussing the leveling effects of modernization, the literature is extensive but one of the best resources is James C. Scott's *Seeing Like a State: How Certain Schemes to Improve the Human Condition Have Failed* (New Haven: Yale University Press, 1998) in which he applies the term "high modernism" to describe large-scale engineering projects supported and implemented by the state. Further, Scott states on page 5 that this ideology "could be found across the political spectrum from left to right [especially] among those who wanted to use state power to bring about huge, utopian changes in people' work habits, living patterns, moral conduct, and worldview." Complementing Scott's work is Paul R. Josephson's *Industrialized Nature: Brute Force Technology and the Transformation of the Natural World* (Washington, DC: Island Press, 2002). This excellent book and its theme of "brute force technologies" was an invaluable resource in understanding Soviet attitudes toward nature.

2. Josephson, *Industrialized Nature,* 3. Literature on water development and modernization is rich with well-known authors such as Arundhati Roy, Maude Barlow, Vandana Shiva, and Tony Clarke, to name a few. One of the best articles that discusses dam building, modernization, and the role of American engineers is Nick Cullather, "Damming Afghanistan: Modernization in a Buffer State," *The Journal of American History* 89, no. 2 (September 2002): 512–537.

3. *Khrushchev Remembers* (New York: Bantam Books, 1970): 487, 489. Egypt and the construction of the Aswan Dam became an important chapter in Cold War politics. Initially, the Eisenhower Administration planned to finance the dam as U.S. interests recognized that "It would respond not only to the physical and economic needs

of Egyptians, but to their national pride and aspirations as well." This made Soviet involvement all the more important as the Soviets even criticized American plans for the dam, emphasizing Soviet hydropower specialists were more experienced. See Silvia Borzutky and David Berger, "Dammed If You Do, Dammed If You Don't: The Eisenhower Administration and the Aswan Dam," *Middle East Journal* 64, no. 1 (Winter 2010): 94; *Khrushchev Remembers,* 488. Not everyone agrees that Nasser invited Khrushchev to the ceremony. According to Asit K. Biswas, Khrushchev requested a formal invitation. See "Aswan Dam Revisited: The Benefits of a Much-Maligned Dam," *D+C Magazine for Development and Cooperation* 6 (2002): 25–27. Accessed 18 March 2006. http://www.inwent.org/E+Z/1997-2002/de602-11.htm.

4. Nikolai Fedorenko, "The Soviet Union and African Countries," *Annals of the American Academy of Political and Social Science,* vol. 354, *Africa in Motion* (July 1964): 1–8.

5. I. Kapranov, "Soviet Aid in the Industrialization of Socialist Countries," *Eastern European Economics* 2, no. 4 (Summer 1964): 33–40.

6. Jane Wolff, "Redefining Landscape," in Tim Culvahouse, ed., *The Tennessee Valley Authority: Design and Persuasion* (New York: Princeton Architectural Books, 2007), 52; David Ekbladh, "How to Build a Nation," *The Wilson Quarterly* 28, no. 1 (Winter 2004): 12–20.

7. David Ekbladh, *The Great American Mission: Modernization and the Construction of an American World Order* (Princeton: Princeton University Press, 2010), 204–205. Ekbladh provides one of the most comprehensive treatments of the role of the TVA in shaping U.S. development policy.

8. Nils Gilman, *Mandarins of the Future: Modernization Theory in Cold War America* (Baltimore: Johns Hopkins Press, 2003), 7, 15. Several notable works on modernization theory include Michael Latham, *Modernization as Ideology: American Social Science and "Nation Building" in the Kennedy Era* (Chapel Hill: University of North Carolina Press, 2000); Shmuel N. Eisenstadt, ed., *Multiple Modernities* (New Brunswick: Transaction Publishers, 2002); Ekbladh, *Great American Mission,* 2010.

9. Arran Gare, "The Environmental Record of the Soviet Union," *Capitalism, Nature, Socialism,* vol. 3, no. 3, 52–72; Zhores A. Medvedev, "Environmental Destruction of the Soviet Union," *The Ecologist* 20, no. 1 (January/February 1990): 24 as cited in Gare, ibid., 53. Adding to Goldman's findings of Soviet environmental pollution were the works of Murray Feshbach and Alfred Friendly, Jr., *Ecocide in the USSR: Health and Nature under Siege* (New York: Basic Books, 1992) and Philip R. Pryde, *Environmental Management in the Soviet Union* (New York: Cambridge University Press, 1991). Enriching the discussion further is Douglas R. Wiener's provocative article, "The Genealogy of the Soviet and Post-Soviet Landscape of Risk," Arja Rossenholm and Sari Autio-Sarasmo, eds., *Understanding Russian Nature: Representations, Values and Concepts* (Saarijarvi: Gummerus Printing, 2005), 209–236, which he argues the acute environmental degradation that resulted under the Soviets was their persistence in continuing Imperial Russia's patrimonial regime in which the resources were under the complete discretion of the tsars. Related to the Soviet Union's record on the environment is Wiener's earlier work in which he reveals the existence of a small but determined opposition group to the excesses of Soviet natural resource planning. See Wiener, *A Little Corner of Freedom: Russian Nature Protection from Stalin to Gorbachev* (Berkeley: University of California Press, 1999).

10. Vincent Lagendijk, (2012) 'How the Model Got Its Mojo. How the TVA Became a Paradigm for Planners' (Conference Paper, European Social Science History Conference, Glasgow, 13 April 2012).

11. Jawaharlal Nehru, Bhakra Nangal Dam dedication, 22 October 1963 as quoted in *The Times of India,* 13 June 2012.

12. During the 1950s, Soviet commitment to industrialization and developing hydropower in as short as time as possible is evident in the report, *Hydroelectric Power Stations of the Volga and Kama Cascade System,* ed. G.A. Russo (Moskvo: GEI, 1960). In the introduction (page 8), the report refers to Lenin's goal of electrification and how this is being pursued as "The ambitious program of electric power construction requires, every year, considerable capital investments; therefore, it is of utmost importance to achieve cost reduction, and to speed up construction." By 1970, Soviet leadership also urged the development of hydropower in order to bring more land under irrigation. As to how this affected the Volga, "The reservoirs of the Volga HES make it possible to provide for the irrigation of land between the Volga and the Ural (4 million ha)." See "Tasks of hydropower workers in the realization of the decisions of the July 1970 Plenum of the Central committee of the Communist Party of the Soviet Union," *Hydrotechnical Construction* 4, no. 11, 993–995.

13. P.A. Warneck, "The Volga-Don Canal" *Russian Review* 13, no. 4 (October 1954): 285–291; "Reversing cost of harnessing the mighty Volga," *RT,* 14 May 2011, http://rt.com/news/volga-hydroelectric -plant-fishing/; David J.M. Hooson, "The Middle Volga. An Emerging Focal Region in the Soviet Union," *The Geographical Journal* 126, no. 2 (June 1960): 180–190.

14. Leonid Brezhnev, "Fifty Years of Great Achievements of Socialism," as quoted in E. Fedorov, *Man and Nature: The Ecological Crisis and Social Progress* (New York: International Publishers, 1972): 90–91. In the same text, Fedorov also discussed concerns regarding the ecological health of the Volga River. Ibid., 95.

15. The proposal to divert water from Siberian rivers to address the shrinking Aral Sea and increase Volga River flow and ultimately the Caspian Sea was still being considered when Mikhail Gorbachev came to power. In part, sensitive to the criticisms of Russian environmentalists, the proposal was shelved. See Bill Keller, "No Longer Merely Voices in the Russian Wilderness," *New York Times,* 27 December 1987, p. A-14. Khachaturov, T. "Natural Resources and National Economic Planning," *The Soviet Review* 15, no. 2 (July 1974): 3–28; Philip P. Micklin, "International Environmental Implications of Soviet Development of the Volga River," *Human Ecology* 5, no. 2 (June 1977): 113–135. Micklin points out those large-scale river diversion proposals were not unique to the Soviet Union in the 1970s as the United States considered moving water from Canada and Alaska to water the desert states in the American Southwest. Ibid., 114.

16. Douglas R. Weiner, *A Little Corner of Freedom: Russian Nature Protection from Stalin to Gorbachev* (Berkeley: University of California Press, 1999). One of the best discussions regarding the effects of a capitalist system on the environment—specifically the California agricultural sector—can be found in Donald Worster, *Rivers of Empire: Water, Aridity, and the Growth of the American West* (New York: Oxford University Press, 1985). While numerous works have been published on the environmental concerns of the Volga River, research by professors in chemistry and ecology at Dubna University

was presented at the Second International Conference on Great Rivers as Attractors for Local Civilizations, Assiut University, 12–14 October 2003.

17. "Reversing cost of harnessing the mighty Volga," *RT,* ibid. Additional select sources include C.X. Li, et al., "Development of the Volga Delta in Response to Caspian Sea-Level Fluctuation during Last 100 Years," *Journal of Coastal Research* 20, no. 2 (Spring 2004): 401–414; "Living Volga Programme," UNESCO, 22 November 2006, http://www.unesco.org/new/en/moscow/about-thi-office/single0view/news/living_volga_pr; *The Volga Vision: UNESCO's Interdisciplinary Initiative for the Sustainable Development of the Volga-Caspian Basin* (Paris: UNESCO, 2004). For an excellent discussion on the difficulties in developing civil society organizations in Russia with specific references to a Volga environmental group, see Jo Crotty, "Reshaping the Hourglass? The Environmental Movement and Civil Society Development in the Russian Federation," *Organization Studies* 27, no. 9 (2006): 1319–1338.

18. *Minneapolis Star Tribune,* 21 April 2004; *Los Angeles Times,* 23 August 2012.

19. *La Crosse Tribune,* 22 August 2004; *Minneapolis Star Tribune,* 21 April 2004. For a concise discussion of contemporary environmental problems in the Upper Mississippi River Basin, see James G. Wiener and Mark B. Sandheinrich, "Contaminants in the Upper Mississippi River: historic trends, responses to regulatory controls, and emerging concerns, *Hydrobiologia* (2010): 49–70, 640; James Wiener, et al., "Mississippi River," in *Status and Trends of the Nation's Biological Resources* ed. M.J. Mac, et al. 2 vols. (Fort Collins: US Department of the Interior, U.S. Geological Survey, 1998). http://biology.usgs.gov/s+t/SNT/; C.R. Fremling and T.O. Claflin, "Ecological History of the Upper Mississippi River" in *Contaminants in the Upper Mississippi River,* ed. James G. Wiener, et al. (Boston: Butterworth Publishers, 1984), 5–25; *Minneapolis Star Tribune,* 21 April 2004.

20. Christopher Morris, *The Big Muddy: An Environmental History of the Mississippi and Its Peoples from Hernando De Soto to Hurricane Katrina* (New York: Oxford University Press, 2012), 206. Morris offers one of the best discussions of the lower Mississippi River Valley from an environmental history perspective with a wide-ranging, interdisciplinary analysis. *Wasting Our Waterways: Toxic Industrial Pollution and the Unfulfilled Promise of the Clean Water Act,* (Environment America, 2007); Jim Wiener and Mark Sandheinrich, "Contaminants in the Upper Mississippi River: historic trends, responses to regulatory controls, and emerging concerns," *Hydrobiologia* (2010): 49–70, 640. In a 2012 report on the health of the Mississippi River, there were some encouraging signs, such as habitat restoration and the return of certain fish species. However, the level of pollutants such as DDT and lead were still areas of concern along with several other alarming findings. See Friends of the River and National Park Service, *State of the River Report: Water Quality and River Health in the Metro Mississippi River* (2012), http://www.mississippiriverchallenge.org/sotr/state_of_the_river_report.pdf.

21. "Full Steam on the Mississippi," *New York Times,* 3 June 2012; The Volga River: Russian Cruises, http://www.allrussiacruiss.com/volga-river/; Volga River Cruises, http://www.valuecruises.net/europe/russia/volga-river-cruises/

Selected Bibliography

Archives/Special Collections/Museums

Dmitrov History and Regional Studies Museum
Muzei Istorii GULAG, Moscow
Muzei kanala imeni Moskvy
National Archives, Kansas City Branch
Oral History Collection, William Alexander Percy Library, Greenville, Mississippi
Russian State Library
Walter Sillers Jr. Papers, Delta State University Library, Cleveland, Mississippi
Smithsonian Digital Collection
State Russian Museum, Saint Petersburg
University of Wisconsin–La Crosse Archives
State Tretyakov Gallery

Books

Anderson, Benedict. *Imagined Communities: Reflections on the Origin and Spread of Nationalism.* London: Verso Books, 1983.

Anfinson, John. *The River We Have Wrought: A History of the Upper Mississippi.* Minneapolis: University of Minnesota Press, 2003.

Applebaum, Anne. *Gulag: A History.* New York: Anchor Books, 2003.

Armiero, Marco. *A Rugged Mountain Nation: Mountains and the Making of Modern Italy.* Cambridge: The White Horse Press, 2011.

Bailes, Kendall E. *Technology and Society under Lenin and Stalin: Origins of the Soviet Technical Intelligentsia, 1917–1941.* Princeton: Princeton University Press, 1978.

Barry, John M. *Rising Tide: The Great Mississippi Flood of 1927 and How It Changed America.* New York: Simon & Schuster, 1997.

Billington, David P., and Donald C. Jackson. *Big Dams of the New Deal Era: A Confluence of Engineering and Politics.* Norman: University of Oklahoma Press, 2006.

Blair, Walter, and Franklin J. Meine, eds. *Half Horse, Half Alligator: The Growth of the Mike Fink Legend.* Lincoln: University of Nebraska Press, 1956.

Blakesley, Rosalind P., and Susan E. Reid, eds. *Russian Art and the West: A Century of Dialogue in Painting, Architecture, and the Decorative Arts.* DeKalb: Northern Illinois Press University Press, 2007.

Blum, Jerome. *Lord and Peasant in Russia: From the Ninth to the Nineteenth Century.* Princeton: Princeton University Press, 1961.

Bonnell, Victoria E. *Iconography of Power: Soviet Political Posters under Lenin and Stalin.* Berkeley: University of California Press, 1997.

Boyle, R.H. *The Hudson River.* New York: W.W. Norton & Co., 1969.

Brooks, Jeffrey. *When Russia Learned to Read: Literacy and Popular Literature, 1861–1917.* 1985. Reprint, Evanston: Northwestern University Press, 2003.

Brown, Richmond F., ed. *Coastal Encounters: The Transformation of the Gulf South in the Eighteenth Century.* Lincoln: University of Nebraska Press, 2007.

Buchanan, Thomas C. *Black Life on the Mississippi: Slaves, Free Blacks, and the Western Steamboat World.* Chapel Hill: University of North Carolina, 2004.

Buck-Morss, Susan. *Dreamworld and Catastrophe: The Passing of Mass Utopia in East and West.* Cambridge: MIT Press, 2002.

Bukharaev, Ravil. *Islam in Russia: The Four Seasons.* New York: St. Martin's Press, 2000.

Burbank, Jane, ed. *Russian Empire: Space, People, Power, 1700–1930.* Bloomington: Indiana University Press, 2007.

Busch, Jason T., et al. *Currents of Change: Art and Life Along the Mississippi River, 1850–1861.* Minneapolis: University of Minnesota Press, 2004.

Chubarov, Alexander. *Russia's Bitter Path to Modernity: A History of the Soviet and Post-Soviet Eras.* New York: Continuum, 2001.

Cioc, Mark. *The Rhine: An Eco-biography, 1815–2000.* Seattle: University of Washington Press, 2002.

Coates, Peter. *A Story of Six Rivers: History, Culture and Ecology.* London: Reaktion Books, 2013.

Colton, Timothy J. *Moscow: Governing the Socialist Metropolis.* Cambridge: Harvard University Press, 1995.

Comment, Bernard. *The Painted Panorama.* New York: Harry N. Abrams, Inc., Publishers, 2000.

Confino, Alan. *The Nation as a Local Metaphor: Wurttemburg, Imperial Germany, and National Memory, 1871-1918.* Chapel Hill: University of North Carolina Press, 1997.

Cooper, Gordon. *Along the Great Rivers.* New York: Philosophical Library, 1953.

Coopersmith, Jonathan. *The Electrification of Russia, 1880–1926.* Ithaca: Cornell University Press, 1992.

Cosgrove, Denis. *Social Formation and Symbolic Landscape.* 1984. Reprint, Madison: University of Wisconsin Press, 1998.

Costlow, Jane T. *Heart-Pine Russia: Walking and Writing the Nineteenth-Century Forest.* Ithaca: Cornell University Press, 2012.

Crandell, Gina. *Nature Pictorialized: "The View" in Landscape History.* Baltimore: The Johns Hopkins University Press, 1993.

Cusack, Tricia. *Riverscapes and National Identities.* Syracuse: Syracuse University Press, 2010.

Dickinson, Sara. *Breaking New Ground: Travel and National Culture from Peter I to the Era of Pushkin.* Amsterdam: Rodopi, 2006.

Dietrich, William. *Northwest Passage: The Great Columbia River.* Seattle: University of Washington Press, 1996.

Dobrenko, Evgeny, and Eric Naiman, eds. *The Landscape of Stalinism: The Art and Ideology of Soviet Space.* Seattle: University of Washington Press, 2003.

Eisenman, Stephen. *Nineteenth-Century Art: A Critical History.* London: Thames and Hudson, 1994.

Eisenstadt, Samuel N. ed. *Multiple Modernities.* New Brunswick: Transaction Publishers, 2002.

Ekbladh, David. *The Great American Mission: Modernization and the Construction of an American World Order.* Princeton: Princeton University Press, 2010.

Ely, Christopher. *This Meager Nature Landscape and National Identity in Imperial Russia.* DeKalb: Northern Illinois University Press, 2002.

Evtuhov, Catherine. *Portrait of a Russian Province: Economy, Society, and Civilization in Nineteenth-Century Nizhnii Novgorod.* Pittsburgh: University of Pittsburgh Press, 2011.

Fedorov, E. *Man and Nature: The Ecological Crisis and Social Progress.* New York: International Publishers, 1972.

Fedorov, N. *Byla li tachka u Ministra?.* Dmitrov: SPAS, 1997.

Ferber, Linda, ed. *Kindred Spirits: Asher B. Durand and the American Landscape.* Brooklyn: Brooklyn Museum, 2007.

Feshbach, Murray, and Alfred Friendly, Jr. *Ecocide in the USSR: Health and Nature under Siege.* New York: Basic Books, 1992.

Figes, Orlando. *Natasha's Dance: A Cultural History of Russia.* New York: Henry Holt and Co., 2002.

Fitzgerald, Deborah. *Every Farm a Factory: The Industrial Ideal in American Agriculture.* New Haven: Yale University Press, 2003.

Fitzpatrick, Sheila. *The Russian Revolution.* 2nd ed. Oxford: Oxford University Press, 1994.

————. *Everyday Stalinism, Ordinary Life in Extraordinary times: Soviet Russia in the 1930s.* Oxford: Oxford University Press, 1999.

Fox, Stephen R., *The American Conservation Movement: John Muir and His Legacy.* Madison: University of Wisconsin Press, 1986.

Fradkin, Philip L. *A River No More: The Colorado River and the West.* New York: Alfred A. Knopf, 1981.

Franklin, Simon, and Jonathan Shepard. *The Emergence of Rus: 750–1200.* London: Longman, 1996.

Franklin, Simon, and Emma Widdis, eds. *National Identity in Russian Culture.* Cambridge: Cambridge University Press, 2004.

Fremling, Calvin R. *Immortal River, The Upper Mississippi in Ancient and Modern Times.* Madison: University of Wisconsin Press, 2005.

Gellner, Ernest. *Nations and Nationalism.* Ithaca: Cornell University Press, 1983.

Gilman, Nils. *Mandarins of the Future: Modernization Theory in Cold War America.* Baltimore: Johns Hopkins Press, 2003.

Goetzman, William H. *New Lands, New Men: America and the Second Great Age of Discovery.* New York: Viking, 1986.

Gold, John R., and George Revill. *Representing the Environment.* London: Routledge, 2004.

Golden, Peter B. *Central Asia in World History.* Oxford: Oxford University Press, 2011.

Goldman, Marshall I. *The Spoils of Progress: Environmental Pollution in the Soviet Union.* Cambridge: MIT Press, 1972.

Goodman, Nancy, and Robert Goodman. *Paddlewheels on the Upper Mississippi, 1823–1854.* Stillwater: University of Minnesota Printing Services, 2003.

Graham, Loren R. *The Ghost of the Executed Engineer: Technology and the Fall of the Soviet Union.* Cambridge: Harvard University Press, 1993.

Hamilton, George Heard. *The Art and Architecture of Russia.* 3rd ed. New Haven: Yale University Press, 1983.

Havighurst, Walter. *Voices on the River: The Story of the Mississippi Waterways.* Minneapolis: University of Minnesota Press, 1964.

Hays, Samuel P. *Conservation and the Gospel of Efficiency.* Cambridge: Harvard University Press, 1959.

Hirsch, Francine. *Empire of Nations: Ethnographic Knowledge and the Making of the Soviet Union.* Ithaca: Cornell University Press, 2005.

Hoops, Richard. *A River of Grain: The Evolution of Commercial Navigation on the Upper Mississippi River.* Madison: University of Wisconsin-Madison College of Agriculture and Life Sciences Research Report, 1993.

Hosking, Geoffrey. *Russia and the Russians: A History.* Cambridge: Belknap Press, 2001.

Hunn, Eugene. *Nch'i-Wàna, "The Big River": Mid-Columbia Indians and Their Land.* Seattle: University of Washington Press, 1990.

Hunter, Holland. *Soviet Transportation Policy.* Cambridge: Harvard University Press, 1957.

Johns, Elizabeth, et al. *New Worlds from Old: 19th Century Australian and American Landscapes.* Canberra: National Gallery of Australia and Wadsworth Atheneum, 1998.

Johnson, Walter. *River of Dark Dreams: Slavery and Empire in the Cotton Kingdom.* Cambridge: The Belknap Press of Harvard University Press, 2013.

Jones, Robert E. *Bread Upon the Waters: The St. Petersburg Grain Trade and the Russian Economy, 1703–1811.* Pittsburg: University of Pittsburgh Press, 2013.

Josephson, Paul R. *Industrialized Nature: Brute Force Technology and the Transformation of the Natural World.* Washington: Island Press, 2002.

Kerner, Robert J. *The Urge to the Sea: The Course of Russian History, The Role of Rivers, Portages, Ostrogs, Monasteries, and Furs.* Berkeley: University of California Press, 1942.

King, Averil, and Isaak, Levitan. *Lyrical Landscape.* London: Philip Wilson Publishers, 2004.

King, David. *The Falsification of Photography and Art in Stalin's Russia.* New York: Metropolitan Books, 1997.

Kluger, James. *Turning on Water with a Shovel: The Career of Elwood Mead.* Albuquerque: University of New Mexico Press, 1992.

Koestler, Arthur. *The Thirteenth Tribe: The Khazar Empire and Its Heritage.* New York: Random House, 1976.

Kotkin, Stephen. *Magnetic Mountain: Stalinism as a Civilization.* Berkeley: University of California Press, 1995.

Lampen, Dorothy. *Economic and Social Aspects of Federal Reclamation.* Baltimore: Johns Hopkins Press, 1930.

Latham, Michael. *Modernization as Ideology: American Social Science and "Nation Building" in the Kennedy Era.* Chapel Hill: University of North Carolina Press, 2000.

Lewin, Moshe. *The Soviet Century.* London: Verso, 2005.

Lincoln, W. Bruce. *The Conquest of a Continent: Siberia and the Russians.* Ithaca: Cornell University Press, 1994.

Love, Katharina Hansen. *The Evolution of Space in Russian Literature: A Spatial Reading of 19th and 20th Century Narrative Literature.* Amsterdam: Rodopi, 1994.

Maher, Neil. *Nature's New Deal: The Civilian Conservation Corps and the Roots of the American Environmental Movement.* New York: Oxford University Press, 2008.

Maiorova, Olga. *From the Shadow of Empire: Defining the Russian Nation through Cultural Mythology, 1855–1870.* Madison: University of Wisconsin Press, 2010.

March, Ray A. *River in Ruin: the Story of the Carmel River.* Lincoln: University of Nebraska Press, 2012.

McCully, Patrick. *Silenced Rivers: The Ecology and Politics of Large Dams.* London: Zed Books, 2001.

McDermott, John Francis. *George Caleb Bingham: River Portraitist.* Norman: University of Oklahoma Press, 1959.

Meinig, D.W. *The Great Columbia Plain: A Historical Geography, 1805–1910.* Seattle: University of Washington Press, 1968.

Milner, George R. *The Cahokia Chiefdom: The Archaeology of a Mississippian Society.* Washington: Smithsonian Institution Press, 1998.

Morris, Christopher. *The Big Muddy: An Environmental History of the Mississippi and Its Peoples from Hernando de Soto to Hurricane Katrina.* New York: Oxford University Press, 2012.

Nash Smith, Henry. *Virgin Land: The American West as Symbol and Myth.* New York: Vintage Books, 1950.

Nehru, J. *Irrigation and Power* 16.1. January 1959.

Nekrasov, Nikolai. *Lyric Poetry.* Moscow: Detskaja Literature, 1976.

Norris, Stephen M. *A War of Images: Russian Popular Prints, Wartime Culture, and National Identity, 1812–1945.* DeKalb: Northern Illinois University Press, 2006.

Olwig, Robert. *Landscape Nature and the Body Politic: From Britain's Renaissance to America's New World.* Madison: University of Wisconsin Press, 2002.

Pálóczi-Horváth, Andras. *Pechenegs, Cumans, Iasians: Steppe Peoples in Medieval Hungary.* Corvina: Hereditas, 1989.

Pauketat, Timothy R. *Cahokia: Ancient America's Great City on the Mississippi.* New York: Viking Press, 2009.

Pauketat, Timothy R., and Thomas R. Emerson, eds. *Cahokia: Domination Ideology in the Mississippian World.* Lincoln: University of Nebraska Press, 1997.

Pearce, Fred. *When the Rivers Run Dry: Journeys into the Heart of the World's Water Crisis.* Toronto: Key Porter Books, 2006.

Perrie, Maureen, et al., eds. *The Cambridge History of Russia.* 3 vols. Cambridge: Cambridge University Press, 2006.

Phillips, Sarah T. *This Land, This Nation: Conservation, Rural America, and the New Deal.* Cambridge: Cambridge University Press, 2007.

Pisani, Donald J. *Water and American Government: The Reclamation Bureau, National Water Policy, and the West, 1902–1935.* Berkeley: University of California Press, 2002.

Pitzer, Paul. *Grand Coulee: Harnessing a Dream*. Pullman: Washington State University Press, 1994.

Pritchard, Sara B. *Confluence: The Nature of Technology and the Remaking of the Rhône*. Cambridge: Harvard University Press, 2011.

Pryde, Phillip R. *Environmental Management in the Soviet Union*. New York: Cambridge University Press, 1991.

Rabow-Edling, Susanna. *Slavophile Thought and the Politics of Cultural Nationalism*. Albany: SUNY Press, 2006.

Radishchev, Aleksandr Nikolaevich. *A Journey from St. Petersburg to Moscow*. Cambridge: Harvard University Press, 1958.

Rassweiler, Anne D. *The Generation of Power: The History of Dneprostroi*. New York: Oxford University Press, 1988.

Rees, E.A. *Iron Lazar: A Political Biography of Lazar Kaganovich*. London: Anthem Press, 2012.

Reichhold, Klaus, and Graf Bernhard. *Paintings that Changed the World: From Lascaux to Picasso*. Munich: Prestel, 2003.

Reuss, Martin. *Designing the Bayous: The Control of Water in the Atchafalaya Basin, 1800–1995*. College Station: Texas A&M University Press, 2004.

Riasanovsky, Nicholas V. *Russian Identities: A Historical Survey*. Cambridge: Oxford University Press, 2005.

Riasanovsky, Nicholas V., and Mark D. Steinberg. *A History of Russia*. 8th ed. New York: Oxford University Press, 2011.

Robinson, Michael C. *Water for the West: The Bureau of Reclamation, 1902–1977*. Chicago: Public Works Historical Society, 1979.

Ruder, Cynthia. *Making History for Stalin: The Story of the Belomor Canal*. Gainesville: University Press of Florida, 1998.

Russell, Bertrand. *The Practice and Theory of Bolshevism*. New York: Simon and Schuster, 1921.

Russo, G.A., ed. *Hydroelectric Power Stations of the Volga and Kama Cascade System*. Moskvo: GEI, 1960.

Sandlin, Lee. *Wicked River: The Mississippi When it Last Ran Wild*. New York: Pantheon Books, 2010.

Saul, Norman E. *Friends or Foes? The United States and Russia, 1921–1941*. Lawrence: University of Kansas Press, 2006.

Scarpino, Phillip V. *Great River: An Environmental History of the Upper Mississippi, 1850–1950*. Columbia: University of Missouri Press, 1985.

Schama, Simon. *Landscape and Memory*. New York: Alfred A. Knopf, 1995.

Schlogel, Karl. *Moscow, 1937*. Cambridge: Polity Press, 2012.

Scott, James C. *Seeing Like a State: How Certain Schemes to Improve the Human Condition Have Failed*. New Haven: Yale University Press, 1998.

Shimotomai, Nobu. *Moscow Under Stalinist Rule, 1931–34*. New York: St. Martin's Press, 1991.

Silverman, Saul N., ed. *Lenin.* Englewood Cliffs: Prentice-Hall, 1972.

Smith, Anthony. *National Identity.* London: Penguin Books, 1991.

Smith, Jeremy, ed. *Beyond the Limits: The Concept of Space in Russian History and Culture.* Helsinki: Studia Historica, 1999.

Smith, William R. *The History of Wisconsin in Three Parts, Historical, Documentary, and Descriptive.* Vol. 3. Madison: Beriah Brown, Printer, 1854.

Solomon, Steven. *Water: The Epic Struggle for Wealth, Power, and Civilization.* New York: HarperCollins, 2010.

Spinei, Victor. *The Great Migrations in the East and Southeast of Europe from the Ninth to the Thirteenth Century, Hungarians, Pechenegs, and Uzes.* Vol. 1. Amsterdam: Adolf M. Hakkert, 2006.

Stefanova, Tatiana, and Tsvetelin Stepanov. *The Bulgars and the Steppe Empire in the Early Middle Ages: The Problem of the Others.* Leiden: Brill, 2010.

Sternin, Grigory. *Ilya Repin: Painting Graphic Arts.* Leningrad: Aurora Art Publishers, 1985.

Stites, Richard. *Revolutionary Dreams: Utopian Vision and Experimental Life in the Russian Revolution.* New York: Oxford University Press, 1989.

Sunderland, Willard. *Taming the Wild Field: Colonization and Empire on the Russian Steppe.* Ithaca: Cornell University Press, 2004.

Swain, Donald C. *Federal Conservation Policy, 1921–1933.* Berkeley: University of California Press, 1963.

Theler, James, and Robert Boszhardt. *Twelve Millennia: Archaeology of the Upper Mississippi River Valley.* Iowa City: University of Iowa Press, 2003.

Tobey, Ronald C. *Technology as Freedom: The New Deal and the Electrical Modernization of the American Home.* Berkeley: University of California Press, 1996.

Tugwell, Rexford G. *The Democratic Roosevelt: A Biography of Franklin D. Roosevelt.* Baltimore: Penguin Books, 1957.

Tyler, Ron. *Visions of America: Pioneer Artists in a New Land.* New York: Thames and Hudson, 1983.

Usner, Daniel H. Jr. *Indians, Settlers, & Slaves in a Frontier Exchange Economy: The Lower Mississippi Valley Before 1783.* Chapel Hill: University of North Carolina Press, 1992.

Valkenier, Elizabeth Kridl. *Ilya Repin and the World of Russian Art.* New York: Columbia University Press, 1990.

The Volga Vision: UNESCO's Interdisciplinary Initiative for the Sustainable Development of the Volga-Caspian Basin. Paris: UNESCO, 2004.

Waldstreicher, David. *In the Midst of Perpetual Fetes: The Making of American Nationalism, 1776–1820.* Chapel Hill: University of North Carolina Press, 1997.

Warnke, Martin. *Political Landscape: The Art History of Nature.* London: Reaktion Books, 1994.

Warren, William H. *History of the Ojibway People.* 1885. Reprint, St. Paul: Minnesota Historical Society Press, 2009.

Watts Folwell, William. *A History of Minnesota.* Vol. 1. 1921. Reprint, St. Paul: Minnesota Historical Society Press, 1956.

Westerman, Frank. *Engineers of the Soul: The Grandiose Propaganda of Stalin's Russia.* New York: The Overlook Press, 2011.

White, Richard. *The Organic Machine: The Remaking of the Columbia River.* New York: Hill and Wang, 1995.

Wiener, Douglas. *A Little Corner of Freedom: Russian Nature Protection from Stalin to Gorbachev.* Berkeley: University of California Press, 1999.

Wolff, Larry. *Inventing Eastern Europe: The Map of Civilization on the Mind of the Enlightenment.* Stanford: Stanford University Press, 1994.

Worster, Donald. *Rivers of Empire: Water, Aridity, and the Growth of the American West.* New York: Oxford University Press, 1985.

Zimonyi, I. *The Origins of the Volga Bulghars.* Szged, 1990.

Articles, Chapters, and Dissertations

Aizlewood, Robin. "Revisiting Russian National Identity in Russian Thought: From Chaadaev to the Early Twentieth Century." *The Slavonic and East European Review* 78, no. 1 (January 2000): 20–43.

Anfinson, John O. "The Secret History of the Earliest Locks and Dams." *Minnesota History* 54, no. 6 (Summer 1995): 254–267.

Arnason, Johann P. "Communism and Modernity." In *Multiple Modernities,* edited by Shmuel N. Eisenstadt. New Brunswick: Transaction Publishers, 2002.

Bassin, Mark. "'I Object to Rain That is Cheerless': Landscape Art and the Stalinist Aesthetic Imagination." *Ecumene* 7, no. 3 (2000): 313–336.

———. "The Greening of Utopia: Nature, Social Vision, and Landscape Art in Stalinist Russia." In *Architectures of Russian Identity: 1500 to the Present,* edited by James Cracraft and Daniel Rowland, 150–172. Ithaca: Cornell University Press, 2003.

Bigony, Beatrice A. "Folk Literature as an Ethnohistorical Device: The Interrelationships between Winnebago Folk Tales and Wisconsin Habitat." *Ethnohistory* 29, no. 3 (Summer 1982): 155–180.

Biswas, Asit K. "Aswan Dam Revisited: The Benefits of a Much-Maligned Dam." *D+C Magazine for Development and Cooperation* 6, (2002): 25–27. Accessed 18 March 2006. http://www.icid.org/aswan_paper.pdf.

Borzutky, Silvia, and David Berger. "Dammed If You Do, Dammed If You Don't: The Eisenhower Administration and the Aswan Dam." *Middle East Journal* 64, no. 1 (Winter 2010): 94.

Boswell, A. Bruce. "The Kipchak Turks." *The Slavonic Review* 6, no. 6 (June 1927): 68–85.

Brain, Jeffrey P. "Late Prehistoric Settlement Patterning in the Yazoo Basin and Natchez Bluffs Regions of the Lower Mississippi Valley." In *Mississippian Settlement Patterns,* edited by Bruce D. Smith, 356–365. New York: Academic Press, 1978.

Brandenberger, D. L., and A. M Dubrovsky. "'The People Need a Tsar': The Emergence of National Bolshevism as Stalinist Ideology, 1931–41." *Europe-Asia Studies* 50, no. 5 (1998): 875.

Christie, Jean. "New Deal Resources Planning: The Proposals of Morris L. Cooke." *Agricultural History* 53, no. 3 (July 1979): 590–606.

Cooke, Catherine. "Beauty as Route to the 'Radiant Future': Responses of Soviet Architecture." *Journal of Design History* 10, no. 2, *Design, Stalin and the Thaw* (1997): 137–140, published by Oxford University Press on behalf of *Design History.*

Crotty, Jo. "Reshaping the Hourglass? The Environmental Movement and Civil Society Development in the Russian Federation." *Organization Studies* 27, no. 9 (2006): 1319–1338.

Cullather, Nick. "Damming Afghanistan: Modernization in a Buffer State." *The Journal of American History* 89, no. 2 (September 2002): 512–537.

Dainina, Katia. "Displaying the Nation and Modernity in Russia: Directions in Museum Studies—Museum and Society in imperial Russia: An Introduction." *The Slavic Review* 67, no. 4 (2008): 907.

Dickinson, Sara. "Russia's First 'Orient': Characterizing the Crimea in 1787." *Kritika: Explorations in Russian and Eurasian History* 3, no.1 (Winter 2002): 3–25.

Dills, Randall. "The River Neva and the Imperial Façade: Culture and Environment in Nineteenth Century St. Petersburg Russia." PhD diss., University of Illinois at Urbana-Champaign, 2010.

Duranti, Marco. "Utopia, Nostalgia and World War at the 1939–40 New York World's Fair." *Journal of Contemporary History* 41, no. 4 (October 2006): 663–683.

Duzs, Elena. "Russian Art in Search of Identity." In *Russia and Western Civilization: Cultural and Historical Encounters,* edited by Russell Bova, 177–210. Armonk: M.E. Sharpe, 2003.

Ekbladh, David. "How to Build a Nation." *The Wilson Quarterly* 28, no. 1 (Winter 2004): 12–20.

Ely, Christopher. "The Origins of Russian Scenery: Volga River Tourism and Russian Landscape Aesthetics." *Slavic Review* 62 (2003): 666–682.

Engerman, David C. "Modernization from the Other Shore: American Observers and the Costs of Soviet Economic Development." *American Historical Review* 105, no. 2 (April 2000): 383–416.

Faller, Helen M. "Repossessing Kazan as a Form of Nation-building in Tatarstan, Russia." *Journal of Muslim Minority Affairs* 22, no. 1 (2002): 81–90.

Fedorenko, Nikolai. "The Soviet Union and African Countries." *Annals of the American Academy of Political and Social Science: Africa in Motion,* 354 (July 1964): 1–8.

Fremling, C. R., and T. O. Claflin. "Ecological History of the Upper Mississippi River." In *Contaminants in the Upper Mississippi River,* edited by James G. Wiener, et al., 5–25. Boston: Butterworth Publishers, 1984.

French, R. A. "Canals in Pre-revolutionary Russia." In *Studies in Russian Historical Geography,* 451–481. London: Academic Press, 1983.

Friends of the River and National Park Service. *State of the River Report: Water Quality and River Health in the Metro Mississippi River.* 2012. Accessed 14 April 2014. http://stateoftheriver.com/.

Gare, Arran. "The Environmental Record of the Soviet Union." *Capitalism, Nature, Socialism* 3, no. 3 (September 2002): 52–72.

Gitlin, Jay. "Empires of Trade, Hinterlands of Settlement." In *The Oxford History of the American West,* edited by Clyde A. Milner II, et al., 79–115. New York: Oxford University Press, 1994.

Graber, Sam J. "The Upper Mississippi River Improvement Association." Master's thesis, University of Wisconsin–La Crosse, 1968.

Hall, Robert L. "Relating the Big Fish and the Big Stone: The Archaeological Identity and Habitat of the Winnebago in 1634." In *Oneota Archaeology: Past, Present, and Future,* edited by William Green, 19–33. Report 20, Office of the State Archaeologist. Iowa City: University of Iowa, 1995.

Hausmann, Guido. "Historic Memory and Culture in the Russian Empire and Soviet Union." International Colloquium, 25–28 June 2007.

Hooson, David J. M. "The Middle Volga: An Emerging Focal Region in the Soviet Union." *The Geographical Journal* 26, no. 2, (June 1960): 181.

Huntington, R. T., and Wayne Franklin. "Expedition to the Mississippi River by Way of the Gulf of Mexico." *Iowa Review* 15, no. 2 (Spring–Summer, 1985): 102–139.

Hydrotechnical Construction 4, no. 11 (1970): 993995.

Ikeda, Yoshira. "Reconstruction of Moscow by Stalin and Waterfront Spaces." Research Meeting of City Core and Bay Area Renovation Project and Oversea Research Project, Hosei University, 18 July 2007.

Kapranov, I. "Soviet Aid in the Industrialization of Socialist Countries." *Eastern European Economics* 2, no. 4 (Summer 1964): 33–40.

Khachaturov, T. "Natural Resources and National Economic Planning." *The Soviet Review* 15, no. 2 (July 1974): 3–28.

Kurat, A. N. "The Turkish Expedition to Astrakhan in 1569 and the Problem of the Don-Volga Canal," *The Slavonic and East European Review* 40, no. 94 (December 1961): 7–23.

Lagendijk, Vincent. "How the Model Got Its Mojo. How the TVA Became a Paradigm for Planners." Paper, European Social Science History Conference, Glasgow, 13 April 2012.

Li, C. X, et al. "Development of the Volga Delta in Response to Caspian Sea-Level Fluctuation during Last 100 Years." *Journal of Coastal Research* 20, no. 2 (Spring 2004): 401–414.

"Living Volga Programme." UNESCO. 22 November 2006. Accessed 14 April 2014. http://www.unesco.org/new/en/moscow/about-this-office/single-view/news/living_volga_programme-1/.

Lubinski, K., et al. *Regulated Rivers: Research & Management* 11, no. 1 (September 1995).

Markov, Vladimir. "An Unnoticed Aspect of Pasternak's Translations." *Slavic Review* 20, no.3. (October 1961): 503–508.

Mastera iskusstv ob iskusstve 7, Moscow, 1970. as quoted in *Levitan* (Leningrad: Aurora Art Publishers, 1981).

Micklin, Philip P. "International Environmental Implications of Soviet Development of the Volga River." *Human Ecology* 5, no. 2 (June 1977): 113–135.

Miller, Angela. "The Mechanisms of the Market and the Inventions of Western Regionalism: The Example of George Caleb Bingham." In *American Iconology,* edited by David C. Miller. New Haven: Yale University Press, 1993.

Mink, Nicolaas. "A Narrative for Nature: Constance Lindsay Skinner and the Making of Rivers of America." *Environmental History* 1, no. 4 (October 2006): 751–774.

Monkhouse, Christopher. "Henry Wadsworth Longfellow and the Mississippi River: Forging a National Identity Through the Arts." In *Currents of Change: Art and Life Along the Mississippi River, 1850–1861,* edited by Jason T. Busch, et al., 140–179. Minneapolis: University of Minnesota Press, 2004.

Moon, David. "Peasant Migration and the Settlement of Russia's Frontiers, 1550–1897." *The Historical Journal* 40, no. 4 (December 1997): 859–893.

Nicollet Island Collection, *Big Price—Little Benefit: Proposed Locks on the Upper Mississippi and Illinois Rivers are Not Economically Viable* (February 2010).

Nivat, Georges. "The Russian Landscape as Myth." *Russian Studies in Literature* 39, no. 2 (Spring 2003): 53.

Noonan, Thomas. "Why the Vikings First Came to Russia." *Jahrbücher für Geschichte Osteuropas,* Neue Folge, Bd. 34, H.3 (1986): 321–348.

Pirogova, Lyudmila. *Vyesti Dubni,* 15 July 1997.

Pisani, Donald. "Beyond the Hundredth Meridian: Nationalizing the History of Water in the United States." *Environmental History* 5, no. 4 (October 2000): 466–482.

Randolph, John. "The Singing Coachmen or, The Road and Russia's Ethnographic Invention in Early Modern Times." *Journal of Early Modern History* 11, no. 1–2 (2007): 33–61.

Skinner, Lee Joan. "Identity, Engagement, and the Space of the River in *Cumandà.*" *Troubled Water: Rivers in Latin American Imagination,* edited by Elizabeth M. Pettinaroli and Ana Maria Mutis, *Hispanic Issues On Line* 12 (2013): 127–144. http://hispanicissues.umn.edu/assets/doc/07_skinner.pdf.

Smith, Anthony. 'The Land and its People': Reflections on Artistic Identification in an Age of Nations and Nationalism." *Nations and Nationalism* 19, no. 1 (2013): 87–106.

Stockdale, Melissa K. "What is a Fatherland? Changing Notions of Duty, Rights, and Belonging in Russia." In *Space, Place and Power in Modern Russia: Essays in the New Spatial History,* edited by Mark Bassin, Christopher Ely, and Melissa K. Stockdale, 23–49. DeKalb: Northern Illinois University Press, 2010.

Swift, Anthony. "The Soviet World of Tomorrow at the New York World's Fair, 1939." *Russian Review* 57, no. 3 (July 1998): 364–379.

Troyen, Carol, "Retreat to Arcadia: American Landscape and the American Art-Union." *American Art Journal* 23, no. 1 (1991): 20–37.

Vasilenko, Petr. H*ydrotechnical Construction* 10, no. 10 (1976): 1053.

Volga River Cruises. Accessed 14 April 2014. http://www.allrussiacruiss.com/volga-river/; Accessed 14 April 2014. http://www.valuecruises.net/eruope/russia/volga-river-cruises/.

Warneck, P.A. "The Volga-Don Navigation Canal." *Russian Review* 13, no. 4 (October, 1954): 285–291.

West, Elliott. "American Frontier." In *The Oxford History of the American West,* edited by Clyde A. Milner II, et al., 115–151. New York: Oxford University Press, 1994.

White, Richard. "Animals and Enterprise." In *The Oxford History of the American West,* edited by Clyde A. Milner II, et al., 237–275. New York: Oxford University Press, 1994.

Whitmore, Janet L. "A Panorama of Unequaled Yet Ever-Varying Beauty." In *Currents of Change: Art and Life Along the Mississippi River, 1850–1861,* edited by Jason T. Busch, et al., 12–62. Minneapolis: University of Minnesota Press, 2004.

Wiener, Douglas R. "The Genealogy of the Soviet and Post-Soviet Landscape of Risk." *Understanding Russian Nature: Representations, Values and Concepts,* edited by Arja Rossenholm and Sari Autio-Sarasmo, 209–236. Saarijarvi: Gummerus Printing, 2005.

Wiener, James G., et al. "Mississippi River." In *Status and Trends of the Nation's Biological Resources,* edited by M.J. Mac, et al., 2 vols. Fort Collins: U.S.

Department of the Interior, U.S. Geological Survey, 1998. http://biology. usgs.gov/s+t/SNT/.

Wiener, James G., and Mark B. Sandheinrich. "Contaminants in the Upper Mississippi river: historic trends, responses to regulatory controls, and emerging concerns." *Hydrobiologia* (2010): 640, 649–670.

Wasting Our Waterways: Toxic Industrial Pollution and the Unfulfilled Promise of the Clean Water Act. Environment America, 2007.

Williams, Rosalind. "The Political and Feminist Dimensions of Technological Determinism." In *Does Technology Drive History? The Dilemma of Technological Determinism,* edited by Merritt Roe Smith and Leo Marx, 227. Cambridge: MIT Press, 1995.

Wolff, Jane. "Redefining Landscape." In *The Tennessee Valley Authority: Design and Persuasion,* edited by Tim Culvahouse, 52. New York: Princeton Architectural Books, 2007.

Zeisler-Vralsted, Dorothy. "The Nile, Ganges, Volga and Mississippi Rivers: Their Portrayal in Art and Literature." In *Water History and Humanity,* vol. 1, *UNESCO History of Water and Civilization.* Paris: UNESCO, 2014 scheduled publication.

———. "The Cultural and Hydrological Development of the Mississippi and Volga Rivers." In *Rivers in History: Perspectives on Waterways in Europe and North America,* edited by Christof Mauch and Thomas Zeller, 63–77. Pittsburgh: University of Pittsburgh Press, 2008.

Newspapers and Magazines

American Lumberman, 12 October 1912

Engineering News-Record, 19 July 1934

La Crosse Tribune, 11 September 1933; 22 August 2004

Los Angeles Times, 23 August 2012

Minneapolis Star Tribune, 21 April 2004

The Moscow Times, 10 March 2011

The New York Times, 27 December 1987; 3 June 2012; 21 July 2013

Kommunisticheskaia partiia Sovetskogo Soiuza v rezoliutsiiax I resheniiakh c"ezdov, konferentsii I plenymov TsK 1898–1953. Izdanie sed'moe. Chast' II (vtoraia (1825–1953)/Gosudarstvennoe izdatel'stvo politicheskoi leteratury. 1953 (This work includes the Plenum of the Central Committee of Communist Party, 11–15 June 1931, pp. 637–669.)

Ploschad Mira (1997)

Pravda, 1931–1937 (selected issues)

Russian Times, 14 May 2011

Time, 26 July 1937

The Times of India, 13 June 2012

USSR in Construction, 1934–1938
Vyesti Dubnia (1997)
Winona Daily News, 21 April 1976
Winona Republican-Herald, 1930–1938 (selected issues)

Government Documents (U.S.)

H.R. Doc. No. 583, 69th Cong., 2nd Sess. (14 December 1926).
Rivers and Harbors Act, 71st Cong., 2nd Sess., Chapter 847, 46 Stat. 918 (3 July 1930).
Cong. Rec., Vol. 72, 71st Cong., 2nd Sess., (25 April 1930.)
Cong. Rec. Vol. 72, 71st Cong., 2nd Sess., Part 2, p. 12645; 7738; 7723.
O'Brien, Patrick, et al. *Gateways to Commerce: The U.S. Army Corps of Engineers' 9-Foot Channel Project on the Upper Mississippi River.* Denver: National Park Service, 1992.
Report of the Mississippi Valley Committee of the Public Works Administration. Washington, D.C.: U.S. Government Printing Office, 1934.

Primary Sources

Avarbach, I. L. "Ot prestupleniia k truda" (From Crime to Labor). OGIZ (Ob'edineni gosudarstvennykh knizhno-zhurnal'nykh izdatel'stv: Gosudarstvennoe izdatel'stvo, 1936.
Bailey, James, and Tatyana Ivanova, trans. *An Anthology of Russian Folk Epics.* Armonk, New York: M.E. Sharpe, 1998.
Belomorstroi [Belomor Construction], 1936.
Beltrami, Giacomo Costantino. *A Pilgrimage in Europe and America, Leading to the Discovery of the Sources of the Mississippi and Bloody River: with a Description of the Whole Course of the Former, and of the Ohio.* London: Hunt and Clark, 1828.
Botkin, B. A., ed. *A Treasury of Mississippi Folklore: Stories, Ballads and Traditions of the Mid-American River Country.* New York: American Legacy Press, 1955.
Bourke-White, Margaret. *Eyes on Russia.* New York: Simon and Schuster, 1931.
Brackenridge, H. M. *Views of Louisiana: Together with a Journal of a Voyage Up the Missouri River, in 1811.* Pittsburgh: Cramer, Spear, and Eichbaum, 1814. As quoted by Barnard Shipp, *The Indian and Antiquities of America.* Philadelphia: Sherman & Co. Printers, 1897.
Bremner, Robert. *Excursions in the Interior of Russia.* Vol. 2. 1839. Reprint, London: Elibron Classics, 2005.
Bulletin of the American Art-Union 2, no. 5 (August 1849): 10–12.

Bulletin of the American Art-Union, no. 9 (December 1851): 137–139. Accessed 14 April 2014. http://www.sil.si.edu/eresources/silpurl. cfm?purl=2152-6125J.

Bunin, Ivan. "The Riverside Tavern." In *The Gentleman From San Francisco and Other Stories*, 216. 1916. Reprint, New York: Penguin Books, 1987.

Burk, Dean. "A Scientist in Moscow." *The Scientific Monthly* 47, no. 3 (September 1938): 227–241.

Carr, Spencer. *A Brief Sketch of La Crosse, Wisc'n*. La Crosse: W.C. Rogers, Printer, Democrat Office, 1854.

Chamberlain, William Henry. *Russia's Iron Age*. Boston: Little, Brown and Company, 1934.

Clayton, Lawrence Al, et al., ed. *The De Soto Chronicles, The Expedition of Hernando de Soto to North America in 1539–1543*. Vol. 1. Tuscaloosa: University of Alabama Press, 1993.

Curry, Jane. *The River's in My Blood: Riverboat Pilots Tell Their Stories*. Lincoln: University of Nebraska Press, 1983.

Dabon, Claudius. "The Voyages and Discoveries of Father James Marquette in the Valley of the Mississippi." In *Discovery and Exploration of the Mississippi Valley with the Original Narratives of Marquette, Allouez, Membre, Hennepin, and Anastase Douay,* by John Gilmary Shea, 2nd ed. Albany: Joseph McDonough, 1903.

Dickens, Charles. "Boz's Description of the Mississippi." *Parley's Magazine* 10 (1842): 390.

Douglas, Charlotte, ed. *Collected Works of Velimir Khlebnikov*. Vol. 1, *Letters and Theoretical Writings*. Cambridge: Harvard University Press, 1987.

Fadlan, Ibn. *Ibn Fadlan's Journey to Russia: A Tenth-Century Traveller from Baghdad to the Volga River*. Translated by Richard Frye. Princeton: Markus Wiener Publications, 2005.

Flint, Timothy. *The History and Geography of the Mississippi Valley*. Vol. 1, 2nd ed. Cincinnati: E.H. Flint and L.R. Lincoln, 1832.

———. *Recollections of the Last Ten Years in the Valley of the Mississippi*. Edited by George R. Brooks. Carbondale: Southern Illinois Press, 1968.

Golitsyn, Sergei. *Memoirs of a Survivor: The Golitsyn Family in Stalin's Russia*. London: Reportage Press, 2008.

Gorky, Maxim. *My Childhood* in *The Autobiography of Maxim Gorky*. Secaucus, New Jersey: Citadel Press, 1949.

———. *Belomor: An Account of the Construction of the New Canal between the White Sea and the Baltic Sea*. New York, 1935.

Guthrie, Woody. "The Grand Coulee Dam," Recorded, 1944.

Herodotus. *The History of Herodotus*. Translated by George Rawlinson. Garden City, NY: The International Collector's Library, 1928.

Hoover, Herbert. "The Improvement of Our Mid-West Waterways." *Annals of the American Academy of Political and Social Science* 135 (January 1928): 17.

d' Iberville, Pierre Le Moyne trans. Richebourg Gaillard McWilliams. *Iberville's Gulf Journals*. Alabama: University of Alabama Press, 1981.

Ickes, Harold L. "Saving the Good Earth: The Mississippi Valley Committee and Its Plan." *Survey Graphic in the Thirties* (February 1934).

Ilin, M. *New Russia's Primer: The Story of the Five-Year Plan*. Boston: Houghton Mifflin Co., 1931.

Kanal imeni Moskvy: 70 let (Moscow: 000Prazdnik, 2007): 50.

Keun, Odette. *A Foreigner Looks at the TVA*. New York: Longmans, Green and Co., 1937.

Khrushchev, Nikita. *Khrushchev Remembers*. New York: Bantam Books, 1970.

Knox, Thomas W. *The Boy Travellers in the Russian Empire*. New York: Harper & Brothers, 1887.

Kohler, Phyllis Penn, ed. *Journey for Our Time: The Journals of the Marquis de Custine*. London: Phoenix Press, 2001.

Komarovsky, A. *The Moscow-Volga Canal*. Moscow: Foreign Languages Publishing House, 1939.

Korobochko, A., and V. Liubovnyi. *Chernetsovy G.G. i.N.G. Puteshestvie po volge*. M., Mysl', 1970.

Lenin, V. I. "Bugun Fishermen's and Workers' Soviet of the Northern Coast, Aral Sea," 7 October 1921. In *V.I. Lenin Collected Works*. Vol. 45. Moscow: Progress Publishers, 1970.

———. "Draft Plan of Scientific and Technical Work," first written between 18–25 April 1918. *Pravda* (4 March 1924) in V.I. Lenin, *On the Development of Heavy Industry*, 39. Moscow: Progress Publishers, 1972.

———. "The Impending Catastrophe and How to Combat It." *Pribol* (October 1917) in V.I. Lenin, *On the Development of Heavy Industry*, 16.

———. "The Immediate Tasks of the Soviet Government," 30 April–3 May 1918. In *Selected Works*, II (New York: International Publishers, 1967), 714–717.

———. "Report of the All-Russia Central Executive Committee and the Council of People's Commissars on the Home and Foreign Policy," 22 December 1920. In *On the Development of Heavy Industry*, 84.

Lenin to G. M. Krzhizhanovsky, 23 January 1920. *Ekonomisheskaya Zhin* no. 18 (22 January 1925) in *On the Development of Heavy Industry*, 49.

Levidov, M. I. *Moscow: Past, Present, Future*. Moscow: Vneshtorgisdat, 1934.

Lilienthal, David E. *TVA: Democracy on the March*. New York: Harper and Row, 1944.

———. *The Journals of David E. Lilienthal*. Vol. 1, *The TVA Years, 1939–1945*. New York: Harper and Row, 1964.

Mason, Philip P., ed. *Schoolcraft's Expedition to Lake Itasca: The Discovery of the Source of the Mississippi*. East Lansing: Michigan State University Press, 1958.

Meijer, Jan M., ed. *The Trotsky Papers, 1917–1922*. The Hague: Mouton, 1971.

Munro-Butler-Johnson, and Henry Alexander. *A Trip Up the Volga to the Fair of Nijni-Novgorod*. Philadelphia: Porter & Coates, 1875.

Moskva-Volgostroi [Moscow Volga Construction] 1936.

Na SHTURM Trassy [Storming the Route] 1936.

Neuberger, Richard L. "The biggest thing on earth: Grand Coulee Dam." *Harper's* (February 1937): 247–342.

Nikitin, Afanasy. *Voyage Beyond the Three Seas, 1466–1472*. Moscow: Raduga Publishers, 1985.

Old Man River Safety Bulletins. 1934–1938. National Archives, Kansas City Branch.

Olearius, Adam. *The Travels of Olearius in Seventeenth Century Russia*. Translated and edited by Samuel H. Baron. Stanford: Stanford University Press, 1967.

Oliphant, Laurence. *The Russian Shores of the Black Sea in the Autumn of 1852*. New York: Redfield, 1854.

Perry, John. *The State of Russia under the Present Tsar*. London, 1716.

Pilnyak, Boris. *The Volga Falls to the Caspian Sea*. New York: Cosmopolitan Book Corporation, 1931.

Plenum of the Central Committee of Communist Party, 11–15 June 1931, pp. 637–669 (Kommunisticheskaia partiia Sovetskogo Soiuza v rezoliutsiiax I resheniiakh c'ezdov, konferentsii I plenymov TsK 1898–1953. Izdanie sed'moe. Chast' II (vtoraia (1825–1953)/Gosudarstvennoe izdatel'stvo politicheskoi leteratury. 1953.

Proceedings of the American Art-Union, 1844–1849.

Ralston, W. R. S. *Russian Folk-Tales*. London: Smith, Elder & Co., 1873.

Roberta Reeder, ed. *Down Along the Volga*. Philadelphia: University of Pennsylvania Press, 1975.

Roosevelt, Franklin Delano. "Campaign Address in Portland, Oregon on Public Utilities and Development of Hydro-Electric Power," 21 September 1932. In *The American Presidency Project*.

———. "Extemporaneous Remarks at Clinch River Below the Norris Dam," 16 November 1934. In *The Public Papers and Addresses of Franklin D. Roosevelt*. Vol. 3. New York: Random House, 1938.

———. "Extemporaneous Remarks at Fort Peck Dam, Montana," 6 August 1934. In *The Public Papers and Addresses of Franklin D. Roosevelt*. Vol. 3. New York: Random House, 1938.

———, "The Fourth 'Fireside Chat'—We Are on Our Way, and We Are Headed in the Right Direction," 22 October 1933. In *The Public Papers and Addresses of Franklin D. Roosevelt.* Vol. 2.

———. "Message to Congress on National Planning and Development of Natural Resources," 3 June 1937. In *The American Presidency Project.* http://www.presidency.ucsb.edu/ws/index.php?pid=15415.

———. "The One Hundred and Sixtieth Press Conference," 23 November 1934. In *The Public Papers and Addresses of Franklin D. Roosevelt.* Vol. 3. New York: Random House, 1938.

———. "Rear-Platform Remarks at Garden City, Kansas," 12 October 1936. In *The American Presidency Project.* http://www.presidency.ucsb.edu/ws/?pid=15171.

Rozanov, Vasily. *Ruskii Nil* M:V. Volgin, *Ataman Kuz'ma Roshchin* (Moscow, 1901).

Rubruck, William. "The Journey of William of Rubruck." In *Mission to Asia: Narratives and Letters of the Franciscan Missionaries in Mongolia and China in the Thirteenth and Fourteenth Centuries,* edited by Christopher Dawson. New York: Harper and Row, 1966.

The Russian Primary Chronicle. Laurentian text, trans. Samuel Hazzard Cross and Olgerd P. Sherbowitz-Wetzor. Cambridge: The Mediaeval Academy of America, 1953.

Sokolov, Y.M. *Russian Folklore.* Hatboro, Pennsylvania: Folklore Associates, 1966.

Solzhenitsyn, Aleksandr I. *The Gulag Archipelago, 1918–1956.* New York: Harper & Row, 1973.

Spalding, Henry C. "The Black Sea and the Caspian." *Van Nostrand's Engineering Magazine* 15, no. 92 (August 1876): 122–127.

Texnika-molodyozhi [Technics of Youth], 1936.

de Tocqueville, Alexis. *Democracy in America.* Vol. 1–2. 1848. Reprint, Garden City, NY: Doubleday & Company, Inc., 1966.

Trotsky, Leon. *Sochinenya.* Vol. 21. As quoted in Issac Deutscher, *The Prophet Unarmed: Trotsky, 1921–1929.* London: Oxford University Press, 1959.

———. Central Committee, April 1926, as quoted in Issac Deutscher, *The Prophet Unarmed: Trotsky, 1921–1929.* London: Oxford University Press, 1959.

———. *Literature and Revolution,* 251–252, 253. 1924. Reprint, New York: Russell & Russell, 1957.

———. *Sochinenya.* Vol. 21. As quoted in Isaac Deutscher, *The Prophet Unarmed: Trotsky, 1921–1929.* London: Oxford University Press, 1959.

Twain, Mark. *Life on the Mississippi.* 1883. Reprint, New York: Signet Classic, 1961.

———. *Mark Twain in Eruption.* Edited by Bernard De Voto. New York: Grosset & Dunlap, 1922.

Von Haxthausen, Baron August. *Studies on the Interior of Russia.* Edited by Frederick Starr. Chicago: University of Chicago Press, 1972.

———. *The Russian Empire: Its People, Institutions, and Resources.* London: Chapman and Hall, 1856.

White, W. L. *Report on the Russians.* London: Eyre & Spottiswoode, 1945.

Williams, Albert Rhys. *Lenin: The Man and His Works.* New York: Scott and Seltzer, 1919.

Volga, Muzukal' naia biblioteka "Pevekovki," December 1936.

Yule, Henry, and Henri Cordier, trans. and ed. *Cathay and the Way Thither, Being a Collection of Medieval Notices of China.* Vol. 3. London, 1916. Cited in http://depts.washington.edu/silkroad/texts/pegol.html.

Zenkovsky, Serge A. *Medieval Russia's Epics, Chronicles, and Tales.* Translated by Serge A. Zenkovsky. New York: E.P. Dutton & Co., Inc., 1963.

Interviews

David Bell. Dubna, Russia. August 2003.

Nikolai F. Fedorov. Dmitrov, Russia, September 2003.

Jerry R. Galm. Professor of Anthropology, Eastern Washington University. March 2012.

Sergey Pipenko. Dubna, Russia. 23 December 2011.

Nikolai Prislonov. Dubna (Russia) International University for Nature, Society and Man. 23 September 2003.

Ivan Y. Shimon. Professor of History, Dubna (Russia) International University for Nature, Society and Man. 6 September 2003; 5 April 2010.

Galina I. Yurchenko. Curator, Muzej Kanala imeni Moskvy. 15 March 2011.

Index